THE BARCELONA

Professor Damian Hughes combines his
practical and academic background within sport,
organization and change psychology to work as
a trusted adviser to business, education and
sporting elite, specializing in the creation of
high-performance cultures. He has written
several successful business texts, including
Liquid Thinking and *How to Think Like
Sir Alex Ferguson*.

Also by Damian Hughes

THE WINNING MINDSET

DAMIAN HUGHES

THE BARCELONA WAY

Unlocking the DNA of a
Winning Culture

MACMILLAN

First published 2018 by Macmillan
an imprint of Pan Macmillan
20 New Wharf Road, London N1 9RR
Associated companies throughout the world
www.panmacmillan.com

ISBN 978-1-5098-0442-9

Copyright © Damian Hughes 2018

The right of Damian Hughes to be identified as the
author of this work has been asserted by him in accordance
with the Copyright, Designs and Patents Act 1988.

All rights reserved. No part of this publication may be reproduced,
stored in a retrieval system, or transmitted, in any form, or by any means
(electronic, mechanical, photocopying, recording or otherwise)
without the prior written permission of the publisher.

Pan Macmillan does not have any control over, or any responsibility for,
any author or third-party websites referred to in or on this book.

9 8 7 6 5 4 3 2

A CIP catalogue record for this book is available from the British Library.

Printed and bound by CPI Group (UK) Ltd, Croydon, CR0 4YY

This book is sold subject to the condition that it shall not, by way of
trade or otherwise, be lent, hired out, or otherwise circulated without
the publisher's prior consent in any form of binding or cover other than
that in which it is published and without a similar condition including
this condition being imposed on the subsequent purchaser.

Visit **www.panmacmillan.com** to read more about all our books
and to buy them. You will also find features, author interviews and
news of any author events, and you can sign up for e-newsletters
so that you're always first to hear about our new releases.

THE BARCELONA WAY

PREFACE

'The true evidence of a culture is how people
behave when no one is watching.'
Anon

The game was forgotten. The lesson was not.

There was a chance, a golden chance, for Barcelona to score
the first goal of the game. The quickly taken shot flashed past
the goalkeeper's desperate dive, past the post and missed by
inches.

Before the crowd had the opportunity to process the events
and react accordingly, Pep Guardiola, in his first season in
charge of FC Barcelona, immediately turned around to look at
his bench. He wanted to take a mental snapshot of the players
that had not been selected. He wished to observe their reaction
to the incident that had just occurred.

Some of the players leapt from their seats in anticipation of
the ball nestling in the back of the net, before holding their
heads in shared frustration that their team had not taken the
lead. Other players neither moved nor reacted to the events,
appearing to be uninterested in what had passed before their
eyes. This detachment conveyed their personal unhappiness at
not being included in the starting line-up.

The following summer, all the players who had failed to
react had left the club.

'A team's culture is about the conduct and behaviour of everyone involved, it's working together towards shared object- ives and, as such, is an immediately identifiable part of the group's identity,' said Pep Guardiola.

INTRODUCTION

In the spring of 2008, Futbol Club Barcelona was a big-name global brand that was losing its lustre. The fortunes of the first team were in decline. Frank Rijkaard, a Dutch disciple of Johan Cruyff and a stellar former player, had helped them scale the heights, winning the league in 2005 and both the league and Champions League (formerly the European Cup) in 2006. But the team – the most talented and expensively assembled crop in the club's history – had faded, winning no major trophies in two seasons. 'A five per cent drop in commitment creates problems,' the then Barcelona CEO, Ferran Soriano, said, 'and Frank didn't know how to re-energise the group.'[1] Rijkaard, it was felt, had lost control of the dressing room. The ideas were running out, the competitive edge had faded, morale was low. New leadership was called for.

The board had a range of options, chief among them a serial winner whose record offered the closest thing to a guarantee of success in a game where, more often than in most other sports, outcomes turn on fortune's tricks.

The authoritarian, charismatic José Mourinho, a coach with a spectacular record of success in his native Portugal, then in England and Italy, seemed just the man to cut big egos down to size and restore drive to a rudderless team. Two board members were dispatched to Portugal to sound him out. Mourinho, who had cut his coaching teeth at the club a decade earlier, gave them a detailed PowerPoint presentation of what he would do to turn Barcelona around.

To the dismay of the majority of Barcelona's 180,000 paid-up members, the board chose Pep Guardiola, a novice with one year's coaching experience with the club's lower-division B team and none in the game's upper reaches. Guardiola had been a great player and captain of Barcelona under Johan Cruyff, but in terms of the new responsibility on his shoulders and the uncharted waters he was being asked to navigate, it was, suggested the sportswriter John Carlin, 'like Sony selecting the manager of a medium-sized regional office to take over as company CEO.'[2]

Nine years – and four coaches – later, Barcelona have established a stranglehold over European football, winning seven league titles, three European Cups and three World Club Championships. In the four years that Guardiola remained at the club, they won fourteen out of nineteen possible leagues and cups, a feat unequalled in the history of the game. Unequalled also are the five Ballon d'Or prizes, the award for the world's best player, granted to Barcelona's Lionel Messi, who has continued to get even better and better. Barcelona have achieved something else, too, something more difficult to win than any official prize: the admiration of the sporting world. The team have revolutionized the 150-year-old sport, while other clubs have peaked and faded from season to season. Coaches from clubs large and small make pilgrimages to Barcelona's training camp, notebooks in hand, hoping some of the gold dust might rub off on them.

Where did it all go right?

The starting point in answering such a question can be found on a single piece of paper, written on by CEO Ferran Soriano, Director of Football Txiki Begiristain (both now at Manchester City) and José Ramón Alexanko, the club's head of youth football. These three men were charged with the task of finding and appointing the next manager. 'Think of Barcelona as a restaurant,' wrote the *Daily Telegraph*. 'Txiki Begiristain is the guy sourcing ingredients and deciding what goes on the menu. Soriano, meanwhile, is the one who's already planning where they're going to open their next restaurant.'[3] What they were looking for was a head chef to combine these elements.

They detailed the criteria their chosen leader would have to meet. Significantly, of the nine-point checklist they employed, just two – the style of play demanded and a wide experience of European football – could be said to centre on the technical skills required to coach a leading football team.

What is particularly fascinating is how little the rest has to do with football and everything to do with the environment in which the players grew up and operated in. The remaining criteria, including a match with the values of the club, the ability to develop leaders and the accepted behaviours, broadly aligned with the principles which Edgar Schein, the world's leading corporate culture expert, outlined as the most important factors of a high-performing culture.[4] In *The Barcelona Way*, we will discover how successful organizations, with no connection to sport, also conform to these same factors. Most importantly, we can learn how to replicate this cultural model and find the template to lead any successful organization.

'To achieve success in any industry, it is vital to understand the logic behind it,' concurs Ferran Soriano. 'You need to go to the roots and put culture at the heart of your business. Combine this with hard work, use good management criteria and apply lots of common sense. Success has absolutely nothing whatsoever to do with good luck but lots to do with a good culture.'

The appointment of the unheralded Guardiola was part of a coordinated plan to re-emphasize the cultural values of the club

– values whose lineage can be directly traced back to Johan Cruyff – which had ebbed and flowed in the order of importance during the intervening years. It was now decreed that it was time to go back to Cruyff's drawing board.

The importance of culture

Laszlo Bock, Senior Vice President of People Operations at Google, has written that, 'culture underpins everything we do at Google.'[5] Culture was Merriam-Webster's word of the year in 2014. In 2015, the world's largest management consultant, Accenture, identified 'optimizing organizational structures for productivity' as one of the key challenges that organizations face. In other words, culture matters. A lot.

In 1994, two business school professors at Stanford University began studying how, exactly, one creates an atmosphere of trust within a company. For years, the professors – James Baron and Michael Hannan – had been teaching students that a firm's culture mattered as much as its strategy. The way a business treats workers, they said, was critical to its success. In particular, they argued that within most companies – no matter how great the product or how loyal the customers – things would eventually fall apart unless employees trusted one another.

Then, each year, a few students would ask for evidence that supported these claims.

The truth was, Baron and Hannan *believed* their assertions were true, but they didn't have much data to back it up. Both men were trained as sociologists and could point to studies showing the importance of culture to making employees happy or recruiting new workers or encouraging a healthy work–life balance. But there were few papers showing how a company's culture impacted profitability. So, in 1994, they embarked on a multi-year project to see if they could prove their assertion right.

First, though, they needed to find an industry that had lots of new companies they could track over time. It occurred to them that the flurry of technology start-ups appearing in Silicon Valley might prove the perfect sample.

The project ended up taking fifteen years and examining close to 200 firms. Their surveys looked at every variable that might influence a start-up's culture, including how employees were recruited, how applicants were interviewed, how much people were paid and which workers executives decided to promote or fire. They watched college dropouts become billionaires and, in other cases, high-flying executives crash and burn.

Eventually, they collected enough data to conclude that most companies had cultures that fell into one of five categories.[6]

One was a culture they referred to as the 'star' model. At these firms, executives hired from elite universities or other successful companies and gave employees huge amounts of autonomy. Offices had fancy cafeterias and lavish perks. Venture capitalists loved star-model companies because giving money to the A team, conventional wisdom held, was always the safest bet.

The second category was the 'engineering' model. Inside firms with engineering cultures, there weren't many individual stars, but engineers, as a group, held the most sway. An engineering mindset prevailed in solving problems or approaching hiring decisions. Engineering-focused cultures are powerful because they allow firms to grow quickly. When everyone comes from a similar background and mindset, you can rely on social norms to keep everyone on the same path.

The third and fourth categories of companies included those firms built around 'bureaucracies' and those construed as 'autocracies'. In the bureaucratic model, cultures emerged through thick ranks of middle managers. Executives wrote extensive job descriptions, organizational charts and employee handbooks. Everything was spelled out and there were rituals, such as weekly meetings, that regularly communicated the firm's values to its workforce. An autocratic structure is similar, except that all of the rules, job descriptions and organizational charts ultimately point to the desires and goals of one person, usually the founder or CEO.

The final category was known as the 'commitment' model, and it was a throwback to the age when people happily worked for one company their entire life. It doesn't mean that the company is stodgy, but it does imply a set of values that prioritize slow and steady growth. Commitment cultures were more hesitant to lay people off. They often hired HR professionals when other start-up companies were recruiting engineers or sales people. 'Commitment CEOs believe that getting the culture right is more important than designing the best product,' says Baron.

In the decade after publishing their results, Baron and Hannan kept close tabs on which start-ups thrived and which ones stumbled. About half the firms they studied remained in business for at least a decade; some became the most successful companies in the world. Baron and Hannan's goal was to see if particular corporate cultures were likely to correlate with success. They were unprepared, however, for how dramatically the impact of culture came through. 'Even in the fast-paced world of high-tech entrepreneurship in Silicon Valley, founders' employment models exert powerful and enduring effects on how their companies evolve and perform,' the researchers wrote in 2002, in the journal *California Management Review*. The enormous impact of cultural decisions 'is evident even after taking account of numerous other factors that might be expected to affect the success or failure of young technology ventures, such as company age, size, access to venture capital, changes in senior leadership, and the economic environment.'

Just as Baron and Hannan had suspected, the star model produced some of the study's biggest winners. As it turned out, putting all of the smartest people in the same room could yield vast influence and wealth. But, unexpectedly, star firms also failed in record numbers. As a group, they were less likely to make it to an initial public offering than any other category, and they were often beset by internal rivalries. As anyone who has ever worked in such a company knows, infighting is often more vicious inside a star-focused firm, because everyone wants to be *the* star.

In fact, when Baron and Hannan looked at the data, they found the only culture producing consistent winners was that of the commitment firms. Hands down, a commitment culture outperformed every other type of management style in almost every meaningful way. 'Not one of the commitment firms we studied failed,' said Baron. '*None* of them, which is amazing in its own right. But they were also the fastest companies to go public, had the highest profitability ratios, and tended to be leaner, with fewer middle managers, because when you choose employees slowly, you have time to find people who excel at self-direction.' Employees in commitment firms wasted less time on internal rivalries because everyone was committed to the company, rather than to personal agendas. Commitment companies also tended to know their customers better than other kinds of firms, and as a result could detect shifts in the market much faster.

One of the main reasons why commitment cultures were successful, it seemed, was because of the sense of trust that emerged among workers, managers and customers, which enticed everyone to work harder and stick together through the setbacks inevitable in any industry. Most commitment cultures avoided layoffs unless there was no alternative. They invested heavily in training. There were higher levels of teamwork and psychological safety.

There is a growing body of evidence to support the commitment culture approach. The Gallup organization reports that companies with engaged employees are 22 per cent more profitable than those in which employees watch the clock. The effect on our quality of life is considerable, too. The Canadian economist John Helliwell and his colleagues found that a 10 per cent increase in employee trust in a company's leaders has the same impact on their life satisfaction as receiving a 36 per cent increase in salary. Creating a commitment culture is exactly where 'doing good' and 'doing well' coincide.[7]

Thousands of miles away from Silicon Valley, on the back of an envelope, the board at Barcelona had intuited almost exactly the same answer. It doesn't require too great a leap of the imagination to jump from the high-tech world of Silicon Valley to the fast-paced world of elite European football and look for comparable cultures.

Star model – Real Madrid

In 2002, Real Madrid celebrated their centenary. It was a year in which the club opened its first theme park, the Vuelta a España cycling race finished at their Bernabéu stadium, and Magic Johnson played with the club's basketball team. The celebrations were all-encompassing, quasi-religious and unavoidable. 'The club had organized some event *every single day*,' remembers Steve McManaman, the affable Scouser who played for them at the time.[8]

The headline event was an exhibition game against a Rest

of the World XI. A full orchestra was arranged on the pitch and Placido Domingo boomed out the club's new anthem. As he did so, the two teams lined up: one in blue, the other in white. The blues were the World XI but the whites had the more glamorous team and more famous faces: Ronaldo, Zinedine Zidane (then the most expensive player in the world), Luís Figo, Roberto Carlos, Raúl, Fernando Hierro, Iker Casillas. There had never been a team like it, not since the club's Alfredo di Stéfano era of the 1950s and early 1960s. 'It was,' said Sid Lowe, the football journalist, 'as if they had cheated at the computer game *Championship Manager*.'[9]

When Madrid's captain, Hierro, said, 'of the ten best players in the world, we have five', it was hardly an exaggeration. Ronaldo had collected the FIFA World Player Award (now merged with the Ballon d'Or) the night before, meaning that of the previous six winners, Madrid now boasted five. They came to be known as the *galácticos*.

The star culture was central to the president Florentino Pérez's vision. His – and, by definition, Madrid's – policy became known as 'Zidanes and Pavónes'; they aspired to a team made up of superstars like Zidane, supplemented with youth-team graduates such as centre-back Paco Pavón, whose commitment to and understanding of the club could be counted upon. It was presented as a philosophy but it was also an economic imperative. The only way to pay the astronomical wages of Zidane et al. was by promoting youth-teamers who were paid far, far less – a 'pittance' as one teammate put it. In turn, the 'Zidanes' carried Madrid's image around the world.

This approach generated great excitement. 'People enjoy just hearing our starting eleven,' commented Michel Salgado, the team's full-back. It was also, ultimately, one of the things that brought about their downfall. The fact that Madrid revelled in their status, humility being a startlingly absent trait, made winning an obligation, but the system was not set up for sustainable success.

In 2000–01 season, Luís Figo's first at the club, they dominated the league from start to finish, winning the title by nine points. The year afterwards, heralding Zidane's arrival, saw them finish third in the league, although they found redemption in Europe by winning their ninth European Cup in Glasgow, beating Barcelona along the way. The following year belonged to the Brazilian superstar Ronaldo, and ended with the league title. But something was shifting. The flaws in Madrid's 'star' model were coming to the fore; tensions, too.

The concerns from outside the club about the eclipse of the 'middle class' – those players like Salgado who were neither superstars nor youth-team graduates – were confirmed in a brutal fashion. Steve McManaman wrote, '[head coach Vicente] Del Bosque effectively told me that his hands were tied.'[10] The coach wasn't allowed to drop the *galácticos*, regardless of their form. Another head coach from the period, Mariono García Remón, recounts an occasion when he omitted the Brazilian striker Ronaldo from the team. 'Yes,' he sighed when discussing the decision, 'it cost me my job.'

The club captain, Fernando Hierro, reprimanded the president for treating players like 'stock'. In 2003, both his and Del Bosque's contracts were not renewed. The lap of honour following the capture of another league title was cut short, and all of the players planned to boycott the club's end-of-season reception, claiming unfair treatment.

'If the most important thing is to put on a circus, then you have less chance of winning things,' Luís Figo once said. 'The rules of a football team are one thing, marketing is another. There was a moment when that balance didn't exist. We reached a point where we left the path a football team should take and we paid for that.'

The rules of sporting success had been subverted, meritoc-racy and structure going out of the window in the name of brand recognition. The *galácticos* were less a football team and more a collection of famous footballers, the embodiment of style over substance, entitlement over effort. One Real Madrid manager from that era declared, 'Everyone wanted to be the maître d', no one wanted to wash the plates.' 'We didn't abide by the normal rules of football and football cornered us and stabbed us for it,' admits Jorge Valdano, the club's former Director of Football.

Despite hiring and firing five coaches between 2003 and 2006, Madrid – and their star culture – did not win a trophy for three years. Not since 1953, before Alfredo Di Stéfano's arrival, had they endured such a drought. The most expensive, most glamorous team ever assembled had been humiliated, and Pérez resigned in February 2006. He had created a culture des-tined for failure, provoking division and inequality. When he fell on his sword, the club's latest head coach, Juan Ramón López Caro, declared, 'From now on, I will play with players, not names.'[11]

Autocracy – Chelsea FC

When you've grown up in the Communist regime of the former Soviet Union, and started your business career import-ing rubber ducks before becoming the twelfth richest person in Russia thanks to owning an oil company, then being accused of 'failing to demonstrate even a minimum amount of man-ners and education' is unlikely to bother you when it comes to the business of getting your own way.

This barbed criticism was delivered by Renzo Ulivieri, the chairman of the Italian Football Coaches Association, who accused Chelsea of approaching the Italian national coach, Antonio Conte, 'without warning' and without seeking permission when Roman Abramovich decided to appoint him as his tenth coach at Stamford Bridge in 2016.

Abramovich, the Chelsea owner, is a self-made billionaire and one of the most high-profile men in European football, yet at the same time probably the least known. He has never given an interview since assuming control of Chelsea in 2003 and those close to him, who could be counted on one hand, have only one-paragraph platitudes to offer. His actions, however, speak far louder.

Arsenal's former vice-chairman, David Dein, once memorably said that: 'Roman Abramovich has parked his Russian tanks on the lawn and is firing £50 notes at us.' The club's policy under Abramovich has been to buy the best players available and rotate the manager at his whim. Stability is an innocent bystander and the theory seems to be that if the players are good enough then it is almost irrelevant who the manager is. Chelsea's impressive collection of silverware under Abramovich tends to substantiate this.

Carlo Ancelotti, one of the Russian's ten full-time coaching appointments (plus two interim appointments), recounts. 'When I first met Abramovich, he told me, "I want to find a manager that gives my team an identity, because when I watch Chelsea I'm not able to find an identity. When I see Barcelona or Manchester United, I find an identity in the team – when I watch Chelsea I cannot find an identity."'[12]

Despite winning the Premier League and FA Cup double in his first season in charge, Ancelotti was under no illusions about the autocratic culture he had joined. 'Abramovich is never happy with "thunderbolt" defeats – defeats that he believes should not happen to Chelsea.' Indeed, the owner would often call emergency meetings to discover the causes.

The most memorable reaction – 'but for all the wrong reasons' according to Ancelotti's assistant, Paul Clement – occurred during the Italian's second season, when the club faced Manchester United in the Champions League quarter-finals. 'The night before the second leg, Abramovich addressed the players, telling them they had to win or there would be huge changes to the team,' Clement remembers. Abramovich then directly addressed Ancelotti. The Italian recalls: 'He told me individually that if we lost then I was not to bother coming back to work. I wasn't sure if he was serious. We lost and I did go back to work, though I felt like a dead man walking.'[13]

He was subsequently dismissed three months later by the club's CEO, Bruce Buck, who was driving away from the stadium when he received the call from the Russian oligarch to say, 'Turn around and tell Carlo he is fired.'

Bureaucracy – Liverpool FC

A camel, so the saying goes, is a horse designed by committee. In the five seasons following the acquisition by American businessman John W. Henry's Fenway Sports Group (FSG), Liverpool signed fifty players, very nearly a team a season. These signings have played under four different managers, each with different, often unconnected tactical plans, yet all overseen by a six-man committee.

'Moneyball' is the moniker employed to describe modern Liverpool's approach to developing its footballing culture. This was the title of the book chronicling the Oakland Athletics baseball team, and in particular its General Manager Billy Beane. Beane used statistics-based scouting techniques and adopted radically different principles on how the game of baseball should be played, and how a team should be built.

His methods got the Oakland Athletics punching above their meagre weight and beating richer, more glamorous rivals. Along the way, 'Moneyball' became not only a book and movie but an adjective for the way many sports teams were run.

A large part of Beane's approach was to search for 'objective knowledge about baseball'. This meant looking purely at statistics, and finding new ways of measuring the game in statistical terms, to inform player recruitment and on-field tactics. This approach identifies players whose contributions are either underrated or overrated by subjective scouts or coaches. One example of moneyball in practice was Beane's decision to fire his traditional scouting team and draft players from schools and universities based solely on statistical analysis.

The Boston Red Sox, owned by Henry, were one of the teams to subsequently adopt these practices, and went on to win the World Series in 2004 – their first in eighty-six years – and repeated the feat in 2007. Given the global reach of the sport's scouting networks and the rapidly increasing volume of statistical analysis the game produces, it stands to reason that such methods could be adopted in football.

The dominant personality in Liverpool's six-man committee is Mike Gordon, a well-respected US stockbroker who is, according to John Henry, 'by far FSG America's most knowledgeable person with regard to soccer'. The other members include the head coach and the club's chief executive.

Footballers, though, are not stocks, and the nature of football makes it far more difficult to isolate the objective statistical value of one player than in baseball. A defender might have the highest pass completion rate on a team, but he might only be passing the ball 18 metres sideways all the time. The committee appears to have created a confusing culture. Former Liverpool coach Brendan Rodgers – one of the four head coaches who have sat on but ultimately worked under the committee – suggests that the confusion lies in the lack of clarity between whether a 'business model' or a 'winning model' is the dominant approach.

He defines the difference. A business model 'is about buying a player, developing and improving them and then selling them on for a much greater fee.' Mario Balotelli, the enigmatic Italian centre forward, is an example of this approach. 'They were thinking this is a fifty million player we could maybe get for sixteen million,' Rodgers said of his signing. Balotelli, a player once deemed 'uncoachable' by José Mourinho, was loaned out within twelve troubled months and eventually given away for free.

Rodgers suggests that a winning model would mean 'trying to get the best possible players that you can, at whatever age they are, it doesn't matter.'[14]

Engineering – Borussia Dortmund

In September 1995, Mainz 05 were bottom of the German 2. Bundesliga table, the country's second tier, with one point and no goals from their first eight games, when they appointed as their manager Wolfgang Frank, a former striker nicknamed 'Floh', Flea, because of his slender frame and great prowess in the air. His tactics, however, were strictly heavyweight. 'We had a decent group of players but we were basically dead as a team,' remembers Mainz 05's solid, unremarkable centre-back, who would eventually take over from Frank as manager. His name was Jürgen Klopp.

Frank won the team's trust by telling them they would be able to beat any opposition with his strategy, a certain lack of individual quality notwithstanding. 'He had us, instantly,' said Klopp. Switching to the new system, educating players where they needed to position themselves at any given moment, took 150 dedicated practice sessions. Frank had his players standing outside, for hours on end, walking round slowly in unison in intricate patterns between poles stuck in the ground. 'In Germany, training was supposed to be fun, all-action: shooting, crosses, piggy-in-the-middle,' Klopp recalls. 'By contrast, the effort that had to go into Frank's system was enormous.'[15]

With the new strategy in place, Mainz picked up thirty-two points in the second half of the season, more than any other team in the top two divisions, to finish in mid-table. 'Until Frank's arrival, we had basically been in the jungle – chasing after everything with a shirt on,' Klopp said. 'He made our results independent of our talent, to an extent. Up until then, we thought that, as the worst team, we would lose. A sense of parity could be achieved by better organization.'[16]

Slowly, silently, this methodical, engineering culture took hold. Klopp honed the approach in his first coaching role at Mainz 05, combining cutting-edge match plans ('with better tactics, you can beat a better team') and his ability to get players to run. It is for his work at Borussia Dortmund, however, that his approach is most feted. In the space of three years, he had taken the Black and Yellows from mid-table mediocrity to the seventh championship in the club's history.

Propelled by limitless energy and a desire to work for each other, Klopp's Dortmund were by far the best and perhaps the only truly German club team of 2010–11: a band of brothers comprised of humble, super-fit players well versed in the theory of the game, prepared to leave their egos outside the dressing room.

'This team is emblematic of a paradigm shift in German football,' wrote *Der Spiegel*. 'Young professionals, technically and tactically well educated, aware of their own strengths but never arrogant.'

'Heavy metal football' is the more prosaic term preferred by Klopp to describe the effects of the culture he creates. One where the opposition were killed by a thousand cuts and where the creation of goal-scoring opportunities was not the result of isolated moments of genius by one or two outstanding players but the logical, mathematically calculated consequence of relentless, frenetic work. A simple example of this approach is his use of still photos rather than match footage to illustrate certain points, such as how great teams celebrate every goal as though it were their first.

'When three players chase in a swarm, it can look chaotic. But this is chaos of a controlled and highly creative kind,' approved Helmut Groß, a structural engineer turned football coach, in *FAZ*.

Commitment – FC Barcelona

There is much discussion as to whether Pep Guardiola's Barcelona is the best football team of all time. However entertaining the debate, it is impossible to resolve conclusively. What we can definitively say is that they marked a watershed in the evolution of the game. There is a before and an after with this team.

In the four years between 2008 and 2012, they redefined the way the game is played and caused the entire football world – from coaches of children's teams to the technical staff of the biggest clubs on the planet – to return to the drawing board and reconsider their most basic premises. Guardiola's team proved that the qualities a footballer most requires to prosper are technical skill and intelligence on the ball. Size doesn't matter; neither does the position of each player on the pitch. Equally significant is the idea that culture, the daily working environment, is a competitive advantage.

It was this final quality that Soriano and Begiristain had sought and then recognized in Guardiola – the promise to stay true to a culture that resided at the very heart of the club. 'It is a much quieter quality than the other, more obvious traits you look for in a leader,' explained Begiristain, 'but it is essential.'[17]

The seeds were sown by one of the sport's great philosophers, Johan Cruyff, who shaped the culture of Barcelona, first as a player and then as manager. As we will see, he identified the key tenets that would bring success to the Catalan club and implemented the structures to ensure they were able to be consistently applied. When Cruyff took over the team's coaching reins in 1988, his first season at the helm was a disaster. Had it not been for his legendary name, and if he had not believed so stubbornly in his own abilities, Barcelona would have sacked him.

Cruyff convinced the president of the club, Josep Lluís Núñez, to forget about the short term and think strategically, allowing time for the Dutch concept of total football – which had captivated the world fifteen years previously during the 1974 World Cup – to permeate every layer of the club. Cruyff wanted his football to be uplifting. He saw winning and beauty as inseparable. When once asked whether he'd be willing to play with a mainly defensive system to win the league, he replied in the negative. 'Imagine having to sit through a season of ugly football – and you might not even win the title!' he mused. 'The whole season would then have been wasted.' This was the path to adhere to, he would argue – this was the cause for which it was worth fighting. It would, he discovered, be easier to dictate the cultural shift from the position of the dugout rather than the pitch.

The Cruyff blueprint became embedded within the club's DNA. The seductiveness of the Cruyff playing style captivated the fans, the Catalan press and the youth players, none more so than the most intelligent and receptive of them all, Pep Guardiola, who rose to the first team captaincy under Cruyff, where he remained after the Dutchman departed in 1996, his trophy haul in double figures. Two Dutch coaches, Louis van Gaal and Frank Rijkaard, perpetuated the club ethos, with varying success. It is significant that when the fidelity to the blueprint wavered, so did the quality of performance and results.

When Guardiola, Cruyff's protégé, ascended to the first team bench in 2008, it coincided with the maturing of a group of players who had been immersed in the in-house philosophy from early adolescence, among them Xavi Hernández, Víctor Valdés, Gerard Piqué, Andrés Iniesta and Lionel Messi. As we will see, Cruyff's other great cultural legacy was La Masia – the renovated farmhouse where players learnt the cultural doctrines from the very moment they arrived at the club, sometimes as young as eleven or twelve years old. What they had been taught, as their chief article of faith, was that the ball was sovereign; possession the primary – practically the only – priority.

Guardiola demanded his players pass the ball low and short, even backwards – an almost scandalous idea at the club at the time – even in defensive extremis, because the cardinal sin is to play a random long ball, to reduce football to an anarchic game of chance. He demands total commitment to the cause. It is a dream that Cruyff had first realized but that faded after his departure, before Guardiola transformed it back into hard, trophy-winning reality.

What Barcelona have done is to invent a new language, or what Cesc Fàbregas has described as the Guardiola 'software'. Even now, some six years since Guardiola left the club, his legacy remains. It is hard to assimilate for those who have not been raised from an early age at the club's La Masia academy. Some, such as Eric Abidal and Javier Mascherano, managed to pick it up, but it is a measure of how tough the challenge is that two superstars such as Thierry Henry and Zlatan Ibrahimović failed to adapt, each ending up as an awkward misfit, only fitfully effective, in the Camp Nou ballet.

This new football idiom was what Sir Alex Ferguson, the Manchester United manager, initially failed to identify after his side's loss to Barcelona in the 2009 Champions League final. Ferguson was convinced his team had lost because they had played below par. When Barcelona inflicted a similarly humbling experience on England's finest at Wembley two years later, Ferguson was forced to proffer his sword in surrender. He understood that he had not just duelled with the best club team in the world but one that also represented a changing of the guard in the history of the sport. Sir Bobby Charlton, England's most revered player, said in an interview with the Spanish sports daily *AS* that 'every club in football should learn to play the Barcelona way'.[18]

Barça imprinted an instantly identifiable picture on football's global consciousness. Physicality and athleticism have bowed to refinement and technique; the warrior spirit remains but has been leavened by intelligence and the killer grace of the matador. It does not matter if a player is tall or short, wide or thin, so long as he knows how to caress the ball. The Barcelona team of Pep Guardiola's reign – the radical extremist of the Cruyff school of philosophy – feeds the dreams of every child who plays football and intrigues those of us who want to understand how we can adapt these lessons to our own, non-footballing, organizations.

In *The Barcelona Way*, we will look at how these individual threads, when woven together, can create the rich fabric of a commitment culture within your own world.

INTRODUCING A COMMITMENT CULTURE: BARCA

Please don't mistake my use of a football club as merely an extended metaphor for running business or other non-sporting organizations. This book shows how the culture which FC Barcelona established is a model, not simply a metaphor, for contemporary business. As such, it provides unique insights into the crucial issues confronting the modern corporate environment.

I will draw from the information I have soaked up in interviews with the leading figures behind this approach, as well as my own academic and working life in leading sports and business institutions, to illustrate how FC Barcelona – and now you – can learn to unlock the DNA of a winning culture.

Not only does football replicate the challenges of business, it intensifies and then accelerates the process by compressing the timescale and sharpening the focus. Mostly, this is a result of the relentless nature of media attention the sport attracts. As Kevin Keegan, the former England manager, once observed, 'If you are Sir Alex Ferguson, there are 70,000 people coming into your business for two hours on a Saturday afternoon and every week they publish a league table – businesses only have theirs published twice a year.'[1]

What football provides is a pure model of corporate management where only the very best practice succeeds. It is, therefore, easier to identify and analyse that best practice. In the unique case of FC Barcelona, where their dominance has been sustained for much longer than the customary four-year cycle of an elite team, lying at the very heart of their success is how they deal with people and the care and attention given to the environment in which those people are nurtured: practices which are of equal relevance to all organizations trying to channel the activities of their talented individuals for the corporate good.

Furthermore, the visibility of this success is total. We cannot easily dissect the behaviour of a leading CEO in real time, because so much remains so secret for so long. By contrast, in football virtually everything is on view; what is not on show is soon revealed by the near-permanent media attention.

My intention is that this book will appeal to people from many different camps. On one level, it is simply a book for all sports leaders – both serving and aspiring. On another, the book is written unashamedly for the sports fan: those who are fascinated by the challenge and want to know how and why Barcelona – and other elite sporting institutions – do what they do. It brings together insights from the collective wisdom of the very best in their profession. Finally, it is written for leaders in all fields of endeavour and in any context where individuals lead other individuals in pursuit of meaning and success.

While there is no 'formula' for such a winning culture – I don't want to overstate the case – in my analysis of the commitment model which lies at the heart of Barcelona's cultural DNA, I have begun to see the same themes, the same principles, reflected in a wide range of other – both sporting and non-sporting – successful commitment environments. Most importantly, these same principles can also be applied to develop your own organization's winning culture.

These five overarching principles – divided into sections – are:

Big Picture

Arc of Change

Repetition

Cultural Architects

Authentic Leadership

An astute observer will note that these can be compacted into the acronym **BARCA**. This is sheer coincidence, of course. Here's our BARCA checklist for creating a winning culture.

1. Big Picture

When Ernest Shackleton was recruiting for his ill-fated 1915 Antarctic expedition, he placed an advert in *The Times* newspaper:

> Men wanted for hazardous journey. Small wages. Bitter cold. Long hours of complete darkness. Constant danger. Safe return doubtful. Honour and recognition in the event of success.

Despite the grim conditions promised, he was deluged by applicants who wished to join him.

Outlining a vision – a big picture – gives a clear direction and destination which everyone can move towards. It's the equivalent of the North Star which the captain of a ship uses to navigate.[2]

FC Barcelona have long been a bastion of Catalan identity. The autonomous region of Spain was persecuted during Franco's dictatorship, its language and culture suppressed, but at Camp Nou it was still embraced on the terraces. The motto, '*Més que un club*' ('More than a club') has a resonance which runs deep. Barcelona represents a people, a nation and a way of life.

This demand, to represent more than a football club, is imparted to those responsible for the footballing culture in the simplest possible terms. The job criteria written by the board's representatives demand that staff 'find the balance between playing the most attractive, most spectacular football possible and efficacy.'

This message – applicable to everybody associated with the club from the players through to the coaches and support staff – creates an understanding that this is a club which is about more than just results: they want to stand for something in the community and among its followers; they want to be a club that entertains as opposed to winning by the bare minimum.

As we have seen, Johan Cruyff built the temple which others have simply, in Guardiola's words, 'maintained'. It was Cruyff who imported and fine-tuned the Dutch philosophy of 'total football' – everybody is comfortable on the ball, everybody attacks and defends as one – and extended it from the pitch to the club's organizational structure.

Cruyff's core message remains the club's today.

In December 1982, Cruyff took a penalty during his second spell with his boyhood team, Ajax Amsterdam, against Helmond Sport. He usually hated penalties and left them to others to dispatch. On this occasion, however, he stepped up and played a little sideways pass for his team mate Jesper Olsen. Olsen drew the startled Helmond goalkeeper before slipping the ball back to Cruyff, who nonchalantly passed the ball into an empty net. It was the first time this daring and innovative manoeuvre had been attempted in elite competition.

In 2016, Lionel Messi and Luis Suárez demonstrated their

adherence to the Cruyff vision of football in Barcelona's 6–1 victory over Celta Vigo. When awarded a penalty, Messi stepped up and slipped the ball sideways for Suárez to run in and score.

It was a memorable moment: the greatest of contemporary players were acknowledging their debt to Cruyff and his continued legacy.

Cruyff, weeks before his death, let it be known he'd loved it.

2. Arc of Change: Cultural Signposts

What does successful change look like?

Many of us grow up believing that we bring about change through determination, that continually improving our performance will lead us in a straight line to our desired outcome.

It's a myth.

Harvard professor Rosabeth Moss Kanter has highlighted how our memories help us recall inspiring beginnings and happy endings, but it is the part in-between we often fail to appreciate – where the hard work kicks in and the tough challenges emerge. This is the Arc of Change. In 1969, Dr Martin Luther King, Jr. vividly described the challenges of leading and navigating people across the arc of change in his book, *Where Do We Go From Here: Chaos or Community?* He wrote:

> You must always realize that the line of progress is never a straight line. It always has its dips and curves, its meandering points. The hopeful thing is to keep moving.[3]

In order to keep moving and lead people along this arc, you need to understand all of the stages you will encounter. Like any story, the arc of change has an identifiable pattern to it. There are five stages: **Dream**, **Leap**, **Fight**, **Climb** and **Arrive**.

Understanding these stages helps create galvanizing moments and signposts the pathway while sustaining the energy and enthusiasm of the group. As we will see, when following and learning from Barcelona and Guardiola's own journey across the Arc of Change, the importance of these cultural signposts is no less pronounced. Progression along the Arc was done mainly through speeches, stories, ceremonies and symbols, all of which hold great meaning.

La Masia, a common Catalan word meaning country house or farm, is one of these central symbols and a pillar on which the success of the modern FC Barcelona is built. It is the home of the finest and most successful football academy in the world. Once again, Johan Cruyff was responsible for the construction of La Masia. When he first left the club – as a player – in 1978, he told the Barcelona president that they needed an academy that was able to produce its own talent in order to compete with Real Madrid and other European rivals. When he returned – as a coach – ten years later, Cruyff was the first man to give the products of La Masia the chance to play in the club's first team. In this first wave of home-grown talent, Josep Guardiola would graduate with honours.

In 2010, La Masia achieved a footballing first. One of the academy's alumni – Lionel Messi, who had joined them from Newell's Old Boys in Argentina at the age of thirteen – won the Ballon d'Or. But that year the two runners-up, Xavi Hernández and Andrés Iniesta, were fellow graduates. Two years later, then Barcelona head coach, Tito Vilanova, another graduate, fielded an entire first eleven comprised of players who had been reared within the footballing hothouse.

When navigating the Arc of Change, we will look at how Barcelona's symbols, speeches, stories and ceremonies were used to signpost the stages of the cultural journey – from the blueprint through to completion – which they travelled.

3. Recurring Systems and Processes

When Sir Alf Ramsey, England's World Cup-winning manager, was once asked about the secret of great coaching and how he was able to get his players to fully understand the vision of how he wanted the game to be played, he offered the reply:

> *Constant repetition gets the message home.*
> *Constant repetition gets the message home.*
> *Constant repetition gets the message home.*
> *Constant repetition gets the message home.*
> *Constant repetition gets the message home.*
> *Constant repetition gets the message home.*[4]

Stelios Haji-Ioannou, the founder of the discount airline EasyJet, would understand the importance of such relentless repetition. In the early days of the company, he would begin his meetings by asking his staff to stand behind their chairs. He then asked each of them to tell him whether the chair before them was empty or not. The obvious reply, 'of course it is empty', would be met by a reminder that the company's mission was offering cheap flights, and therefore depended on planes being full. Their mission meant focusing their efforts on 'putting bums on seats'.

Within the cultural DNA of FC Barcelona, the most import-ant daily activities, repeatedly enforced, soon become standard practice. Players are expected to arrive an hour before they are due to train. 'Punctuality, as a representation of being mentally prepared, is strictly enforced,' recounts Guardiola's assistant, Manuel Estiarte.

In footballing terms, it is the club's relentless application of the rondo – a demanding, quick-fire passing game of piggy-in-the-middle – which directly translates the demands of the club's Big Picture into everyday habits and routine. It is the main feature of all training sessions, obliging players to learn how to pass, pass and pass again under pressure.

Xavi, until recently the most decorated Spanish player in history, offers this explanation:

> It's all about rondos. Rondo, rondo, rondo. Every. Single. Day. It's the best exercise there is. You learn responsibility and not to lose the ball. If you lose the ball, you go in the middle. Pum-pum-pum-pum, always one touch. If you go in the middle, it's humiliating, the rest applaud and laugh at you.[5]

For this team, rondo isn't a mere drill. It's more like their identity.

4. Cultural Architects and Organizational Heroes

'All animals are equal, but some animals are more equal than others.'

When George Orwell wrote this statement, he was referring sardonically to the post-revolutionary society in his novel *Animal Farm*, not to elite sport. But there is another, more constructive, way of reading Orwell's dictum, one that highlights an important aspect of shaping a winning culture.

In any culture, every individual brings a unique set of attributes to the group and there will be some who will possess more social influence than others. Willie Railo, the late Norwegian psychologist, called these people 'cultural architects'. These are the players who the rest of the team respect; this respect enables them to set the attitudinal and behavioural 'norms' for the rest of the group. While Orwell was satirizing the Soviet elite's hypocrisy in preaching complete equality while reserving privilege to the chosen few – much like the 'Star model' identified earlier – in a commitment culture, this social influence is harnessed for the betterment of any group, or in our case, sports team.

'Cultural architects are people who are able to change the mindset of others,' Railo said. 'They are able to break barriers, they have visions. They are self-confident and able to transfer self-confidence to other players. At least three, and not more than five, such figures in a squad are needed by a coach to extend the "shared mental model" that a team needs for success.'[6]

Alex Ferguson, not yet a 'Sir', anointed Eric Cantona as his cultural architect at Manchester United in the early 1990s. When Cantona arrived at United, he started staying behind after morning training to take extra practice. The group of younger players coming through – Scholes, Beckham, Butt and the Nevilles – saw the talismanic leader doing extra training and thought, *If it's good enough for the best player in the club then it's good enough for us.* This attitude endured throughout the silver-plated decade in which they defined English football.

At Barcelona, the promotion of Xavi, Iniesta, Puyol, Valdés and Piqué from the club's own youth system is a continuation of the tradition started by Johan Cruyff and of which Guardiola and his successors – Tito Vilanova, Gerardo Martino, Luis Enrique and Ernesto Valverde – were all direct beneficiaries. The importance of cultural architects – and their positive influence on their teammates through the promotion of the required behaviours and attitudes – caused Gary Neville to reflect on the associated cultural impact: 'When seven of the Barcelona players came through the ranks of their club, understanding what it means to be a part of it, this helps make them an unstoppable force.'

5. Authentic Leadership

A good drummer will tell you it's knowing when not to hit the drum that marks out good drummers from the average; the silent spaces between the action are, in fact, a part of the action, in the same way that utilizing negative space is a key part of good design. Similarly, a good leader knows that a *to don't* list is as important for success as a *to do* list. What you don't do defines you – and the culture – as much as what you do.

Sir Richard Branson, the British entrepreneur, says that authentic leadership is all about where you make your stand. 'The best leaders make it clear what they stand for and constantly reinforce that with what they do and what they choose not to do.'

When Pep Guardiola was first unveiled as head coach, he was quizzed on the future of his three star – and most richly rewarded – players, men who had briefly scaled the footballing heights but had been unable to sustain such a dazzling trajectory thereafter.

He appeared to have no compunction in answering questions about Ronaldinho, Deco and Samuel Eto'o with a tone which matched the funereal black suit and tie he wore to his first press conference:

> These three are not in my mind for the future; in fact, we will go on without them. My view is that it's all about performance and what players can give to my squad. What I will not tolerate is a lack of effort to rebuild the success of the team. I want the talented, inspired players to understand that, individually, they are worth much less than when they invoke team values.

Within weeks, Ronaldinho and Deco – and within a year,

Eto'o – were all shipped out at a considerable financial loss. The positive cultural impact, however, was immense.

A willingness to work hard, with humility, diligence and attention to detail, were the team values Guardiola was keen to establish. When Zlatan Ibrahimović, the mercurial Swedish striker, joined the club as its most expensive signing in 2009, Guardiola's first words were, 'Here at Barça, we keep our feet on the ground.' He instructed the fast car-loving Swede, 'We don't turn up to training in Ferraris and Porsches. We come here to work.'

Ibrahimović, as we will see, is a rare but powerful example of Guardiola failing to appreciate the importance of cultural fit. The Swede struggled to adapt to the culture and left after one, unhappy year. He recalls his teammates as 'looking like school boys' eager to please their demanding leader. 'The best footballers in the world stood there with their heads bowed, and I didn't understand it. It was ridiculous,' he reflected.[7]

This is a book to help you understand how the approach adopted by the leaders of FC Barcelona to creating a sustainable winning culture can be adapted for your own world. Usually these topics are treated separately – there is 'change management' advice for businesses, 'self-help' advice for individuals and 'change the world' advice for activists. That is a shame, because all cultural change has something in common: for anything to change, someone has to start acting differently.

There is no obligation for you to agree with or do everything suggested in this book. While I want you to finish the book being able to apply the ideas directly to your own culture for immediate effect, I also want to give you more than just a set of prescriptions. I want to make you think.

BEFORE COMMITMENT:
THE POWER OF CHOICE

Fuentealbilla is a village of La Mancha, deep in Don Quixote country. It has a population of just 1,864. In 1996, twelve-year-old Andrés Iniesta left there for Barcelona. When he first arrived, the diminutive boy cut a sorry sight. 'He was pale, tiny and sad,' recounts José Bermudez, one of his classmates. 'The canal that runs through my village is not enough to hold the tears my grandson cried,' lamented Andrés Lujan, his maternal grandfather. Young Iniesta wanted to turn straight around again. 'I had a feeling of abandonment, of loss, as if I had pulled something from inside, deep inside of me,' the player, who would surpass his teammate Xavi to become Spain's most decorated ever, explains.[1]

He admits that when his parents came to visit he wouldn't just sleep in the same hotel room as them, he would sleep in the same bed. The rest of the time he slept in La Masia, the stone-built, Catalan-style farmhouse that stands alongside the Camp Nou, looking out the window and wondering.

'Those days were the worst of my life,' he says. 'You're five hundred kilometres away from home, you're without your family. You're from a small place where you can walk everywhere and the change is huge. There were lots of nights I thought: *I want to go home*. Very hard moments. I'd think I was never going to make it. But you have to be strong.

'I have to fight. I've come this far, there's no going back.'[2]

These words contain the key to understanding why a twelve-year-old boy would willingly agree to leave the safe cocoon of family life and, equally, how to begin to create a winning culture: give people a choice which allows them to exert control.

The choices that are most powerful in generating motivation are decisions that do two things: they convince us that we are in control and they endow our actions with a sense of purpose – a larger meaning. Such control is established when we develop a mental habit of transforming decisions into meaningful choices; when we assert that we have authority over our lives.

Self-help books and leadership manuals often portray this kind of drive as a static feature of our personalities or the outcome of a neurological calculus in which we subconsciously weigh up efforts versus rewards. But we now know that motivation is more complicated than that. It is more like a skill, akin to reading and writing, which can be learned and honed.

Scientists have found that people can get better at self-motivation if they practise the right way. The trick, researchers say, is to feel like we have our own answer to the most fundamental question: why?

'The need for control is a biological imperative,' a group of Columbia University psychologists wrote in the journal *Trends in Cognitive Sciences* in 2010.[3] When people believe they are in control of their decisions, they tend to work harder and push themselves more. They are, on average, more confident and overcome setbacks faster. This instinct for control is so central to how our brains develop that infants, once they learn to feed themselves, will resist adults' attempts at control even if submission is more likely to get food in their mouths.

One way to prove this sense of control to ourselves is by making decisions. 'Each choice – no matter how small –

reinforces the perception of control and self-efficacy,' the Columbia researchers wrote. 'I wanted to be at Barcelona and as bad as it got,' remembers Iniesta, 'there was no way I wanted to go home.' Even if making a decision delivers no benefit, people still want the freedom to choose: 'Animals and humans demonstrate a preference for choice over non-choice, even when that choice confers no additional reward,' researcher Mauricio Delgado noted in the journal *Psychological Science* in 2011.

'You know when you're stuck in traffic on the freeway and you see an exit approaching, and you want to take it even though you know it'll probably take longer to get home?' said Delgado. 'That's our brains getting excited by the possibility of taking control. You won't get home any faster but it feels better because you feel like you're in charge.'[4]

'If there's one characteristic all Barça players have it's precisely that,' Iniesta says. 'They all have made a choice, a commitment. It might look easy to reach the top and stay there, to play for your country and win things, but it isn't. All players that have achieved those things have that: the big ones, the small ones, the good-looking ones, the ugly ones, the nice ones, the not so nice ones . . . they all have that will to succeed.'[5]

Simon Sinek, the author of *Start With Why*, argues that, because of the limbic system – a nerve centre buried deep within the pre-linguistic core of our brain – the way we feel about something is more important than what we think about it. 'What I'm interested in,' says Sinek, 'is what gets people up every single day to do something, maybe pay a premium, maybe suffer inconvenience, because they are driven by something else. What is that thing? What I've learned is it's that question, "why?" It has a biological imperative, it drives us, it inspires us.'[6]

Before we can begin to look at the requirements of creating

a winning culture, we also have to be able to answer this same question: why do you want to?

EXERCISE: WHAT'S YOUR LEVEL OF COMMITMENT?

You want to create a high-performing culture? Then commit.

Many successful entrepreneurs I have worked with in business do not, contrary to popular belief, have a headful of ideas, nor are they creative geniuses. They have just one idea which they fully commit to. They have a level of focus and a conviction that drive them on until their endeavour bears fruit. You can't guarantee success with commitment. But you can be sure of giving yourself the best chance.

Commitment can be strangely liberating. Once we commit, we fully focus on what we are trying to achieve. It frees us up from distractions.

Think about all the roles you play in your life: parent, partner, sibling, colleague, mentor, friend. Our problem is, we mix them all up. We're playing with our children while on the phone dealing with a work issue; we are listening to our partner while writing an email to a friend. When we commit to one of those roles at any given time, we are free to focus – to devote ourselves to that particular role at that moment. Distractions are like a fruit machine in a bar – the ringing bells and flashing lights that catch the corner of your eye and turn your attention.

Try holding your hands wide around your eyes, as if you were holding a pair of binoculars, and focusing on something ten feet away and about the size of a ten-pence piece. Usually, in less than a minute, you'll notice other things in the peripheral areas: someone or something moving or appearing to do so. If you start to bring your hands in until you are looking with just one eye, as if holding a telescope, you'll find it easier to focus on the same spot for longer. The narrowing of focus holds your attention.

Before we begin anything – reading this book, creating a winning culture, starting your daily routine – we must understand that there are three essential levels of commitment.

Level 1: You show up. You do the job exactly as you're told to do it; nothing more, nothing less. You get a little better.

Level 2: You show up. You do the job, and you target certain tasks that'll help you towards your goal. You push yourself, think about the detail of what you are doing. You get a lot better.

Level 3: You show up, having thought about how today's activity fits into the larger goal you are working towards. You work *very* hard, pushing yourself into the discomfort zone over and over, with full commitment. Later, you reflect and analyse your performance with a cool, objective eye. You get a *lot* better, creating what Vern Gambetta, a well-known coach and athletic consultant, calls 'the quantum leap'.[7]

One reason I like this concept is that it takes us into the more targeted idea of *deliberate choice* and *commitment* – deciding and measuring the total amount of time and energy put into the process of getting better or, in this case, understanding how to create a winning culture.

I also like it because it embraces the idea that some of the most vital work happens away from the workplace, in the time we use to reflect, strategize, plan and figure out honest answers to those three simple but immensely difficult questions we face every day: where are we right now? Where do we want to be tomorrow? Why do we want to get there?

I use this exercise with elite sports teams, who have embraced it by regularly asking athletes to rate which level they were aiming for before the session and to afterwards assess which level they reached – and why.

It is a great way of forcing them to make clear, considered choices about their own approach, and also facilitates constructive conversations between athlete and coaches. It emphasizes the control they have over their performance – so beloved by the human brain – as well as what they can't control, and it does so far more effectively than a one-sided critique from a coach.

Before reading any further, ask yourself: what is your own level of commitment?

1. BIG PICTURE

Més que un club
(More than a club)

Imagine you were building a new house. In the beginning, an architect creates a blueprint for your home, and then the construction stage begins. At each stage of this process, you can feel pretty confident that by following the plans carefully, you'll eventually have a home that realizes the architect's original vision.

Throughout this book, we will look at how to get a team of people to psychologically commit to making this vision of a commitment culture – the Big Picture – become reality.

There are four factors in creating this culture:

1. **Imagination** is where you sell a vision of what you are trying to achieve and why. By capturing people's imaginations with 'what might be', you can obtain an emotional commitment.

2. **Illustration** is the part where you show people how you're going to do it. This is all about strategy and tactics. This is where you demonstrate that there is a method and approach geared towards achieving the goals you've stated.

3. **Participation** is allowing people to contribute. This isn't necessarily about being democratic; more about consultation and co-authorship. Encouraging people to participate in the plan and tactics is a great way to get

such buy-in. Having ideas align is key to gaining support and understanding.

4. **Integration** is about making the vision a reality and ensuring that your way of doing things is embedded. This is as much a cultural shift as it is an operational one; establishing a way of doing things is directly reflective of the type of environment you wish to create.

We'll spend this section on steps one and two – Imagination and Illustration – and the rest of the book on steps three and four.

1.i   THE POWER OF ASKING 'WHY?'

The emotional glue of any culture – be it religion, nation or team – is its sense of identity and purpose. What we as human beings identify with most closely are the things that we recognize as being important to ourselves – specifically to our deepest values. And this kind of personal significance has the emotional power to shape behaviour.

This fusion of personal meaning to public purpose is a concept that all great teams focus on – almost to the point of obsession. Personal meaning is the way we connect to a wider team purpose. After all, if our values and beliefs are aligned with those of the organization, then it stands to reason that we will work harder towards its success. If we don't, our individual motivation and purpose will suffer, and by extension so will the organization.

Good leaders understand this idea and work hard to create a sense of connection, collaboration and communion within their organization. Purpose relates to an overarching goal – something beyond the daily practicalities of the organization. This larger purpose drives an individual's intrinsic motivation, and establishes both a sense of belonging and a reason to make sacrifices to achieve the goals of the individual and the organization.

So big is the concept of 'identity' in organizational culture that brand consultancies, advertising agencies and engagement specialists all vie for the opportunity to define and deliver it. It takes a significant investment of time and thought to get this right, but clarifying the 'Big Picture' for your own organization brings its own reward: everything else – business strategy, vision, values and purpose – flows from it. When this is merged with corporate identity, design, advertising and communications, it can deliver powerful shifts of mindset and behaviours within teams and organizations.

The neuroscientist Wolf Singer reported an interesting finding in the mid-1990s: he had identified a particular pattern of brain waves whose purpose appeared to be geared towards connecting different activities within the mind to create a sense of coherence. Specifically, he found that when people perceived something as meaningful, clumps of neurons in disparate parts of the brain mysteriously engaged in synchronized firing. These high-level oscillations were, for example, seen when a meaningful word was sounded out to people but was absent when something meaningless was said. It seems that these waves have the key function of making the flood of data hitting our brains meaningful. Interestingly, when people arrive at new insights, there is a jump in the frequency of these 'mean ing waves'. This form of brain activity is very different from the serial firing of neurons associated with other mental activities. Our brains, therefore, are constantly searching for a sense of meaning – of coherence – in our everyday activities.[1]

Around the same time, the neurologist V. S. Ramachandran found that when people were asked to think of areas of their life that were meaningful to them, a particular part of the temporal lobes in their brain was activated. In addition, he established that when this area of the brain is activated, people experience a strong sense of connection and unity with others.[2]

For years, clinicians have known that patients suffering from temporal lobe epilepsy sometimes experienced an overwhelming sense of spirituality and, at times, grandiose ideas about themselves and their goals – but the new research identified that a deep sense of meaning, purpose and unity could be produced in just about anyone when this particular area was stimulated. In our case, this effect can be achieved through infusing daily routines and activities with a clear link towards contributing to the Big Picture destination.

Spend ten to fifteen seconds, no more, studying the letters below. Then close the book, pull out a sheet of paper, and write down as many letters as you can remember.

JFKFBINATOUPSNASAVAT

If you're like most people, you probably remembered about seven to ten letters. That's not much information.

Now try the exercise again. There's a twist this time. I haven't changed the letters or the sequence. All I have done is change the way the letters are grouped. Once again, study the letters for ten to fifteen seconds, then close the book and test your recall.

JFK   FBI   NATO   UPS   NASA   VAT

Chances are you did much better this time around. Suddenly the letters meant something, which made them easier to remember. In round one, your brain was working hard to remember raw data. In round two, you could see the bigger picture: John F. Kennedy, the FBI, the North Atlantic Treaty Organization, United Parcel Services, National Aeronautics and Space Administration and Value Added Tax. Grouped like this, the letters become familiar acronyms.

The human brain, it seems, is designed to both work hard to produce a sense of coherence and meaning and then to respond positively to this sense when it arises. This is why investing time in painting the Big Picture is so essential to the creation of a high-performing culture.

The emerging consensus is that, from an evolutionary point of view, the drive for contextualisation and coherence is an essential tool for dealing with a complex and bewildering environment. Seeking meaning through a positive feeling of purpose also creates a sense of dissatisfaction with the status quo, which in turn leads us to break new ground and make something more of ourselves and the world.

None of this would have surprised the famed psychoanalyst, Viktor Frankl, who wrote more than sixty years ago that it is people's search for meaning – not pleasure, power, status or wealth – that defines them as human beings. By this, Frankl means that people are, in a fundamental sense, motivated to make sense of their lives and find a purpose that goes beyond thinking about their own basic needs. People want to find the answers to the questions 'Why?' and 'What for?' Frankl believed that, if they could answer these questions, individuals could bear many of the challenges that life would inevitably throw at them.

Nazi authorities seized the manuscript for Frankl's first book on this topic, *The Doctor and the Soul*, as he was taken to a concentration camp. In the unlikely – and hostile – environment of a concentration camp, Frankl truly learned to test his ideas. He found that even in a situation where some of the most fundamental human needs – for security, shelter and food – were left unsatisfied, it was the creation of meaning which helped people survive. Frankl created personal meaning by giving himself the task of 'administering mental support to the needy'. He encouraged people to focus on the thought that 'for everyone, something or someone is waiting'. Even for those who believed that they would not survive the camp, he endeavoured to create a sense of meaning by asking them to think about how others, who might be waiting for them, would expect them to behave. He also encouraged people to visualize life beyond the camp and to consider what they could learn from the experience and how they could put that to good use.

In his book, published in 1946, he encouraged people to reframe their lives by telling them to 'think less about what to expect from life but rather ask yourself what life expects of you'. Frankl survived the concentration camp and put his learning to good use by creating logo therapy – a technique aimed at overcoming psychological problems through focus on the creation of meaning.

A significant part of Frankl's thinking is that meaning doesn't simply appear as a sudden revelation, but rather as something that people have to continually create and work towards. The creation of meaning is founded on how people think about their activities. Frankl is fond of quoting one of his patients: 'A person who assumes that life consists of stepping from success to success is like a fool who stands next to a building site and shakes his head, because he cannot understand why people dig deep when they set out to build a cathedral.'[3] As we will see, the foundations of the FC Barcelona cathedral are buried deep within their history.

The psychologist Abraham Maslow took up some of Frankl's theories and developed them further. In his seminal paper on the hierarchy of human needs, Maslow argued that there is a certain set of base needs that people need to satisfy, namely sustenance, security and shelter. Beyond these, however, they also strive for companionship and belonging – and, then, ultimately, for self-actualization. It is the satisfaction of these latter needs that Maslow felt generated a sense of true meaning and fulfilment. Self-actualization, for Maslow, occurred when people connected with the unique aspects of themselves and were able to contribute to society in a distinctive way: 'A musician must make music, an artist must paint, a poet must write; if he is to be ultimately at peace with himself, what a man can be, he must be.'[4]

According to Maslow, meaning comes from stretching yourself to be what you can be. It's not about having quiet time or creating the right work–life balance. If you ask people about those times when they have felt best about themselves, they frequently pick situations where they felt most challenged and had to dig deep to find answers. It's also interesting to note that a common feature of many of the Fortune 'best companies to work for' is that they impose cultures where people must stretch themselves.

In *Good to Great*, his study of how great organizations emerge, Jim Collins described this as the 'extra dimension' – a guiding philosophy that consists of core values and core purpose beyond just making money. He believes that, when authentic and rigorously adhered to, a dramatic and compelling purpose is a fundamental driver of the companies that go from good to great.[5] As we will see, the appointment of Pep Guardiola was part of Barcelona's deliberate plan to reconnect with their own sense of purpose, with dramatic results.

This is why conversations about meaning have gone from being side issues to taking centre stage. Here are some examples of the kinds of purpose statements that companies have produced:

GlaxoSmithKline: to improve the quality of human life and enable people to do more, feel better and live longer

Walt Disney: to make people happy

The John Lewis Partnership: the happiness of its members [all staff are shareholders] through worthwhile and satisfying employment

Microsoft: to enable people and business throughout the world to realize their full potential

Google: to organize the world's information, making it universally accessible and useful

FC Barcelona is driven by perhaps the most motivating purpose of them all: they play for Catalonia; they play for freedom.

FC Barcelona – more than just a football club

To understand this purpose, we need to go back to 11 September 1714, a date which marked the end of the siege of Barcelona, when the city fell to King Philip V of Spain. In short, the Catalans had chosen the wrong side in a war of royal succession, but the battle has come to be seen as a central moment for the 'nation' – the point at which 'independence' was lost. At every home game, chants for Catalan independence go up when the clock reaches seventeen minutes and fourteen seconds. The date is still used to mark the National Day of Catalonia, and can be seen as 'celebrating' defeat – a fact that is not lost on many both inside and outside Catalonia. It is seen as somehow symbolic of the Catalan mindset, and as such reinforces the idea of Madrid as the natural enemy.

Philip V abolished Catalonia's political institutions and banned the Catalan language in schools, virtually ending Catalan aspirations until the Renaixença, or cultural renaissance, of the mid-1800s. A Catalan parliament, the mancomunitat, was set up in 1914, but abolished by the dictatorship of General Miguel Primo de Rivera just over ten years later, in 1925.

With Primo de Rivera's fall from power in 1930, the arrival of the Second Republic, Spain's first real democracy, ensured that Catalonia was granted autonomous government. However, the brutal Spanish Civil War between 1936 and 1939, and the subsequent dictatorship of General Francisco Franco, brought those ambitions of autonomy to a sudden end. Franco's Spain was based on centralization and ethnic, cultural and linguistic homogenization, and anyone who dared challenge this – such as the people of Barcelona, who demanded their dialects, cultures and individual identities be officially recognized – was suppressed. Since Franco's death in 1975, Catalonia has re-established significant autonomous powers, but recent polls suggest that over 50 per cent of Catalans still want total independence from Spain.

In October 2017, the Spanish government declared the independence referendum, called by the Catalan government, illegal and national police and civil guard were brought in to dismantle it. The violent images – police in riot gear firing rubber bullets and smashing through the doors of polling stations – travelled around the world. The Catalan government claimed 850 people had been hurt. 'We did what we had to do,' declared the Spanish president Mariano Rajoy. Josep Maria Bartomeu, the club president, decided to play their game against Las Palmas behind closed doors, as a way of making their point. 'Voting is democracy!' the former Barcelona player Carles Puyol said.

FC Barcelona is an extension of the Catalan identity. In many people's minds, this political battle is now played out on the football pitch. The Barcelona defender Gerard Piqué once said that Barcelona versus Real Madrid – perceived to be Franco's favourite team – is Catalonia versus Spain. Joan Laporta, the former president of the club, has no doubts: 'At one level, that's true,' he says. 'It's a sporting confrontation with political connotations. Madrid has always represented Spain and we have always represented Catalonia.'

You won't catch many in Catalonia insisting, as others in Spain do, that sport and politics should not mix. Like it or not, sport and politics do mix, especially here. The symbolism is inescapable and no match is so infused with politics as the *Clásico*, when Real Madrid and Barcelona meet. 'They are the two biggest teams in the world,' says Pichi Alonso, a Barcelona player who later became the Catalan 'national' team coach. 'But Barcelona have a social significance. At Barcelona, you have a sense of complete identification with the club. It means a massive amount for Catalan society.'

'Every time Madrid and Barcelona meet, it becomes a rebellion against the establishment,' says the former Barcelona striker Hristo Stoichkov. When Barcelona face Madrid it is, according to many *cules* – Barcelona's loyal fans – the nation against the state, freedom fighters against General Franco's fascists, the Spanish Civil War's vanquished against its victors; a confrontation represented by the assassination of FC Barcelona's president, Josep Sunyol i Garriga, at the start of the Civil War in 1936. Bobby Robson, who managed the club in the 1996–97 season, once claimed, 'Catalonia is a country and Barcelona is its army.' This is the cause – the 'why' element of the Big Picture – that all FC Barcelona recruits are obliged to sign up to.

The message is delivered early: a children's history of FC Barcelona, complete with a prologue from president Rosell, has an explicitly political narrative. Cartoon illustrations depict armed Spanish civil guards closing the club's stadium, scenes from the Civil War and Franco's police running on to the Camp Nou pitch, truncheons in hand. Powerful images which are intended to embed the sense of purpose deep within the consciousness as early as possible.

Former Barcelona president Joan Gaspart says, 'History has transformed us into something more than just a football club:

Barcelona is the defence of a country, a language – a culture. Barcelona felt persecuted.' Joan Laporta, the man who followed Gaspart into the presidency, describes Barcelona as the unofficial Catalan national team.

From the first moment a young player arrives at the club, the required attitudes are reflected in and maybe even encapsulated by the famous phrase *Més que un club*, more than a club. The Big Picture is there to guide every activity.

The origins of the motto itself may lie with former president Narcís de Carreras, who, in January 1968, was reported to have said, 'Barcelona is something more than a football club, it is spirit that is deep inside us, colours that we love above all else.' The phrase was given greater currency when the advertising executive Javier Coma was asked to come up with a slogan that expressed what Barcelona was for the World Football Day held at Camp Nou in 1974. The full-page ad ran on page two of *La Vanguardia* newspaper, with the headline, written in Castilian, reading, *El Barça es mas que un club*. 'Barça is more than a club: it has an emotional and cultural significance beyond what is normal for a sporting association,' ran the text.

The slogan came to be the embodiment of FC Barcelona, and remains so today. Written in Catalan, *Més que un club* is now a trademark, present in official club literature, from communiqués to team sheets, and splashed across press room backdrops and stadium meeting points. Asked how he would define Barcelona, Laporta sits back on the sofa in his offices and smiles with the satisfaction of a man who is about to deliver the perfect answer: 'Més que un club.'[6]

EXERCISE – WHAT'S YOUR POINT?

Your cause, your Big Picture, may not have the historical or political resonance of FC Barcelona's, but I have established six other types of purpose that can still truly inspire others. Which one do you – and your team – most identify with?

1. Universalization – A purpose based on universalization is essentially a set of aspirations aimed at bringing things enjoyed by some people or a particular section of the world's community to those who have previously missed out. Walmart's purpose – 'To allow ordinary folk to experience the same things as rich people' – is an example of universalization. Similarly, Henry Ford wanted to make the motor car accessible to everyone and Sergy Brin and Larry Page's driver at Google was to enable free access to searching the web; they only thought about making money at a much later stage.

2. Innovation – Being cutting edge, breaking new ground and developing things that no one else has developed can significantly enhance people's motivation. Think of Apple's desire to break the rules of convention and go where no one has gone before, memorably captured in their 'Think Different' campaigns.

3. Global responsibility – A purpose based on global issues has been embraced by some companies to give their activities greater meaning. Environmentalism and the needs of disadvantaged sections of society are two key aspects of this. Both are at the heart of BP's redefinition of itself as 'Beyond Petroleum' and its desire to seek mutual advantage in dealings with producer countries.

4. Excellence – Companies such as Toyota and BMW frame their purpose on a drive for perfection. Being truly brilliant at one's craft propels people at all levels within these companies. Toyota frames its purpose as 'to contribute to society through the practice of manufacturing high-quality goods and services.'[7] This seemingly innocuous statement, when taken to its logical conclusion, leads to a culture which is obsessive about quality and continuous improvement.

5. *Fresh challenge* – A purpose based on being the underdog that brings fresh challenges can be equally compelling. When a company is fighting the forces of arrogance, complacency and anti-competitive tendencies displayed by larger, more established players, it can whet the appetite of all employees. It can even do so if your company wins a seat at the top table.

Indeed, fresh challenge is the key driver at Virgin. David Silverberg captured the essence of Richard Branson and his Virgin group of companies in an article for Digital Journal. Silverberg noted that when Branson compiled evidence that the much larger British Airways was 'smearing' Virgin Airlines, he 'defended his company like he was protecting his child from a pack of bullies.' When he won a settlement, he divided up the windfall among all of his staff. 'Branson,' notes Silverberg, 'has defined Virgin as a David fighting corporate Goliaths.'[8] And he's continued to do so even as they've grown into a Goliath themselves.

6. *Human values* – A purpose based on treating people well has increasing resonance today. This was at the centre of the Body Shop's mission in its early years. Similar in its approach is Starbucks, which not only talks about the primacy of its employees – 'We are a people business serving coffee not a business serving people coffee,' Howard Schultz, the company founder, clarified – but also how well it treats its suppliers. As evidence of its values, Starbucks provides equal benefits to its part-time workers.

The danger of ignoring the Big Picture

It was Charles Handy, the organizational behaviour expert, who reminded us of the need to constantly monitor and refresh the Big Picture before the curve peaks and turns downward. Handy suggests that a flat-on-its-side, S-shaped curve governs most things in life. There is a little wiggle at the start, and then a significant rise to a (rounded) peak, followed by a downward tail-off. The key, Handy suggests, is to refresh the situation just before the absolute peak occurs.[9] Where organizations, including FC Barcelona, are concerned, a failure to do this with the Big Picture usually precedes wider cultural problems.

The two most common symptoms of people losing sight of the Big Picture as the central reference point of their culture tend to manifest themselves as variations on a theme of complacency. The first telltale sign is a growing tendency for self-parody. It was Errol Flynn who said: 'The trouble with Humphrey Bogart is that, after eleven o'clock at night, he thinks he's Humphrey Bogart.' This can happen to every leader: people respond to the things you do, positively and negatively, and gradually you provide them with more of what they want – maybe unconsciously. But it happens. You become what people think you are, rather than what you want to be.

In business, it may be a behavioural mannerism, a style factor or a particular way of going about your work – but what was once intuitive now becomes a formula. It's a mixture of pull and push – the leader provides it, the people react positively and expect more of the same. So more is provided, even if the circumstances are not quite as appropriate, and the cycle is repeated until the distortion becomes apparent. The superficial substitutes for the substantial, and dogma substitutes for analysis.

The Disney organization succumbed to its own version of

this myopia in the years after Walt Disney's death. The company's Big Picture purpose – 'To make people happy' – was always too general a statement to be their true corporate driver. It could more accurately have been described as a 'deep-seated drive to innovate in providing family entertainment'. It was this radical spirit that led Walt Disney to create the first full-length animated films and the innovative attractions of the Disney theme parks. This ceaseless innovation, and willingness to reinvent before the progress curve turned south, gave rise to one of the company's mottos.

After Disney's *The Three Little Pigs* won the 1933 Academy Award for Best Animated Short Film, it continued to break box-office records as the most successful cartoon that had ever been released up to that time. *Variety* magazine declared: 'Three Little Pigs is proving the most unique picture property in history. It's particularly unique because it's a cartoon running less than ten minutes, yet providing box office comparable to a feature, as demonstrated by numerous repeats.' Disney was repeatedly asked whether he would take advantage of the commercial opportunities and make a sequel. 'You can't top pigs with pigs,' was the pithy retort.[10]

Throughout his time on the company's board, Walt's nephew Roy regularly complained that the company's performance problems were due to the original sense of purpose being replaced by a more machine-like drive for commercial success. Repetitive products – effectively attempts to top pigs with pigs – as well as a preoccupation with rewards for key executives seemed to be more of a priority and slowed innovation. 'I just felt, creatively, the company was not going anywhere interesting. It was very stifling,' he said.

A consequence of this was Disney allowing Pixar, the small Californian animation studio, to supersede its role as the innovator in family entertainment in the digital age; an oversight that the company had to correct eventually through an expensive acquisition of the studio in 2006.

As we shall see, FC Barcelona, at various points in their history, have allowed their sense of purpose to drift. These periods, characterized by bitter infighting and backstabbing, often manifest themselves in a decline in the team's perform-ance. The focus of the Big Picture – playing beautiful football for Catalonia – has at times become blurred by a preoccupation with playing the victim to Real Madrid's apparently unfair strength and success, a condition diagnosed by Johan Cruyff as 'Madriditis'.

The second symptom is the search for comfort zones. 'The opposite kind of thinking,' according to Barry Gibbons, the former head of Burger King, 'that moved Michelangelo to paint the Sistine Chapel ceiling instead of the floor.'[11]

Theodore Levitt, a Harvard business professor, investigated comfort zones in a widely quoted and anthologized *Harvard Business Review* article, first published in 1960.[12] He reminds us of the need for an organization's leaders to either refresh or re-invent the sense of purpose just before the absolute peak occurs.

The kerosene industry serves as an example of an industry whose failure to grow was due to a limited market view. In the early twentieth century it was one of the world's most powerful and wealthy industries, yet it became virtually extinct within two decades. The industry leaders believed that they were in a market sector all of their own, and as long as they continued doing what they did, they would remain successful. Instead, if they had taken the time to reflect on their thinking and identify the real Big Picture, they would have recognized that they were, in fact, part of a wider illumination industry (the bulk of kerosene was used to light oil lamps). When cheaper, cleaner methods of illuminating a house emerged – namely gas and electricity – the leaders were not in a position to adapt and evolve, either by marketing their product for new uses or by evolving into power conglomerates.

Levitt explores a number of other industries which struggled because they were too short-term in their visions. The railway companies struggled because they were in the railway industry rather than the transportation business. In the 1930s, Hollywood slumped for a while because it remained convinced that it was in the movie business and not popular entertainment. If they had got it right, the leaders of the railways would have developed cars and planes and Hollywood studios would have bought into television.

After a ten-year run on Broadway, with box-office receipts showing no sign of dropping off, Cameron Mackintosh, the producer of *Cats*, stunned the world of showbusiness by firing more than a third of the cast. He said he'd spotted signs of long-run-itis, the kind of familiarity which means you set complacent performance targets which you know will be accomplished – both by yourself and your team – pretty much by just turning up for work.

Long-run-itis is a charge that could be levelled at the Barcelona team during Frank Rijkaard's last season in charge, 2007–08. The task of representing Catalonia in the right manner – through teamwork, humility and passing football – had begun to be eroded, with personal agendas and destructive behaviours becoming increasingly prevalent. The collective Big Picture had been replaced by individual portraits. As Txiki Begiristain has said, 'Frank admitted that he loved the group of players who had done so much for him. He was reluctant to break up the team.' 'The problem wasn't about talent, but about commitment,' agrees Soriano. 'We had to change the leader.'[13] If leaders lose sight of or simply do not know what the true cause driving an organization is, purpose-drift is common.

EXERCISE – WHY? WHY? WHY? WHY? WHY?

If you can recognize one or both of these symptoms creeping into your own world, this is an exercise used by the ground-breaking design firm IDEO and offers a simple way to connect the purpose – or the why – of any given task to the Big Picture.

Instructions:

1. *Before starting any task, ask the person responsible for it to describe their most important objective in one sentence.*

2. *Whatever the answer, ask the person 'why?' (and really listen to the answer).*

3. *Then in response to that answer, ask 'why?' again (and again, really listen).*

4. *Repeat until you have asked the question, 'why?' at least five times.*

Yes, this activity might annoy everyone in the room but you might also be surprised by what you uncover. As IDEO explains it, 'This exercise forces people to examine and express the underlying reasons for their behaviour and attitudes.'

The original technique was developed and fine-tuned within the Toyota Motor Corporation as a critical component of its problem-solving training. Taiichi Ohno, the architect of this method, describes it in his book *The Toyota Production System: Beyond Large-Scale Production*: 'By repeating "why" five times, the nature of the problem as well as its solution becomes clear.'[14]

The simplicity of this technique can be illustrated with an example from the sports world, where I was helping the executive leaders identify how they could arrest a decline in participation levels.

Problem: Participation in our sport is falling

1. *Why is participation in our sport falling?*
Because there are fewer and fewer young people replacing the older participants leaving the sport through natural attrition.

2. *Why are fewer young people taking up our sport?*
The sport is not seen as being exciting enough.

3. *Why is the sport not seen as being exciting? We have revolutionized our sport's presentation and our elite events to make them more attractive to this target audience.*
Because this generation is not aware of this new and exciting approach to our events and to our sport.

4. *Why are they not aware?*
Because they are not being reached by our communications detailing these new initiatives.

5. *Why are they not being reached by our communications?*
Because younger individuals are not consuming the type of media we're active in. They are engaging far more with newer forms of media and consume their sports news through them.

Solution: We need to divert our resources away from communicating via traditional media channels and invest in social media platforms.

FC Barcelona's Big Picture, lost and rediscovered

As alluded to above, FC Barcelona has lost focus on the Big Picture numerous times in its history, including towards the tail end of the Rijkaard era. But the problem was even more pronounced as the 1987–88 season drew to a close, Barcelona had a lamentable record of winning the Spanish title only twice in the previous twenty-eight years, and Madriditis seemed chronic. 'You cannot be a victim and still remain a winner,' remarked Johan Cruyff. Real Madrid were enjoying a stranglehold on the title, and were set to clinch the third of what would become five in a row. Barça were limping towards a sixth-place finish, despite having been European Cup finalists under Terry Venables just two years previously. The club had parted company with Venables the previous year and the success of his tenure was fast receding into memory. 'A feeling of stagnation had begun to settle on the club,' recalls the journalist Sid Lowe.[15]

The Spanish government was also clamping down on tax evasion, and investigations revealed that the majority of Barcelona's players had agreed contracts that illegally minimized the amount of tax they paid. When the club was ordered to pay back the shortfall, the president Josep Lluís Núñez insisted it should be the players who coughed up, not the club. The players were furious, insisting that it was the club's responsibility, and that they'd entered into the contracts in good faith.

On 28 April 1988, the bulk of the Barça team held a press conference at the Hotel Heredia, calling on President Núñez to resign. It came to be known as 'the mutiny of Heredia'. 'Núñez has deceived us as people and humiliated us as professionals,' the players said in a joint statement.

Two days after the mutiny, the Barça players met Real Madrid in a league match at Camp Nou. Of all the many extraordinary encounters between the two teams, this was probably the most surreal. The home team was loudly whistled as it came out on to the pitch, the membership showing its disgruntlement even when they went ahead. Banners were held up accusing the players of being *peseteros* – money-grubbers. The Real Madrid team was applauded when they entered the field and throughout the first half. Despite Barcelona's eventual victory, the bitterness lingered.

It was in these circumstances that Núñez delivered a masterstroke. He brought the one person who could seem to guarantee the success and spectacle that so many *cules* pined for back to the club: Johan Cruyff.

EXERCISE – THE DEPARTMENT OF WHY

When I first started coaching, one of my tutors introduced me to a magical formula – adapted from the world of journalism – called 'Five Ws and an H'.

'A coach's job,' he said, 'is to explain to athletes who, what, where, when, why and how they are going to succeed.' Five Ws and an H. The talismanic power of those six letters has remained with me since.

Indeed, I've discovered that the notion applies with particular force to the world of business. Just consider the structure of the modern firm. The training and development department takes care of the H – how employees do things. The human resources department, along with some outside recruiters, handles the 'who'. Meanwhile, the CEO, often flanked by a few high-priced consultants, devises the strategy – the 'what'. The 'where' and 'when' of products is the domain of the logistics and supply chain team, the 'where' and 'when' of people the province of the facilities and administrative staff.

And the 'why'? Well, that's handled by, er . . . hmmm.

At most companies, it's Four Ws and an H.

It's a costly mistake to make.

Adam Grant, a researcher at the University of Pennsylvania's Wharton School, led a fascinating research study to prove this very point.[16] Grant visited a call centre at a large American university, where each night employees made phone calls to alumni to raise scholarship funds. With the permission of the university, Grant and his team randomly divided the call centre representatives into three groups. For a few days, before they made calls, people in the first group read brief stories from previous employees about the personal benefits of working in the job – how they developed communication skills and sales know-how that later helped them in their careers.

The second group also read stories before hitting the phones, but theirs were from people who had received scholarships from the funds raised and who described how the money had improved their lives. The aim of these stories was to remind workers of the purpose of their efforts.

The third group was the control group; they read nothing before dialling. Participants were also told not to discuss what they'd read with the recipients of their calls. Then, a month later, Grant measured the performance of the three groups.

The people in the first group, who'd been reminded of the personal benefit of working in a call centre, did no better than those in the control group. Both groups earned about the same number of weekly pledges and raised the same amount of money as they had in the weeks before the experiment.

However, the people in the second group – who took a moment to consider the significance of their work and its effect on others' lives – raised more than twice as much money, in twice as many pledges, as they had in previous weeks, and significantly more than their counterparts in the other two groups.

In other words, reminding employees about that missing W – the 'why' – doubled their performance.

It's more difficult to do something well if we don't know the reasons we're doing it to begin with. People at work are thirsting for context, yearning to know that their efforts contribute to a larger whole. And a powerful way to provide that context is to spend a little less time monitoring who, what, where, when and how – and a little more time considering why.

Here are two simple ways to do that.

First, find out whether the people on your team even have a 'why'. At your next staff meeting, ask this question: 'What's the purpose of this organization?' Then hand everyone a blank index card and ask them to write their answer anonymously. Collect the cards and read them aloud. What do you hear? People needn't recite the same lyrics, but they should be playing the same basic tune. If they're not – if answers range all over the place or people don't have answers at all – you might have a problem, no matter how good you are at the where, when, what and how.

Second, keep the 'why' alive. Once a week, at that staff meeting, spend a few minutes revisiting the question. Talk about the purpose of the week's activities. Discuss your efforts' effect on other people's lives. Remind each other why you're doing what you're doing in the first place.

1.ii   THE WHAT

In *Built to Last*, Jim Collins and Jerry Porras's great study of long-lived business organizations, they coined the memorable term BHAG: a Big, Hairy, Audacious Goal.[1]

Henry Ford's BHAG early in the twentieth century was to 'democratize the automobile'. In 1990, Wal-Mart set the goal of quadrupling in size to be a $125 billion company by the year 2000. Collins and Porras defined a BHAG as 'an audacious ten- to thirty-year goal to progress towards an envisioned future', and their research showed that setting these big, motivating goals was a practice that distinguished lasting companies from less successful ones.

To understand how FC Barcelona used this, I'm interested in goals that are closer at hand – the kinds of things that can initially be tackled in months or years, not decades. Goals which offer a vivid picture of a near-term future that could be possible. This is often the missing piece of the Big Picture jigsaw, because it can be difficult to step back from the detail and assess the direction of travel.

We've seen the importance of knowing why you are pursuing the mission, and we'll discuss the importance of instructing people how to behave; but we haven't answered some very basic questions: where are we headed in the end? What's the destination?

The Bengal tiger illustration

During Disney's drift in focus away from the original sense of purpose which had propelled the company, there were people who fought to keep Walt Disney's original pioneering spirit and mission alive. This was fabulously illustrated by an unusual boardroom meeting in 1995.

Walt Disney created a team of Imagineers to come up with new and exciting creations for his studios and theme parks, and this group are still a much-valued part of the organization today. One of their ideas was Animal Kingdom, which was an improvement on the traditional zoo.

Joe Rohde, a senior creative executive at Disney and an explorer who sports a handlebar moustache and an elongated earlobe, stretched by a string of shells and bones collected from his visits to tribal villages in Africa, Thailand and Nepal, had twice presented to the Disney board a thick, bound proposal for a new park that featured live animals. Twice, the proposal was thrown out by Michael Eisner, the CEO, on the grounds that, 'People don't want to see live animals. Where's the "wow" in that?'

The third time he presented, Rohde didn't bring a thick proposal into the boardroom with him. He brought in, on the end of a chain, a six-foot-long, 400-pound Bengal tiger, to illustrate the allure of live animals. 'Now do you get it?' he asked. They got it. Animal Kingdom, the fourth theme park at Walt Disney World in Orlando, was the result.[2]

Collins and Porras knew that goals should have an emotional component – a BHAG shouldn't just be big and compelling, it should 'hit you in the gut'. When you describe a compelling destination, you're helping to correct one of our mind's great weaknesses – the tendency to get lost in analysis. Our first instinct, when we are faced with a situation that requires us to embrace change, is to offer up data: here's why we need to change. Here are the tables, graphs and charts that prove it. The rational part of our brains loves this; poring over the data, analysing it and poking holes in it – debating the various conclusions that you've drawn. To our rational brain, the analysing phase is often more satisfying than the 'doing' phase, and that's dangerous when effecting real, long-term change.

At FC Barcelona, the Bengal tiger equivalent was a slender Dutchman who personified the Big Picture: a man who clearly understood and represented the club's sense of identity; a charismatic figure who reminded them of what the club could achieve if they remained true to their purpose.

EXERCISE – THE POWER OF DREAMING

We all daydream. We all spend hundreds of hours in a pleasantly dozy state.

Science has now weighed in, leaving no doubt that daydreaming can be a good thing for our brains. The deeper question is, are some daydreams more useful than others when it comes to producing motivation and real-world results? In other words, is there a smarter, more *controlled* way to daydream?

One fascinating answer can be found in *Top Dog*,[3] a book about the science of competition by Po Bronson and Ashley Merryman. Here's the key point: daydreaming works best when you focus *both* on the goal and on the obstacles between you and the goal.

In other words, you shouldn't daydream about the payoff, but about the whole process.

For example, one scientist studied German children who

were about to learn English. Some students fantasized only about the benefits they'd get ('I'll make my father proud!' 'I'll talk to the members of my favourite American band!'), while others fantasized about both the barriers and the benefits. After a semester, the first group averaged a C-grade; the second averaged an A.

Another scientist studied hip-replacement patients. Some patients daydreamed about all the wonderful stuff they'd do after surgery, like running marathons and dancing; others focused on the fear, pain and difficulty of recovery as well as the benefits. After surgery, the second group had significantly more mobility and less pain.

Why? The peril of high expectations. Our brains are easily seduced by the sweetness of anticipated benefits, which means that we get demoralized by any setbacks – *wait, this isn't what's supposed to happen!* But the process of obstacle–benefit daydreaming, on the other hand, prepares you emotionally and tactically for the challenge ahead.

One nice way to apply this idea is the Zander Letter – named after the music educator Benjamin Zander. It works like this: before he begins teaching a new class, Zander asks the students to take out a sheet of paper, date it three months in the future, and title it: *I Succeeded in this Class Because* . . . In the letter, they're asked to detail the concrete steps they will take that will lead to their success.[4]

I like this method, because it can be applied to just about any project and it puts the learner in the right mindset for effective daydreaming. They can't just focus on the seductive sweetness of the outcome. They also have to figure out exactly how they're going to get there.

Can you start to harness the power of dreams within your workplace?

The Significance of Johan Cruyff

Without Johan Cruyff, there would be no Pep Guardiola, no Lionel Messi, no Xavi Hernández, no Andrés Iniesta, no treble-winning nights and no adoration of the sporting world. The players would have been judged too slow, too small and the football deemed too lightweight. Cruyff's bold brush strokes added glorious colour to FC Barcelona's Big Picture.

The genius from Amsterdam painted such a vivid picture of what success looked like, sowing the seeds that allowed these incredible players to be recognized and to become central to FC Barcelona's story. Without Cruyff, this story wouldn't exist. Even the latest, greatest Barcelona era has his DNA running through it: the way they train, the way they play, how they recruit their cultural architects and staff and why entertainment falls only just behind victory in their list of priorities.

He understood the three main criteria to cover when explaining the 'what' element of the Big Picture in a culture:

— **Credibility**

— **Clarity**

— **Cojones**

Credibility

A journalist once chased Gandhi through a busy train station, hoping to get an interview for his newspaper. Despite the man's impressive persistence, Gandhi politely declined to respond to his questions. Finally, as the train was pulling out of the station, the reporter called out to Gandhi, 'Please give me a message for the people!' Without hesitation, Gandhi leant out of the window and shouted back, 'My life is my message!'[5]

Johan Cruyff could arguably make the same claim; that his life's work embodied his message of how to play beautiful football and win. Cruyff's contribution to Barcelona dwarfs that of any other individual. 'The most important figure in football history,' suggests Ferran Soriano.[6] The Dutchman twice created a lasting legacy at the Camp Nou, first as a player between 1973 and 1978, and again as a coach from 1988 to 1996. As discussed, the club has intermittently strayed from his path, before finding success again when they got back to it.

Cruyff's father, Manus, was a fruit seller and died when Johan was just twelve. Johan's mother cleaned the dressing rooms at Ajax's stadium, and the club had been at the heart of his life from a very young age. He made his debut for the first team at seventeen, and would lead Ajax to three successive European Cups, winning the Ballon d'Or in 1971 (he would win two more as a Barcelona player). He was different; graceful, elegant, clever. He had a swagger about him, drive – a natural leader. He was recognized as the world's best player even before he illuminated the 1974 World Cup, and Barcelona were determined to have him. As his teammate Juan Manuel Asensi puts it: 'With Cruyff, everything changed – the club as well as the team.'

When Cruyff made his debut, Barcelona were fourth from bottom in the Spanish league; at the end of the season, they were champions for the first time since 1960. Cruyff missed just one game that season and didn't lose a single game that mattered. At last, Barça could look Madrid in the eye; the fatalism was washed away. Temporarily, at least.

'They were always thinking about inferiority; they had Madriditis,' Cruyff recalled. 'We were always thinking we were the victim, but in my way of thinking there was no victim. I said, "Let's look at ourselves, let's think about how we can be better. Let the rest do whatever they want; we know what we want."'

Asensi vividly remembers the new way of thinking: 'This change in mentality was brutal. Suddenly from always losing we saw that we could win, it was as if we had been drowning and now we were pulled out of the water. We could swim.'

Cruyff's playing time at Camp Nou was less trophy-laden than his subsequent time as a coach. However, it did contain many remarkable, enduring moments. One such was on 17 February 1974, when a Cruyff-inspired Barça claimed a historic 5–0 win over Real Madrid at the Santiago Bernabéu. Less than two years before the death of General Franco, the despot who had ruled Spain with an iron fist since 1939, this match was, for many Catalans, a nail in the coffin of his regime and of their own subjugation. The *New York Times* even declared that the result had done more for the Catalan cause than any politician or resistance figure ever could.

What made it even better was that Cruyff had been able to play only after he and his wife had decided to bring forward the birth of their son. Jordi Cruyff, originally due on 15 February 1974, was born on the ninth. 'Jordi' is also the patron saint of Catalonia, the dragon slayer of legend whose saint's day is celebrated every year with stalls springing up all over the city of Barcelona, draped in the red and yellow stripes of the *Senyera* flag.

Today, there are countless Jordis in Barcelona; back then, there were none below the age of forty, and even those over forty usually found themselves forced to adapt their name to Jorge. Under Franco, it was forbidden to name a child by a non-Castilian name, so when Cruyff went to register his son he was told he would have to call him Jorge. Cruyff was having none of it. He'd already registered Jordi in the Netherlands, and simply would not back down, practically bullying the Barcelona registrar into writing his son's name the Catalan way.[7]

Cruyff's actions drew displays of gratitude from Catalonia. The world's best player calling his son Jordi was met as if it was a small victory for Catalonia against the dictatorship; beating Madrid 5–0 ten days later was a big one. 'Cruyff represented a revolution,' Joan Laporta insists.

'You know what most struck me?' Cruyff asked journalists Frits Barend and Henk van Dorp as they strolled around Camp Nou conducting an interview for Dutch television in 1977. 'They didn't say "congratulations", they said "thank you". That was really something. That will always stay with me. It was all they said, "thank you", everywhere. One time, we were shopping on the Costa Brava and an old woman came up to me and said over and over again, "thank you, thank you". That made a very deep impression and taught me a lot about Barcelona and probably involved me with this club for the rest of my life.'

Cruyff was the living embodiment of the Catalan spirit: where he went, others would follow. He was able to do so because of the immense credibility he had at the club and among its fans. This credibility stemmed from the clear link between the manner in which he lived his life and the club's sense of purpose. When he returned as coach in 1988, his example and his message steered the club back towards the Big Picture, a picture which, as we have seen, had become increasingly blurred.

Clarity

While he played and coached, trophies were won, but it is almost as much for the ripples as the splash that Cruyff is venerated. 'His greatest achievement,' suggests the journalist Graham Hunter, 'has been to install not only a mentality at the Camp Nou, but to fuse a backbone as well.'[8] No matter who comes and goes – players, coaches, presidents – if FCB select players as they do now and train them as they do now, they won't be far away from being attractive, successful and hard to play against. 'Some clubs have an identifiable style. Barcelona could turn up in orange with pink polka dots and after five minutes that cover would be blown. You would know you were watching Barcelona,' says the sports writer Martin Samuel.[9] This is down to Cruyff's insistence of clarity and consistency in playing style and developmental structure.

When he died in March 2016, Cruyff hadn't held a formal post at the club, with salary and a contract, since he was sacked as coach in May 1996 (two years after, by his own admission, he had run out of new ideas and should have walked away to concentrate on his Cruyff Foundation charity), but the clarity of his vision, advice and criticism had steered the club for vast chunks of the intervening years. It was Cruyff who had encouraged the club to hand the torch to Pep Guardiola and who then served as the young coach's mentor.

However, the structural decisions he took when he returned to the club as a coach remain his most important legacy – ahead of the solitary league title he won as a player in 1974, or even the great psychological liberation he gave the organization by leading them to their first European Cup in 1992, beating Sampdoria in the final.

The trophies? They live in history. Leagues often won on the last day of the season and usually at the cost of massive humiliation to Real Madrid. Four European trophies, the most important of which being that European Cup. The creation of a clear and repeatable football philosophy is his most important achievement – Cruyff embedded beliefs which remain not only part of Barcelona's DNA but are now part of the wider footballing culture of Spain and Europe. This is all the more

remarkable when we consider that these beliefs, so fundamental to Barcelona's success, were completely alien when he
introduced them.

When he arrived from coaching Ajax in 1988, Cruyff immediately began laying down some vital foundations that would
be intrinsic to both the immediate and long-term future. His
assistant, Charly Rexach, explains, 'When Cruyff and I arrived
to take over at Barça, we decided to install the football which
inspired us.

'We inherited a culture at the club where the fans whistled
and jeered at a defender if he passed the ball back to the goalkeeper, or if a winger reached the byline but didn't cross the
ball – whether there was anyone there to take advantage or not.

'Our original task was to go out and find players who had
the correct philosophy and skill set and to educate the ones
we inherited, but a by-product was that we educated the fans.
Everything flowed once we taught everyone that there was a
baseline philosophy and we would not bend from it.'[10] Indeed,
the power of Cruyff's vision would eventually oblige many in
the football world to bend to his ways.

Neither Cruyff nor Rexach ever claimed to be inventing
anything new. Pablo Picasso once declared, 'good artists
borrow, great artists steal' and both were open about the fact
they were adapting and evolving concepts that they themselves
had been taught. Cruyff fostered an atmosphere where experi-
mentation, risks and lateral thinking were all encouraged – all
so long as the basic template of touch, technique, maintaining
possession and stretching the pitch with quick circulation of
the ball was maintained at the same time.

When Cruyff arrived, it took him little time to discover that
he disagreed with the way the club's youth system was being
run. He insisted that it was nonsensical that the age-category

teams were being trained in a style and system that was particular to their specific coach. 'It was a big club but it didn't have a specific football culture,' recounts Pep Guardiola. 'We had one Argentinian coach who played an Argentinean style, then came a German coach who played a German style.'[11] In short, there was no common credo. Thirteen youth levels under the first team could mean thirteen different playing styles and kids having to re-learn every year as they moved up the ladder.

Cruyff had a different vision, and insisted on a number of conditions:

1. Every youth level must be trained based on the same concepts and in the same formation.
2. The top kids needed to be pushed out of their comfort zone and played at an age group one or even two years ahead.
3. Those *perlas de la cantera*, the jewels of the youth system, require accelerated promotion into the first team.

All youth teams worked on positional play, one- or at most two-touch circulation of the ball, squeezing space – all principles which have subsequently thrived under Guardiola. This strategy, plus adherence to all teams playing attacking, creative, rapid football based on pressing and accurate passing, is Cruyff's most enduring legacy.

'When I was there, you would see seven-year-old kids doing the same training session, with the same patterns, as the first team. He created something from nothing and you have to have a lot of charisma and personality to do that. Everybody knows about football but you need the charisma to say: "You must go in that way", and everybody follows. That's so difficult to find,' marvels Guardiola.[12]

The ethos of how to play football had been planted at Camp

Nou and La Masia by Cruyff. His promotion, coaching and education of Pep Guardiola the player contributed massively to the beliefs and behaviours of Guardiola the manager, who faithfully adhered to the Big Picture idea, while adding his own flourishes. 'I will forever remain indebted to Cruyff,' Guardiola declared, 'because he is the one who gave me the opportunity and he has taught me a great many things.'

Cruyff explained in 2009, 'When he was young, Guardiola didn't have the physique to make it at the top and without such intelligence as he possesses, he'd not even have made it to our Juvenil [under 18] side.

'Over his career, this has been a great advantage to him. We talked at great length about his vision and his organizational skills and, thanks to them, our team won many prizes. We also talked about how to minimize his deficiencies and he handled all that process just magnificently. After his Barça career, he spread his wings and learned elsewhere. Now, he's back with experience, huge intelligence and that tendency to work obsessively. He is the perfect model for Barcelona.'[13]

'When Guardiola was appointed as coach, it was with a confidence that he would continue to develop the inherited cultural blueprint laid down by Cruyff,' said Ferran Soriano.[14] In other words, Guardiola was identified as a leader who would remain faithful to the Big Picture idea.

On the day Cruyff left as manager, sixteen-year-old Xavi Hernández was already part of the youth system, with five years of La Masia training under his belt. Andrés Iniesta was being scouted. Victor Valdés had spent four years in the system and a seventeen-year-old called Carles Puyol had just been scouted and signed – to play as a winger. Each of these young players – identified even then as cultural architects – would play an important role in the future culture of Barcelona. Cruyff's system was not only to train players brilliantly once the right ones were selected, but to change the criteria used to scout them in the first place. As a result, the club was now consistently choosing the best young players, or at least the right ones for their system.

Cruyff's next important gift to Barça was perhaps more indirect. Cruyff was able to detect which of his former pupils possessed the qualities to invigorate the club. Speaking in 2011, he said that for so-called 'inexperienced' coaches, such as Rijkaard and Guardiola, there were particular criteria to take into account.

'The coach of any world-class club needs to be aware of so many things, including what the club stands for and how to convey that to the public and the press. He also has to know his public, as well as managing the dressing room. In truth, the football really only accounts for forty per cent of his work. All the decisions relating to who plays and how they will play are affected by all the other knowledge the coach already has. And what does experience consist of? Experience of the dressing room, of working under intense pressure, facing a big game. If you have dealt with all of that as a player, then you have a huge amount of experience.'[15]

Cojones

'My father,' recalls Jordi Cruyff, 'had an "irritating" habit of being right most of the time. Even with things like driving. He would know the right route, and more than that, he would go all these different ways to make sure he got as many green lights as possible. He would calculate that if this one was red, the next two would be green. He was always trying to find the quickest way, the best way. He was a step ahead. His brain was never sleeping.

'He was part of the one per cent who will always be remembered.'[16]

Even after his Dutch side lost the 1974 World Cup final to Germany, Cruyff had the courage to maintain his basic principle that there is a right way and a wrong way to play football. 'There is no better medal than being acclaimed for your style,' he once said. To him, it was essential that the game must be played with intelligence, style, technical skill and vision. His bible preaches that if your first touch and your use of possession are top-class, then winning games or trophies will naturally follow.

Cruyff said of the 1974 World Cup, 'I don't mind [getting beaten]. We played beautiful football all the way to the final, we brought Holland and the Dutch style of football to the attention of the world and, because we lost, it generated huge amounts of sympathy and support for our brand of how to play. Perhaps there was more good than bad in losing that way.'[17]

'He was the most courageous coach I ever met,' Guardiola confesses. 'When he smells the talent it doesn't matter if the age is sixteen or seventeen because he believed in, what in Spain we call, the *efecto mariposa* [butterfly effect].'[18]

When Rijkaard was dismissed in 2008, Cruyff was asked to assist Guardiola for his first season. He refused, because to have interfered would have been to disturb the butterfly effect: Guardiola was ready.

If there was one criticism of Cruyff, a charge which he accepted when he claimed that he should have left the club in 1994, it was that he could be incredibly brusque with those who failed to adhere to the Big Picture. 'Cruyff is the trainer who has taught me the most. But he is also the trainer who made me suffer the most. With just a look he gave you shivers that could chill your blood,' said Guardiola, who recounts the occasion he made his debut for the Dutch master and received a severe rollicking at half-time. 'You were slower than my granny,' Cruyff told the callow teenager.[19]

Txiki Begiristain similarly recounts one occasion when Cruyff insulted him and Bakero, two of his key players, and an hour later asked them to organize a meal for all the squad and their wives the following night. 'He was demanding a lot and knew when you needed to be pushed or protected,' Begiristain laughs, 'I could forgive him most things.'[20]

It was Cruyff's courage – to maintain adherence to drive the change and keep everyone on the right course – which ensured the Big Picture and its implementation could be realized.

What is essential when creating the Big Picture, though, is to marry your long-term goal – the what – with short-term critical moves – the how. The Big Picture risks being empty talk without lots of behavioural-level execution. You have to back up your vision with a good behavioural script. At Barcelona, it was deemed that Pep Guardiola was the leader to do precisely this.

EXERCISE – WHAT'S UP?

When I work with leaders who are preparing to share the 'what' element of their Big Picture, I ask them to write a short advert advertising for people to join them, avoiding bullet points or buzzwords. What would you say? What do you offer and why? How would it appeal to others?

To illustrate the importance of this, let's use the example of Winston Churchill's first speech after becoming Prime Minister during the Second World War. He famously stood before the nation and declared that, 'I have nothing to offer you but my blood, toil, tears and sweat.' Now imagine if you stripped it of all emotion and put into a company-approved PowerPoint presentation:

My offer:

— Blood

— Toil

— Tears

— Sweat

It loses something doesn't it?

Instead, I find that asking these three questions can help them take care of the detail:

After someone hears your explanation . . .

1. What do you want them to know?

2. What do you want them to feel?

3. What do you want them to do?

If you've solid answers to these three questions, the particulars of the 'what' will often take care of themselves.

1.iii   THE HOW

Date: Wednesday, 26 May 2010
Time: 9.45 p.m.
Location: Camp Nou, Barcelona

Imagine that you are Zlatan Ibrahimović as he makes the steep
ascent from the tunnel into the evening sunlight that bathes
Camp Nou. You are there to greet the 70,000 fans who have
come especially to herald your arrival – the most expensive
footballer ever acquired by the club and the second most costly
of all time. You pause for a moment and think about what that
really means, when a pantheon of great players, some of whom
are your heroes – like Maradona, the Brazilian trio of Ronaldo,
Rivaldo and Ronaldinho, the Frenchman Thierry Henry – are
included in the list.

'This is giving me the chills,' you say to your friend and
agent Mino Raiola, with an involuntary shudder.

It has been a hectic few days since you signed and agreed
to move from Internazionale, the Milanese club where you
have spent two happy and successful years. In your mind,
you replay the events since your plane landed at quarter to five
that afternoon.

'It was chaos. Hundreds of fans and journalists were
waiting for me, and the papers wrote pages and pages about
it. People were talking about "Ibramania". It was crazy. If I

hadn't fully understood how big a deal this was before, I did now.'

When you arrived at the stadium, you were further shocked by the number of journalists waiting to question you. 'I've never seen so many reporters,' you said to President Juan Laporta as an aside, before attempting to answer their questions and recall some of the simple Catalan phrases you had learned for this very occasion. Your attention, however, was distracted by the volume of the roar which was emanating from the stadium.

Once you had left the press room, you were presented with your new kit, learning that you had been given the number nine, 'The same number Ronaldo had when he was here at the club,' you said. You cast your mind back to the early days on the notorious Rosengaard estate, east of Malmö, Sweden, when you would watch him on television performing in this same shirt and then go and practise those same skills. Now things really were getting emotional. You take a couple of gulps of air in order to calm the nerves.

'Let's go,' instructs Raiola. 'I will never be able to describe it,' you think as you stride towards the stage set up in the middle of the pitch. It seems like everyone is screaming your name from the top of their lungs.

The press officer hands you a ball and points towards the phalanx of press photographers. 'Say "Visca, Barça!",' he reminds you – 'Go, Barça'.You trot in the direction of the flash-bulbs, which capture the simple tricks, honed in Sweden, polished in Holland and Italy, and now showcased in Barcelona.

The press guys are going crazy. 'Kiss the badge, kiss the badge,' they urge, and at that moment, you recall later, you are 'like a little boy. I obeyed and kissed the badge on the shirt.' You will get shit for that later.[1]

Ten months later, Ibrahimović was ignominiously sold by the club – who were prepared to accept a loss of £20 million to offload him back to Italy.

Climbing the Behavioural Ladder

Where did it all go wrong? To answer that question, we can turn to Fred Lee, a senior vice president of a major medical centre and – most intriguingly – a 'graduate' of Disney University, the training programme the company uses to develop its employees, or 'cast members'. Lee learned a lot from his time at Disney University, which took Walt Disney's bold vision to 'put smiles on faces' and moulded it into clearly understandable and easily replicable behaviours that would make his vision a reality.

'It was Peter Drucker, the management guru, who once observed that "Culture eats strategy for breakfast every day of the week",' Lee recounts. 'After a stint working for Disney, I know exactly what that means. I was joining a culture, not getting a job.'[2]

After his training at Disney University, Lee moved into running hospitals with incredible success. The lessons he learned within the House of Mouse were then assimilated into the medical industry.

At the start of the very first day's training, the opening question from the instructor charged with the induction of new members into Disney's traditions was, 'What is the primary focus of every cast member at Disney?'

'We all quickly answered with variations on the concepts of courtesy and customer service. But we were wrong,' Lee recalls. '"The primary focus of every cast member is safety," said our instructor. '"Every one of you must be constantly aware of guest safety."'[3]

The instructor had paused for dramatic effect and then illustrated his point. 'If you see a child climbing over a fence, you drop everything else you are doing and stop that potentially hazardous activity. If somebody falls down or faints, rush to their aid. Nothing at Disney is more important than safety.'

Once he was satisfied that this was understood, the instructor unveiled the four key behaviours at Disney. Safety and courtesy and efficiency are clear enough. The fourth, 'show', relates to everything that makes a sensory impression. It means how well an area 'shows' to a guest. For Disney's front-line cast members, it refers especially to their personal appearance and how neat and tidy every area of the park looks. The key message in these four behaviours was still to come. Lee explains, 'There are four areas of constant quality focus at Disney and each of these has an order of priority. When you are faced with two conflicting demands, understanding these priorities will help you know exactly which concern takes precedence.'

The order is:

1. SAFETY

2. COURTESY

3. SHOW

4. EFFICIENCY

When an employee is faced with a cultural question like, 'Should I ignore this customer to stop that child playing in the fountain?' it is almost always a dilemma, because the employee is faced with two or more competing values – often not hierarchized by the organization. If he or she does the one thing – courtesy to a guest – he or she could be in trouble for not doing the other – observing safety procedures. 'The value of Disney's ladder of priorities is that it resolves such a dilemma immediately,' Lee reasons. Safety is number one – stop the child then return to the customer.[4]

According to the scientific method, for a theory or model to be considered 'elegant' it must have clarity, simplicity and completeness. Disney's ladder of priorities has all three. First, each of the concepts is discrete and clear. The words chosen are made instantly unambiguous to employees and there is no fuzzy overlap in meaning between them. Second, the prioritizing eliminates confusion about expectations when equally good alternatives confront the chooser. Third, it is complete, because it defies the observer to find any conflict of interest that is not settled by the words and priorities chosen on the ladder.

Decision paralysis

Let's contrast this with the more popular approach to creating high-performing cultures. Imagine working in a hospital which states its 'values' are:

SERVICE   PEOPLE   QUALITY

FINANCIAL STRENGTH   GROWTH

Now, let's look at this through the eyes of a frontline employee; think about some of the obvious questions which arise when trying to determine how to behave.

What is the difference between service and people, or service and quality? Isn't there also some fuzzy overlap, at first glance, between financial strength and growth?

Why isn't there any mention of safety?

What about processes – the engine for efficiency?

Where is teamwork, a vital part of process improvement and quality? If they are all part of quality, then too much appears to be captured under quality, and probably too little under growth.

How can a frontline caregiver distinguish clearly between the values through the words we have chosen? What this confusing approach creates is a state of decision paralysis. Multiple options, even good ones, can freeze us and make us revert to the default plan. This behaviour is not rational, but it certainly is human.

Decisions are the rational brain's turf, and because they require careful supervision and self-control, they also tax our strength. The more choices we are offered, the more exhausted we get. Have you ever noticed that shopping is a lot more tiring than other kinds of 'light' activity, such as watching television or going for a walk?

Now you know why – it's all those choices. This is important, because we encounter excess choice all around us. Consider three real examples of decision paralysis.

Scene 1: a deli. The store managers have set up a table where customers can sample imported jams for free. One day, the table showcases six different jams. Another day: twenty-four jams. As you'd expect, the twenty-four-jam display attracts more customers to stop by for a sample. But when it comes time to buy, they just can't make a decision. Your conversion analysis shows that shoppers who saw only six jams on display are ten times more likely to buy a jar.

Scene 2: the office. The employees of a large company read over the materials relating to their pensions. The human resources department has thoughtfully provided many investment options: domestic growth stock funds, domestic value stock funds, municipal bond funds, real estate investment funds, emerging market funds, developed market funds, money market accounts, and more. Each category might have several choices within it. The extra options backfire, however, because for every ten options offered, the employees' rate of participation goes down by two per cent. Decision paralysis deters people from saving for their own retirement. And because many companies match employees' contributions, employees may also be walking away from free money.

Scene 3: a local bar. It's speed-dating night. Singles meet a series of other singles one-on-one, spending perhaps five minutes with each person, in the hope of making a romantic connection. But decision paralysis thwarts even Cupid. Young adults who meet eight other singles make more 'matches' than those who meet twenty.

Bottom line: decision paralysis disrupts medical treatment and retail decisions and investment decisions and dating decisions. Let's go out on a limb and suggest that it might affect decisions in *your* job and life, too.

As Barry Schwartz puts it in his book *The Paradox of Choice*, as we face more and more options, 'we become overloaded. Choice no longer liberates, it debilitates. It might even be said to tyrannize.'[5]

Maintaining the status quo feels comfortable and steady because much of the choice has been squeezed out. Within a familiar culture, you have your routines, your ways of doing things. For most of your day, your brain operates on autopilot. But when you attempt to integrate someone into your culture, their autopilot doesn't work any more, as choices suddenly proliferate. For example, when you're on a diet, the habitual daily trip to the vending machines is disqualified, and in its place is left a decision. When you've got a new manager, the way you communicate stops being second nature and starts being a choice.

Change brings new choices that create uncertainty. Let's be

clear: it's not only options that yield decision paralysis – like picking one doughnut from a hundred flavours. Ambiguity does, too. In times of change, you may not know what options are available. And this uncertainty leads to decision paralysis as surely as a table with twenty-four jams.

Ambiguity is exhausting to our brain because the thinking brain is tugging on the reins of the emotional part, trying to direct it down a new path. But when the road is uncertain, our brain will insist on taking the default path – the most familiar path.

Why?

Because uncertainty makes us anxious. (Think of how, in an unfamiliar place, you gravitate towards a familiar face.) And that's why decision paralysis can be deadly for a culture – because the most familiar path is always the status quo.

Ambiguity is the Enemy

Many leaders pride themselves on setting high-level direction: 'I'll set the vision and stay out of the details.' It's true that a compelling vision is critical, but it's not enough. Big Picture, hands-off leadership isn't likely to work in a cultural change situation, because the hardest part of change – the paralysing part – is actually in the details.

This was the situation that Guardiola inherited when taking over from Frank Rijkaard. In August 2006, Rijkaard's team sat at the summit of world football. The 2006–07 season kicked off with a show of appreciation for his side at the UEFA Club Football Awards in Monaco. Many felt, in fact, that this team was on the brink of becoming the greatest in the club's history. But as the influential Catalan journalist Lluís Canut explains in his book *Els Secrets del Barça*,[6] the ceremony and Super Cup that followed, supposedly the coronation of that team's achievements, paradoxically heralded the beginning of the end, as the first signs of indiscipline became apparent.

At the hotel where the team were based before the Super Cup, against Sevilla, Frank Rijkaard had, to the astonishment of everyone, invited a Dutch pop group to join him at his table for dinner the evening before the game. He allowed the players the freedom to go to bed at a time of their choosing, inevitably resulting in a late night for the usual wayward suspects. The team's preparation was reflected in the scoreline at the end of the match: a 3–0 victory for Sevilla. That defeat served as the first of many warning signs that were to surface throughout the following season; the coaches and players had stopped enforcing and reasserting the culture that had brought it success, and it culminated in Real Madrid winning the league by eighteen points and FC Barcelona players being obliged to offer a guard-of-honour to the newly minted champions. Things continued to stall during the following season, and in the summer of 2008 Soriano and the club's directors turned to Pep Guardiola to revitalize the Big Picture and the club's behavioural culture.

Ambiguity is the enemy.

Any successful change requires a translation of ambiguous goals into concrete behaviours. In short, to make a switch, you need to script the critical moves. Change begins at the level of individual decisions and behaviours, but that's a hard place to start because that is where the friction is. Inertia and decision paralysis will conspire to keep people doing things the old way. To trigger movement in a new direction, you need to provide crystal-clear guidance. That's why scripting is important – you've got to think about the specific behaviour that you want to see in a tough moment, whether the tough moment takes place in a team meeting or the last minute of a crucial game. You can't script every move though – that would be like trying to foresee the seventeenth move in a chess game. It's the critical moves that count.

In a pioneering study of organizational change, described in the book *The Critical Path to Corporate Renewal*,[7] researchers divided the change efforts they studied into three groups: the most successful (the top third), the average (the middle third) and the least successful (the bottom third). They found that, across the spectrum, almost everyone set goals: 89 per cent of the top third and 86 per cent of the bottom third. A typical goal might be to improve sales by 50 per cent. But the more successful change transformations were more likely to set behavioural goals: 89 per cent of the top third versus only 33 per cent of the bottom third. For instance, a behavioural goal might be that the sales team meets once a week and each team includes at least one representative of every area of the business.

Guardiola's hierarchy of priorities

To return to the case of Zlatan Ibrahimović, the individual behaviours which had propelled him to footballing success and glory would soon prove to be incompatible with his new club's behavioural ladder. In a clash between an individual's prodigious talent and the Big Picture, when viewed through the lens of a high-performing culture, there can only be one winner.

Guardiola's ladder of behavioural priorities were:

1. HUMILITY

2. HARD WORK

3. TEAM PLAYER

Every member of the team was expected to adhere to them, including new recruits like Ibrahimović. But in his case, reconciling individual and cultural behaviours proved impossible.

1. Humility

Before he had actually signed for the club, the Swede was given his first lesson on the importance of humility. 'I'd spoken with the Barcelona gang on the phone,' he recounts, 'and, as you know, Barcelona and Real Madrid are at war with each other. They're arch-rivals, and a lot of it is to do with politics – Catalonia against the central power in Spain, all that stuff – but the clubs also have different philosophies.' He was instructed how he would travel from Italy to Barcelona – and just as importantly, why.

'"We're not like Real. We travel on regular planes," they told me, and sure, that sounded reasonable. I flew with Spanair rather than a private jet.'

This message was reinforced on his first day at the training ground, when Pep Guardiola came up to him, looking a little self-conscious:

'Listen,' Guardiola said, 'Here at Barça, we keep our feet on the ground.'

'Sure,' I said. 'Fine!'

'So we don't turn up to training sessions in Ferraris or Porsches.'

I nodded, didn't go off on one and say things like, What the hell business is it of yours what cars I drive? At the same time though, I was thinking, What does he want? What kind of message is he sending here? Believe me, I don't need to make a big deal of looking tough any more and drive up in some flash car and park it on the pavement or something. That's not what it's about. I do love cars. They're my passion and I could sense something else behind what he was saying. It was like, Don't think you're anybody special!

I'd already got the impression that Barcelona was a little like school, or some sort of institution. The players were cool – nothing wrong with them. To be honest, though, none of the lads acted like superstars, which was strange. Messi, Xavi, Iniesta, the whole gang – they were like schoolboys. The best footballers in the world stood there with their heads bowed, and I didn't understand any of it.

Here everyone did as they were told. I didn't fit in, not at all. I thought, Just enjoy the opportunity. Don't confirm their prejudices. So I started to adapt and blend in. I became way too nice. It was mental.

I said what I thought people wanted me to say. I drove the club's Audi and stood there and nodded my head the way I did when I was at school. I hardly yelled at my team-mates any more. I was boring. Zlatan was no longer Zlatan.

I was the second-most-expensive transfer in history and unfortunately, I was feeling the pressure of everything – that here at Barça we don't make a show and stuff, and I guess I wanted to prove I could do it too.[8]

Despite his initial understanding, Ibrahimović deliberately transgressed this particular behavioural code as his relationship with the club, and Guardiola in particular, deteriorated:

When I realized I was going to be on the bench for the game against Almeria, I remembered that line: Here at Barcelona we don't turn up to training sessions in Porsches or Ferraris. What kind of nonsense was that, anyway? I'll take whatever car I want, at least if I can wind up idiots. I jumped in my Enzo, put my foot on the gas and parked up right in front of the door to the training facility. Of course, it was a huge circus. The papers wrote that my car cost as much as the sum total of all the Almeria players' monthly wages. I didn't give a damn. The rubbish in the media was small potatoes in this context. I'd made up my mind that I was going to have my say.[9]

Strike one!

2. Hard Work

In June 2008, Guardiola had wasted no time in making his mark on his new charges. Under the new manager, the players' weight was immediately scrutinized – it was no longer acceptable to gain even a pound or two. Guardiola was normally first to the training ground every morning – usually not long after 8 a.m. Punctuality, as a representation of being mentally prepared, became strictly enforced. Guardiola's rules were simple. There were fines for lateness, plus a stint of lone training for offenders was thrown in for good measure. Players being unprepared to work hard in any way, whether this was tying up their laces on the training pitch or not arriving for training at all, was forbidden.[10]

In Ibrahimović's case, the 2009 Christmas break, four months after he had joined the club, brought him into conflict with the trademark behaviours that had brought the club immense success in Guardiola's first season. Ibrahimović was injured following a snowmobile accident in northern Sweden, an activity strictly forbidden by club management.

'I always drive like a maniac,' he recalls. 'I've done so much mental stuff I don't even want to think about it and now in the mountains I was ripping it up on my snowmobile. I got frostbite but had the time of my life.'

Soon after returning to Spain, he had another accident, crashing his club car into a concrete wall during heavy rain, wrecking its entire right axle. 'A lot of the guys in the team had crashed their cars in the storm, but nobody did it quite as massively as I did. I won the crashing-your-car tournament.'[11]

Both of these avoidable injuries forced him out of training and prevented him working hard for the betterment of the team.

Strike two!

3. Team Player

Throughout his first season in charge, Guardiola would test for team-orientated behaviour. As we saw in the preface, if the team missed a clear opportunity on goal he would immediately turn around to look at the bench. Some footballers leapt from it in anticipation of the ball nestling in the back of the net, while others neither moved nor reacted. He determined that the latter behaviour illustrated that their personal agendas were more important to them than the team's collective success. By the end of the following summer, all the players who consistently failed to react had left the club.

By the end of his first season, Guardiola's behavioural standard of putting the team first was gold-plated, and he often enjoyed illustrating it with the example of Seydou Keita, the versatile Malian midfielder. In the days before the 2009 European Cup final, Guardiola approached the midfielder and asked him to fill in as a full-back. The coach was stunned by the response. 'Don't play me there,' he begged. His reasoning, however, was selfless rather than selfish. 'I would do anything for you, boss, but I have never played there. My teammates will suffer.'

The player was putting the collective needs of the team ahead of any individual desire to play. He knew he wouldn't be picked for the final unless he was prepared to play as a makeshift right-back. Guardiola assented to Keita's request and marvelled, 'I have never met such a good and generous person as Keita.'

As the 2009–10 season progressed, Ibrahimović was asked to adapt his usual style of play to accommodate Lionel Messi, who was establishing himself as the greatest player in the world, and perhaps of all time.

'Within the team, play centres around Messi, which is natural – he's brilliant,' the charismatic striker recounts. 'He went up to Guardiola and told him, "I want to play in the centre." Guardiola swapped it around and I ended up in the shadows. Guardiola sacrificed me.'

Within weeks of this decision, Ibrahimović's circle began to openly question Guardiola. 'If Guardiola doesn't play Ibra, it's best if you send him to a psychiatric hospital,' said Mino Raiola, his outspoken Italian agent.

Encouraged by Raiola and other friends, Ibrahimović approached Guardiola to express his dissatisfaction. 'With all due respect,' he offered the coach, 'this isn't working. It's as if you bought a Ferrari but you're driving it like a Fiat.' He instructed the manager that he would rather not play than be utilized in the manner Guardiola preferred.

Strike three!

Clarity counters Resistance

'Talent will always get you into the dressing room,' explains Txiki Begiristain, 'but how you behave within the culture will determine how long you remain there.'[12]

By translating the club's Big Picture into clearly understandable, everyday behaviours, Guardiola was able to apply a standard to all the players, regardless of their dizzying football talents. No matter how good, a refusal to climb the behavioural ladder will result in those who guard the culture choosing to reject you.

Joan Laporta, the Barça president, understood the cultural importance of these behaviours when he later reasserted the reasoning for Ibrahimović's short stay at the club. 'He never really got on the same page as the rest of the team,' he told *la Repubblica*. 'Football is all about the collective. Solidarity is even more important at Barcelona than anywhere else.'

In your own culture, until you can ladder your way down from an idea to a specific behaviour, you're not going to easily lead a cultural change. To create movement, you have to be specific and be concrete. You've got to emulate the humility, hard work and team-orientated behaviours and flee from empty clichés.

EXERCISE – CLIMB THE BEHAVIOURAL LADDER

Ric Charlesworth, who coached the Australian women's hockey team – the Hockeyroos – to two Olympic golds, would regularly ask his players to describe the perfect game. He would get them to work through hypothetical situations in groups and describe how the perfect team would behave during that game.[13]

Most players and coaches will quickly and easily outline the physical, tactical and technical aspects they consider essential. The best, however, will then extend their description to include the winning behaviours on display. These are people who have often witnessed games where the difference has been the superior behaviours of the winning team.

Although no game is ever perfect, this exercise is useful because it considers the end point of their work and allows a discussion about how a perfect player or coach would react to the many challenging situations that can occur.

In my experience, there are a few rules that make this exercise effective:

1. Limit the behaviours to three

Choosing just three 'trademark behaviours' forces teams to identify the essential ones; the ones that differentiate them. Equally, this stops it becoming a shopping list of 'nice to have' behaviours, which are both impossible to recall and tend towards blandness.

2. See something, say something

This simple rule prevents general phrases ('be nice') or jargon ('stay professional') creeping into the discussion. The behaviours have to be something that can be observed and, therefore, commented on – positively and negatively.

3. Rank them

This rule is very powerful. Creating it may take time. But you'll get that time back many times over, as you and your team have the confidence that the decision-making process will be (a) easy (b) consistent (c) fast and – most importantly – (d) *right*.

Imagine if your own team had equally clear criteria for how they made decisions. All that extra time you would save; the extra understanding and respect for others' decisions you would have; the extra alignment it would bring.

1.iv   BIG PICTURE SUMMARY

When creating the Big Picture, there is a triangle of performance which must be addressed. To ensure optimum performance you need to have all three.

How

Why   **What**

Asking what seem to be three very basic questions – 'why', 'what' and 'how' – can, in an instant, remove many of the barriers that hinder or block forward progress towards creating a culture.

Although all three are important, whenever people tell me they can't get their team to do something, I always ask, 'Is the "why" big enough?' You see, the 'why' is the first and the most important question to address. If you can create a big enough 'why', people don't necessarily need to know how. In extreme circumstances, when the 'why' is important enough, people just find a way.

As a leader, it's important to cover these three areas with your whole team, but as the example of Zlatan Ibrahimović illustrates, it's equally critical to invest time in understanding an individual's 'why'. This may seem time-costly, but understanding an individual's motivations will save you doing it later and in more difficult circumstances.

In this section we've established how addressing these

questions and qualifying them with repeatable methods, the change towards creating a high-performing culture can begin to be made. The Big Picture is in place – it's time for the Arc of Change.

2. ARC OF CHANGE: CULTURAL SIGNPOSTS

'Winning doesn't happen in straight lines.'
Sir Alex Ferguson

In order to lead people towards the Big Picture, you need to understand the Arc of Change: the five stages you and your colleagues will encounter along the way. After studying successful movements in business, sport and society, I've identified five stages that every change journey contains:

Dream   **Leap**   **Fight**   **Climb**   **Arrive**

Understanding these stages will help you create galvanizing moments that shape how your fellow travellers experience the journey, as well as sustaining their energy so you all arrive at and achieve the Big Picture.

You'll appreciate this sentiment if you have ever experienced the swell of enthusiasm when setting a New Year's resolution before battling the waves of apathy and despondency just weeks later, when the hard work sets in. Eventually, the hard work is rewarded with signs of progress and the levels of enthusiasm begin to return.

We've already seen – in the Big Picture section – how leaders need to communicate the why, what and how in a way that galvanizes the hearts and minds of your team at critical junctures, such as when they first launch an idea or celebrate its completion. But the real trick is to sustain the interest and commitment of these same people over the long haul with an ongoing stream of meaningful and timely communications.

Imagine if you could fly overhead, study the topography and anticipate the obstacles, and then use that insight to map out a clear path. Providing cultural signposts that point travellers to where they have been, where they are at and where they are going along the Arc of Change is crucial.

In this section, we will look at four ways to provide these signposts. **Speeches, Stories, Ceremonies** and **Symbols** can be employed within your cultural change toolkit to help communicate your Big Picture purpose in a compelling and desirable way, helping your travellers long for and help achieve it.

2.i   STORIES

Location: Team meeting room,
Joan Gamper Training Ground, Barcelona
Date: March 2011

'Right lads, sit down,' instructed Pep Guardiola, the head coach, his hands simultaneously indicating a request for silence. 'We have a special guest here, today. I would like to introduce you to Fernando Parrado. Nando is going to tell you a story; his story. I'd like you to give him your full attention.'

The sixty-one-year-old Uruguayan man stood up, cleared his throat and began to recount the events of October 1972, nearly forty years earlier.

Bound for Chile, the twin-engine plane was carrying four crew members and forty-one passengers, most of them members or supporters of Nando's rugby team in Montevideo, Uruguay. The team was flying to a match in Santiago, and their plane had taken off on an ominous date in October 1972 – Friday the 13th. Deep in the Andes, the pilot encountered bad weather, went off course and struck a ridge, causing the plane to break apart in mid-air.

'Most of us lived by the sea at home,' he said. 'We'd never been in mountains before, or touched snow. One minute we're laughing and joking, and then we're covered in blood and are freezing on this mountain at 11,000 feet with no clear way out.'

For ten days, the survivors drank melted snow and scavenged stale bits of food from the scattered luggage. Nando spent three days nibbling his way through a single chocolate-covered peanut, savouring first the chocolate and then each half of the nut.

But when the food ran out and the threat of starvation loomed, the survivors had only one horrific option. They used shards of glass as cutting tools, and ate the bodies of the crew members first. Later, however, they were forced to take flesh from the corpses of their friends.

Among the few women on the plane – all of whom died – were Nando's mother and sister. From the start, everyone agreed not to touch the bodies of Xenia and Susy. Nando, however, worried that as food grew more scarce, someone would be tempted to eat them. He wasn't going to let that happen. After two months on the mountain he volunteered to go and seek help.

'I thought, if someone doesn't go for help soon, we will die here one by one. I couldn't blame anyone for doing what was necessary to survive. But, I wondered, who will be the last one alive? What will he eat? The mountain was stone. Nothing grew there. What else could we eat but our dead friends?'

With his close friend and teammate Roberto Canessa, Parrado left the crash site and made his way across some of the most rugged mountains in the world without a map or compass, aiming for the Chilean border, braving the cold and the darkness on a journey that covered seventy miles in ten days and carrying only a sock full of 'meat' to sustain him. He says the word 'meat' so casually that the players – sitting listening with a silent intensity – have to remind themselves he's talking about human flesh.

'If we were going to die anyway, I wanted to die trying to get out. We were climbing on instinct. On hope.'

After reaching a shepherd's hut below the snow line, Nando and Roberto were eventually able to lead rescuers back to the fifteen survivors, who had been stranded for seventy-two days.

'Just two – Roberto and I – saved everyone else,' he says in a matter-of-fact voice.

The bodies of his mother and sister remained where he had left them. They were given a proper burial at the site, their graves marked by a simple steel cross.[1]

When Nando finished his story, the FCB players – who he described on Uruguayan television as 'sensitive young men, they were like an amateur team' – sat in stunned silence, reflecting on the incredible tale which was captured in the 1993 Hollywood film *Alive* before breaking into a spontaneous – and heartfelt – round of applause.

'It helped us realize that awful things happen that can destroy anyone, but there are people who rebel against it and fight for their lives,' Gerard Piqué commented on the talk.

Pep Guardiola watched his team and listened to their incisive questions with a growing sense of satisfaction. The parallels between the life and death struggle they had just heard about and their own journey was becoming evident to them. 'We could identify with the qualities required to achieve the objectives,' agreed Victor Valdés.[2]

The Arc of Change

Imagine if you were to plot Nando Parrado's death-defying adventure on a graph. There is little doubt that the line detailing the events would be a bumpy one, eventually reaching a high point where Parrado and his fellow survivors are rescued. It would, in fact, be following the same story arc you follow leading people through any change.

As detailed in the introduction to this section, I've identified five stages that every successful arc of change contains:

Dream   Leap   Fight   Climb   Arrive

This arc of change echoes what Joseph Campbell, the American writer and academic, called the 'monomyth'. Campbell had studied myths and religious stories from across the world and noticed they all essentially followed the same structure. In 1949, he published his book on the subject, *The Hero with a Thousand Faces*.[3]

These stories feature an ordinary-seeming boy (it's usually a boy) from a modest background who is 'called to action'. The young hero travels from his humdrum little world to a 'region of supernatural wonder' and encounters fabulous forces, has various helpers and wins a great victory. He then returns to 'bestow boons' on his home community.

Folk and fairy tales tend to be structured in much the same way, as are many adventure films. *Star Wars*, for example, was built on explicitly Campbellian lines, with George Lucas designing Luke Skywalker to be a classic monomythic hero.

Sport is a world rich in symbolism and metaphor, too, so our favourite stories about sporting heroes tend to follow the same pattern. Both Johan Cruyff and Pep Guardiola tick most of Campbell's boxes, which helps to enhance their status as credible cultural leaders to guide the club's progress.

They were both from humble beginnings and their talent made inevitable the call to a lifetime of action in various sporting arenas designed for wonder. Their careers were long, challenging journeys, during which they both endured many great trials. Cruyff and Guardiola had brought back loads of 'boons', including league titles, cups galore and the gratitude of the Catalan nation, not least for the psychological liberation of the 1992 European Cup victory.

Guardiola's invitation to Parrado was based on an understanding that stories have the power to orientate people during times of change. This was a lesson he had learned during his own playing career.

In 1992, when Guardiola stood on the balcony of the Generalitat Palace in Barcelona, which houses the Catalonian presidential offices, and declared: 'Ciutadans de Catalunya, ja tenui la copa aqui' – 'Citizens of Catalonia, you have the cup here' – it was no accident that Barcelona's returning heroes presented their first European Cup to the city from the exact spot where, almost fifteen years earlier, the former Catalan president Josep Tarradellas had used a similar expression to announce his return from exile: 'Ciutatans de Catalunya, ja soc acqui' 'Citizens of Catalonia, I am finally here.'

Guardiola, a Catalan reference point of the team, of the club, understood both the significance of the team's coronation as a European superpower and his role as an iconic symbol of the nation. 'I had the phrase prepared,' he admitted afterwards.

As we will see in this chapter, Guardiola would frequently – and skilfully – employ stories to ease transition and keep his team engaged and motivated.

Relatable Stories

If you want to make a point to someone, it tends to make a much stronger impression if you can use a story to illustrate it. Guardiola's behavioural ladder – detailing how to behave to enhance the Big Picture – was redolent with stories, such as Seydou Keita's willing sacrifice of his place in the team to embody the 'team first' ethos.

Ingvar Kamprand, the founder of IKEA and once the fourth richest man in the world, has deliberately allowed stories to grow and circulate around him which help to reinforce his company's vision. He regularly travels to the airport by bus and only ever stays in cheap motels rather than luxurious five-star hotels when he is on business. This simple story, which freely circulates among his staff, is consistent with his purpose, which is to 'help create a better life for many people by providing cheap but quality furniture for their homes'. The story shows a man who is still in touch with reality and is still concerned with getting the best value for money. His bus trips are a metaphor for his own company's journey.[4]

This same lesson can be learned from probably the most widely read book in history: the Bible. What is the Bible 'about'? Different people will, of course, answer that question differently. But we can all agree that the Bible contains perhaps the most influential set of behavioural rules in human history: the Ten Commandments. They became the foundation of not only the Judaeo-Christian tradition but of many societies built on that tradition. So surely most of us can recite the Ten Commandments front to back, back to front, and every way in-between, right?[5]

All right then, go ahead and name the Ten Commandments. I'll give you a minute to jog your memory.

Okay, here they are:

1. *I am the Lord your God, who brought you out of the land of Egypt, the house of bondage.*

2. *You shall have no other gods before Me.*

3. *You shall not take the name of the Lord your God in vain.*

4. *Remember the Sabbath day, to make it holy.*

5. *Honour your father and your mother.*

6. *You shall not murder.*

7. *You shall not commit adultery.*

8. *You shall not steal.*

9. *You must not bear false witness against your neighbour.*

10. *You shall not covet your neighbour's house, nor your neighbour's wife . . . nor anything that is your neighbour's.*

How did you do? Probably not so well. But don't worry – most people don't. A recent study found that only 14 per cent of US adults could recall all Ten Commandments; only 71 per cent could name even *one* commandment. The best remembered commandments were numbers 6, 8, and 10 – murder, stealing and coveting – while number 2, forbidding false gods, was in last place.[6]

If we have such a hard time recalling the most famous set of rules from perhaps the most famous book in history, what *do* we remember best from the Bible?

The stories. We remember that Eve fed Adam a forbidden apple and that one of their sons, Cain, murdered the other, Abel. We remember that Moses parted the Red Sea in order to lead the Israelites out of slavery. We remember that Abraham was instructed to sacrifice his only son on a mountain. These are the stories we tell again and again and again, even those of us who are not remotely 'religious'. Why? Because they stick with us, they move us, they persuade us to consider the constancy and frailties of the human experience in a way that mere rules cannot.

When you are leading people through the Arc of Change, particularly the fight stage, stories are powerful ways to remind them to persevere and retain faith in the methods chosen to realize the Big Picture. Guardiola chose the tense moments before the biggest match of his coaching career to reinforce the importance of teamwork in his players' minds.

On 27 May 2009, two hours before kick-off of the Champions League final, the team arrived at the stadium in Rome.

Guardiola then ignored his usual custom of allowing his players to spend time alone. He had a surprise up his sleeve.

Throughout the season, he had engaged with the players emotionally before games, but on this occasion he had prepared something different, something that would not require any additional words.

Guardiola has said, 'What I have learned over the years – I am aware tactics are very important, but the really, really great coaches are coaches of people and that human quality is what makes them better than the rest. Choosing the right people to look up to and give them authority in the dressing room is one of many selections a coach has to make.'

Guardiola felt the final was an occasion which called for something out of the ordinary to help set the tone. His plan got under way a couple of weeks before the final, with a text message to Santi Padro, a TV producer for the Catalan channel TV3: 'Hola Santi. We have to meet. You have to help me with the Champions League.'

When Santi came up with the goods a few days later, Guardiola watched the end result on the laptop and the film the producer had put together brought a tear to his eye. Santi knew straight away that he had achieved exactly what Guardiola had asked him to. Guardiola then called for Manuel Estiarte, part of the FCB backroom team, telling him he had to watch this DVD. His friend's reaction was equally resounding:

'When and where will you show it to them?'

'Just before the game,' replied Guardiola.

To which his friend could only reply, 'Wow!'[7]

The players were surprised when their warm-up session at Rome's Olympic Stadium was brought to an end a little sooner than they expected. There was emotion and tension in the air as they headed down the tunnel to the dressing room.

Guardiola spoke. 'Lads, I want you to watch this. Enjoy this. This is the teamwork which has taken us to Rome.'

The lights in the dressing room went off as a big screen illuminated the room and the theme from the movie *Gladiator* filled the space with sound. 'My name is Gladiator . . .' were the first words the team heard as they watched a montage of the film of the same name and aerial shots of the stadium where they were about to play the final. They then watched a rousing seven-minute video that merged images from the Hollywood blockbuster with footage of the entire Barcelona squad, all set to the film's epic soundtrack. Every single footballer, even those who played a more peripheral role in the season, was honoured in the film: the two reserve goalkeepers, Alexander Hleb, even Gabriel Milito, the defender who had been injured for much of that campaign. It featured everyone. Except Guardiola – the coach had stipulated that under no circumstances did he want to be eulogized in the footage. It was all about his players.

'We've got a better chance of survival if we fight together,' comes the battle cry from behind the helmet that covers the gladiator's face; the voice of Russell Crowe resounding in the darkness of the dressing room.

'There was once a dream that was Rome,' says Crowe, before he goes out to do battle in the Coliseum. An image of Andrés Iniesta then appeared on screen, pressing the palm of his hand against Xavi's in the tunnel before a game. They smile at each other.

When the film finished, there was a silence in the room. Nobody moved, firstly because of the surprise, then the emotion. Players were shyly looking at each other. Tears were shed. Unthinking, unconsciously, players had put their arms around each other's shoulders. It was an intense, special moment.

The number of those players who have subsequently recounted the effect of this film, and cited its influence in sticking together during a torrid opening blitz from their opponents – Manchester United – suggests the message certainly hit the mark.

EXERCISE – THE PIXAR APPROACH

Ever since Pixar made its first feature-length film, *Toy Story*, in 1995, it has been capturing the world's imagination with hit movies like *Monsters, Inc.*, *WALL-E* and *Up*.

The studio has won twenty-seven Oscars and brought in more than $8 billion in gross revenues. And while Pixar is known for establishing the CGI animated feature and pushing graphics boundaries, it is as much known for its brilliant storytelling that appeals to people of all ages.

Former Pixar story artist Emma Coats[8] shared some of the wisdom she gained working on the films *Brave* and *Monsters University*, including how they use just six sentences to structure a story:

1. Once upon a time there was ___.

2. Every day, ___.

3. One day, ___.

4. Because of that, ___.

5. Because of that, ___.

6. Until finally ___.

The Pixar-inspired six-sentence format builds stories in a way which is both appealing and supple. It allows leaders to take advantage of the well-documented persuasive force of stories – but within a framework that forces conciseness and discipline.

You can even summarize this book with a Pixar story:

Once upon a time, the story of FC Barcelona's dominance was viewed with a mixture of admiration and wonder. Every week, we watched them play football with a rare style and panache and assumed that it was down to pure talent and dazzling skills. The challenges they faced in order to deliver these performances were somehow different to ours and so, while we enjoyed watching them operate, we knew there was nothing we could learn. One day, you picked up this book and began to read about the replicable methods employed to create a culture which produced such consistently impressive results. Because of that, you understood the parallels between their world and yours and because of this understanding you were able to incorporate some of the practices into your own culture. Finally, you and your team are now seeing the benefits of a commitment culture and its associated success.

When you know the message you want to convey, think of a story you want to share and fill in the blanks using Pixar's story structure above. After you have filled in the blanks, rewrite and expand your story.

2.ii   RITUALS AND CEREMONIES

One Saturday morning in November 2008, barely five months after Guardiola's arrival as coach, Juan Carlos Unzué, the team's goalkeeping coach, discovered that his father had died suddenly. That evening the team played a league match, won and immediately afterwards boarded a charter flight Guardiola had requested to take the entire sporting staff, star players not excluded, to Pamplona for the funeral the next morning. 'He'd have made the same gesture for anybody,' said Unzué, who will be forever grateful to Guardiola but is cold-eyed enough to see that behind his generosity lay a deeper purpose. 'He sent out a message that day to all of us that we'd be together as a team in bad times and good. On the field that translates into a spirit of fierce solidarity. Eleven players attack and eleven players defend.'[1]

Like stories, ceremonies depict where we are at moments of change and transition. For thousands of years, almost all cultures have used rite of passage ceremonies to mark changes that humans undergo at critical moments in our lives: bar and bat mitzvahs, debutante balls, graduations, baptisms, weddings, coronations and inaugurations.

The advertising agency Saatchi & Saatchi has its spirit statement, 'Nothing Is Impossible', embedded in the stone steps outside its office in Charlotte Street, London. It's another form of ritualization: when you enter the building you cross the threshold into a place where 'anything can happen'.[2]

Something similar happens at Liverpool Football Club. As they walk onto the pitch, both sides pass underneath a sign, close to the mouth of the players' tunnel, which bears the words 'This Is Anfield'. The home players will pause and touch the sign as they pass. This is a ritual with different meaning depending on the colour of your playing kit.

Symbols and ceremonies can help make the transition between stages of the Arc real and tangible – they make them a 'thing'. They 'actualize'. In the case of FC Barcelona, these ceremonies were often employed to indicate the dream of the Big Picture and the successful arrival stages of the Arc of Change.

In his four years in charge, Guardiola symbolized his adherence to the Big Picture by giving nineteen *canterano* (academy-trained youngsters) their debuts. 'When the young players were introduced to the first-team training sessions, we told them they were expected to continue the responsibility of representing the club in the right way,' explained Victor Valdés.[3] This was enforced through young players joining the other home-reared La Masia graduates in the traditional games of rondo. 'We all need these rituals,' acknowledges the celebrated Dutch footballer Ruud Gullit. 'You have to go through them in order to get to what really matters.'[4]

One of the most important roles of these ceremonies within the FC Barcelona Arc of Change is to affirm solidarity. Ceremonies demonstrate sentiments such as 'we are serious', 'this is over' and 'I'm committed'. Some ceremonies may even be so meaningful that they can never be duplicated, instead becoming cherished experiences that deeply bond a group. French sociologist Émile Durkheim proposed that ceremonial rituals not only maintain social order but also develop group cohesion and strong interpersonal relations, all consistent with the trademark behaviours of Guardiola's leadership approach.[5]

A study by the Royal Melbourne Institute of Technology found that ceremonies also enhance communication by 'eliciting arousal, directing attention, enhancing memory, and improving associations'. In short, ceremonies help people understand where they are on their change journey and process new messages and ways of thinking, making the moment more likely to be remembered.[6]

As we have identified, some ceremonies communicate the anticipation of a new beginning and others demarcate an arrival. This was plainly evident in what defender Carles Puyol identified as the 'most special moment' of his fifteen-year career in the Barcelona first team.

The team were stunned in 2011 when they learned that Eric Abidal, the popular French defender, would need an operation to remove a cancerous tumour from his liver. The head coach struggled to get the words out past the tears when he rang Manuel Estiarte to tell him the news.

Abidal recounts Guardiola's input: 'Pep was amazing, sending me messages saying, "Keep going, we are all counting on you to be there."' Guardiola also used the defender's struggle as a metaphor for his own team. 'Gentlemen,' he addressed the players, 'do you realize when you feel tired and we believe that life is difficult that one of your teammates has played thirteen games with a monster that would eat him inside? Okay, we're tired, there are excuses, but there are priorities: we are in good health and Abi is an example for all of us.'

Just seventy-one days after his operation, Abidal played the full ninety minutes as Barça swept aside Manchester United in the Champions League final at Wembley. In one of the most touching acts seen in modern football, Barcelona's talisman and captain Carles Puyol, a fiercely proud Catalan, gave up the chance of hoisting the most coveted club trophy in world football above his head and instead bestowed the honour on Abidal. It was a reward for the determination that he had displayed in his return to action. Puyol recollected: 'When Abidal lifted the Champions League trophy, the implications were significant. He gave us the example of fighting, he didn't give up and he was with the team and he could live a very special moment, a moment he deserved more than anyone.'[7]

This unscripted gesture is possibly the most powerful symbol of Guardiola's Arc of Change, because it captures the behaviours he had sought to embed and the uplifting message that FC Barcelona is 'more than a club'. It was a very real symbol that Guardiola's methods had become inculcated within the club's DNA.

Throughout the Arc, whether it is at points of triumph or in moments of disappointment, it's important to use ceremonies to keep people motivated. Victories should be celebrated, but even dark passages – whether slight missteps or utter disasters – must also be acknowledged so people can move on.

After every trophy success, Guardiola, his squad and staff would put their arms around each other's shoulders and dance around the centre circle in a version of the Catalan *sardana*. The staff would then form a guard of honour at the tunnel, the blue-collar workers slapping and cuffing the superstar heroes as they pass through. After winning their sixth trophy of Pep's reign – the 2009 World Club Championship against Estudiantes de la Plata – the players wore a T-shirt bearing the motto '*Todo Ganado, todo por ganar*' ('Everything won, everything to aim for') to signal that they had arrived but, most significantly, they continued to climb. Tito Vilanova, Guardiola's successor, believed that these moments create 'a wonderful sense of union that is almost more valuable than winning the trophy.'[8]

EXERCISE – RITUALIZE TO ACTUALIZE

When basketball coach Pat Riley moved from the championship-winning Los Angeles Lakers to the New York Knicks, he found a team battling against itself. Cohesion had broken down and the players operated either alone or in small groups.

When the players arrived for their first meeting with Riley, he had organized the room into groups of chairs representing the players' friendship groups. Each player was directed to a specific chair and then Riley asked the players to look around the room. He explained that a team divided cannot win, and then told them he was going to leave the room for fifteen minutes and allow them to consider their options.

When he returned, the players had reformed the room into a semi-circle of chairs with one left for the coach. 'In just one meeting,' Riley later recounted, 'we had moved the players from a "me" to a "we" culture and begun the process of building team cohesion and winning.'[9]

As we have seen, these symbols and rituals can be used to reinforce the Big Picture. They make it real in a vital, visceral way. From induction ceremonies to first caps, from the club song to the hierarchies – they are the framework that holds the belief system in place. When the players drive their club cars to training – or watch the video of every one of their teammates – they are connecting to something greater than themselves. They are making the metaphor their own, connecting their personal story to that of the team.

Symbols, ceremonies and rituals can be organizational: drinks on a Friday night; the annual Christmas party. IKEA staff subvert the casual Friday idea and dress up in their smartest clothes to celebrate the end of the working week. Whenever his team won four consecutive games, Guardiola would foot the bill for a team meal at one of the city's most exclusive restaurants.

Symbols can be societal: red poppies, the giving of gifts or flowers, the wearing of diamonds, the invention of the word 'hello' to answer the phone, Christmas itself. The chanting of Barcelona's club anthem to symbolize Catalan independence. Barça fans flocking to the Canaletes, the fountain where all Barcelona victories are enjoyed.

And they can be personal: Guardiola would habitually lock himself in his office forty-eight hours before a game until he experienced 'that special moment, that feeling of pure joy and satisfaction', when he worked out his plan to defeat his opponents. 'It's these wonderful moments that make the job worthwhile. I love my work because of that moment.'

How can you use symbols and ceremonies in your environment to emphasize your position along the Arc of Change?

2.iii   SPEECHES

One of Guardiola's closest friends is David Trueba, a Spanish novelist and film director whom he met at a poetry reading in 1995, when he was twenty-four. Trueba wrote this about his friend: 'He is curious about a lot of things beyond football. But you get the sense sometimes that he codifies them in his own special way. That he "footballizes" them.' In other words, he finds a lesson applicable to football everywhere.

According to Trueba, his friend followed the 2008 American elections closely: 'He stayed up until the final result was in, peppering me with information all night on the phone, following Obama.'[1]

He has no doubt been 'footballizing' Barack Obama too; learning what he can from an expert in another field and applying it in his own. This was a method of learning employed by Cruyff, who once had an opera singer give his team lessons in breath control. Guardiola surely drew lessons in how to bring people with you along the Arc of Change from the campaign, and in particular from the storytelling ability which allowed Obama to connect so effectively with voters and convince them to join his cause.

When he was running for the Democratic nomination for president, Obama came under attack because of the fiery comments of his pastor, Reverend Jeremiah Wright. When he found himself firmly entrenched in the fight stage of his change arc – his poll ratings falling, his opponent Hillary Clinton criticizing his judgement (she dismissed Obama's loyalty by saying, 'I wouldn't have Wright as my pastor') and the campaign losing momentum – he delivered a speech which reconnected to his own Big Picture – of a fairer, more tolerant America – to persuade people to keep faith.

Obama's remarkable speech defused the issue, reignited his campaign and led many Americans to see a better future for their country. The speech is packed with rich, passionate language which points to the hope for a better America. He concluded his speech in the following way:

> There is one story in particular that I'd like to leave you with today – a story that I told when I had the great honour of speaking on Dr King's birthday at his home church, Ebeneezer Baptist, in Atlanta.
>
> There is a young, twenty-three-year-old white woman named Ashley Baia who organized for our campaign in Florence, South Carolina. She had been working to organize a mostly African-American community since the beginning of this campaign, and one day she was at a round table discussion where everyone went around telling their story and why they were there.
>
> And Ashley said that when she was nine years old, her mother got cancer. And because she had to miss days off work, she was let go and lost her health care. They had to file for bankruptcy, and that's when Ashley decided that she had to do something to help her mom.
>
> She knew that food was one of their most expensive costs, and so Ashley convinced her mother that what she really liked and really wanted to eat more than anything else was mustard and relish sandwiches. Because that was the cheapest way to eat.

She did this for a year until her mom got better, and she told everyone at the round table that the reason she joined our campaign was so that she could help the millions of other children in the country who want and need to help their parents too.

Now Ashley might have made a different choice. Perhaps somebody told her along the way that the source of her mother's problems were blacks who were on welfare and too lazy to work, or Hispanics who were coming into this country illegally. But she didn't. She sought out allies in her fight for injustice.

Anyway, Ashley finished her story and then goes around the room and asks everyone else why they're supporting the campaign. They all have different stories and reasons. Many bring up a specific issue. And finally, they come to this elderly black man who has been sitting there quietly the entire time. And Ashley asks him why he is there. And he does not bring up a specific issue. He does not say health care or the economy. He does not say education or the war. He does not say that he was there because of Barack Obama. He simply says to everyone in the room, 'I am here because of Ashley.'

'I'm here because of Ashley.' By itself, that single moment of recognition between that young white girl and that old black man is not enough. It is not enough to give health care to the sick, or jobs to the jobless, or education to our children.

But it is where we start. It is where our union grows stronger. And as so many generations have come to realize over the course of the 221 years since a band of patriots signed that document in Philadelphia, it is where the perfection begins.[2]

Two stories, one within another, beautifully told, entwined together to touch a nation. At the heart of it is the story of Ashley helping her mother, but around it is the story of the quiet, elderly black man. Above all, it offers a picture of the kind of society which America could become.

Obama's evocation of Martin Luther King, his linking of the small events with the national perspective and his use of passion, hope and universal experiences to create a connection make up a rhetorical juggernaut it's hard to dodge.

The first poll published after the speech, conducted by the *Washington Post* and ABC News, showed the impact of Obama's rhetorical choices. His ratings began to rocket again.

Around the same time as Obama's Arc was in the climb stage towards the Presidency, Guardiola was beginning his own journey. In June 2008, Guardiola had no compunction about delivering his own 'Leap' stage message on a pitch in Fife, Scotland, where he'd gathered his team to begin training for the new season. It was important to articulate his dream and indicate the start of the process.

'It is time for a "restart" in the dressing room,' he announced. 'I don't know if there are bad habits, but the past is gone.

'What I can promise is that I will not tolerate a lack of effort put into this project to rebuild the success of the team. Sure, you can be guaranteed that you are going to run and run and run, but my primary intention is to convince you with my words. I want your involvement in my plan, I want to inspire your faith in what we are doing and above all, I want even the talented, inspired players to understand that, individually, they are worth much less than when they invoke team values.'[3]

Xavi, returning with his fellow Spain internationals from winning the European Championship, explained the impact Guardiola had: 'Pre-season had already started when I re-joined training and the squad were working their butts off. The coaches, the physical trainers, Pep: they were on us like hawks, pushing for repetitions, pushing for the intensity.'

The call to Leap was explicitly understood. 'Carles Puyol, Andrés Iniesta and I all looked at each other, thinking, *Woah! What's going on here, these guys are absolutely full-on.* More importantly, I thought to myself, *This is one of those moments where you either jump right on the train or it's leaving without you.*'

When you deliver a speech, you have the opportunity to explain your ideas and directly address any resistance to change. By contrasting your current situation (*what is*) with the improved reality your people will enjoy if they embrace your – Big Picture – dream (*what could be*), you'll be able to make the future more alluring than the present. Speeches motivate continued forward movement because the gap between *what is* and *what could be* creates a tension that your team will naturally want to resolve. The aim is to distance them from the current reality and keep them focused on the Big Picture that people long to see come true.

Speeches often contain some of the stories, ceremonies or symbols we have addressed in order to amplify ideas and heighten emotion. Speeches differ from stories because stories unfold in a chronological sequence, whereas speeches aren't bound by the constraints of time and place. A speech offers a freedom to unveil insights in the order that conveys information in the most persuasive and engaging manner possible.

EXERCISE: LESSONS FROM MARK ANTONY, OBAMA AND OTHERS

'*Friends, Romans, countrymen, lend me your ears; I come to bury Caesar, not to praise him.*'

In just sixteen words, we see Shakespeare's Mark Antony deploy three of the greatest rhetorical techniques. These same three practices can be used whenever you need to deliver a speech to orientate others along the Arc of Change:

1. Opening with a three – *Friends, Romans, countrymen.*
    Guardiola: *My players are going to run and run and run.*

2. Ending the opening line with an interaction that commands attention: *Lend me your ears.*
    Guardiola: *I want your involvement in my plan.*

3. The use of a contrast that gets the audience on your side (in the case of Mark Antony, they have just heard an anti-Caesar speech) – *I come to bury Caesar, not to praise him.*
    Guardiola: *An individual talent is worth much less when they don't invoke team values.*

When I work with leaders, I often use a comparison between Barack Obama and Gordon Brown to illustrate the importance of this speech structure. Read both and decide for yourself which has a bigger impact.

On Tuesday, 4 November 2008, Barack Obama delivered his victory speech (the Arrive stage on the Arc) in Chicago.

He employed all three techniques in his address. '*It has been a long time coming, but, tonight, because of what we did on this day, in this election, at this defining moment, change has come to America,*' he said to a long roar.

Let us contrast this with a speech delivered by then-UK Prime Minister Gordon Brown. He chose these words to close his speech at the Labour Party conference in 2009 – his last speech before the General Election in 2010. And, on that most important occasion, in his most important speech, at that most important point, the very end, he chose to use a far less elegant four points. He said:

'Because we are the Labour Party and our abiding duty is to stand. And fight. And win. And serve.'

When delivering speeches to orientate people along the Arc of Change, tell stories that are relevant to your audience and use the power of three.

At a UEFA conference, French coach Gérard Houllier once shared an insight into the myriad tasks an elite-level coach needs to carry out, and the demands made of him. He described the unrelenting pressures coaches face, stresses which eventually caused him to retire with heart problems.

He said that his twenty-five years' experience had taught him a particularly valuable lesson: the importance of the five-minute rule. More specifically, 'The five minutes when a manager stands in front of the cameras are the most important five minutes of a manager's week, because the players, fans and your employers are watching for positive or negative signs.'[4]

From the day he took over at FC Barcelona until the evening he finally walked away, Guardiola held 546 press conferences. He refused to do any individual press interviews throughout his four years in charge. This was the advice proffered by Guardiola's mentor, Argentine Marcelo Bielsa, who insisted that it was wrong to give priority access to a big television company over a small newspaper. Guardiola introduced a new rule whereby he refused to give one-to-one interviews so as to avoid favouritism and getting drawn into media politics. He knew that newspaper politics – one journalist may feel slighted by lack of access, for example – could cause them to deliberately misinterpret his words. Paco Aguilar, the deputy director of Catalan newspaper *El Mundo Deportivo*, explains, 'In all his years in charge, he maintained this and didn't give a single one-on-one interview. That's why his press conferences were always so long.'[5]

By his own estimate, Guardiola sat in front of the media for 272 hours, or eleven full days. That amounts to around 800 questions a month. Every word scrutinized, every gesture picked up on, every utterance interpreted and extrapolated by the world's press. He frequently used these occasions as opportunities to orient his players on where they were positioned on the Arc of Change.

When his players are asked to recount the moments which resonate during their journey, they tend to recall two significant speeches. Each one was a clear demarcation of a significant stage of the change journey: the dream – the speech he delivered in Scotland – and the fight.

In April 2011, Barcelona and Real Madrid had a run of four *Clásicos* in eighteen days. These games were characterized by Madrid players playing with an aggression bordering on violence, and more than one Barça player indulging in diving and other unsportsmanlike conduct. In the Copa del Rey final, the referee had, rightly, disallowed a goal by Pedro for offside. Guardiola said later: 'A two-centimetre decision from a linesman who must have had a very good view ruled out Pedro's goal.'

The day before the two teams subsequently met in the first leg of the Champions League semi-final, Guardiola and his players were having lunch in the private restaurant of their hotel. The television was showing José Mourinho's press conference. Guardiola had his back to the screen when one of his assistants suggested he turn around and listen.

'We have started a new cycle,' Mourinho was saying. 'Up until now there was a very small group of coaches who didn't talk about referees and a very large group, in which I am included, who criticize referees. Now, with Pep's comments, we have started a new era with a third group, featuring only one person, a man who criticizes the referee when he makes good decisions. This is completely new to me.'

Guardiola's players were also listening by this stage and were furious at Mourinho's words and his mocking tone. It appeared to be a signal that the fight stage had been reached for Guardiola. 'The time has come!'

A few months earlier, Guardiola had confessed to his closest colleagues: 'I know Mourinho and he's trying to provoke me into a reaction, but it won't work. I'm not going to react. I'm not going to answer back. Only when I think the time is right.'

Now his – and the team's – moment to enter the fight stage had come. At 8 p.m. on the day before the match, the players left their training session at Madrid's Bernabéu stadium sensing that their leader was about to respond to Mourinho. Even senior management had heard that he was preparing a strongly worded statement. Leaving the dressing room, one of the players closest to Guardiola wished him luck with the press conference, as did sports director Andoni Zubizarreta, who surprised him by saying: 'We don't answer back, eh, Pep? We don't answer back. We like a low profile. A low profile.'

He decided to ignore management's advice and go ahead anyway.

'Señor Mourinho has permitted himself the luxury of calling me Pep, so I will call him José,' he said. 'Tomorrow at 8.45 p.m. we face each other on the pitch. He has won the battle off the pitch. If he wants his own personal Champions League trophy away from the pitch, let him take it home and enjoy it. In this room [the Bernabéu press room] Mourinho is the fucking chief, the fucking boss. He knows all about this and I don't want to compete with him in here. I'd just like to remind him that I worked with him for four years [at Barcelona]. He knows me and I know him.

'If he prefers to value the views of the journalist friends who take their information in a drip feed from [Real Madrid president] Florentino Pérez more than the relationship we had for four years then that's his choice. I try to learn from José on the pitch, but I prefer to learn as little as possible from him off the pitch.'

Manuel Estiarte recounts: 'The team were travelling back from training to the hotel when mobile phones started bleeping – mostly SMS messages like: "The boss has really started something this time".' When Guardiola arrived back at the team hotel, his men were waiting to give him a standing ovation. 'His speech proved that he was our first defender,' said Victor Valdés. 'It was important to the players that he defended us.' His teammates considered the response long overdue. These were players who had also been accused of a range of transgressions, including doping, dirty tricks, play-acting and exerting undue influence over referees. Now Guardiola had stepped in. And he'd done it in the right place at exactly the right time. 'It was one of the most special nights of the last three years,' Estiarte added.[6]

Guardiola's team, taking their lead from the head coach, delivered two performances of grit and defiance to defeat Madrid and progress to the Wembley final against Manchester United and, ultimately, their second European cup in three seasons.

EXERCISE – SPEAKING TO CONNECT

People talk all the time about what makes a great leader, teacher or coach. The vast majority of these conversations focus on the daily business of the craft: methods, information and strategies. And this makes perfect sense.

But every once in a while, we get a glimpse of what leading through change really is. Guardiola's speeches strike such a chord with his players because they are a perfect case study of *relationship-based leadership*. It's an approach where the leader puts his effort and focus on building relationships – creating identity, trust and a sense of belonging.

A conventional leader focuses first on skills. A relationship-based leader, on the other hand, focuses first on creating a sense of belonging. A conventional leader asks: what can I do to help them win? A relationship-based leader asks: what can I do to help us nurture connections and create a culture? A conventional leader views his team through the lens of performance. A relationship-based coach views his team through the lens of connections – which, not coincidentally, tends to make the teaching all the more effective. People work hard for a team. They work even harder for a team that truly feels like family.

This is not conventional leadership. These speeches are all about relationship-building.

You might call these 'soft skills', but as this shows, they are anything but 'soft' in their application. They're a product of a relationship-based approach that has four core principles:

1) Seek to create belonging by establishing a clear, vivid identity.

2) Be vulnerable. Notice how he talks openly about emotions, especially his own. This creates safety and trust.

3) Speak to the whole person. Connect in ways beyond the field.

4) Tell the truth. The strength of the relationship is in its honesty and trust.

2.iv   ARC OF CHANGE SUMMARY

Many of us instinctively spend a lot of time and energy seeking the big breakthrough: that magical moment when, after a lot of effort, everything finally clicks; when you win the big game, get the promotion, nail the presentation. While those moments are incredibly satisfying, they're also a problem.

Here's why: focusing on the big breakthrough can create a steady diet of disappointment (after all, breakthroughs are rare, by definition). Worse, you stop focusing on the smaller, incremental steps of the journey that really matter.

Psychologists say that when we attempt to change, it can be like entering a dark room, feeling around for the furniture and memorizing its location, so you can move through the room ever more swiftly. In a word, the orientation techniques in this section are about cultivating awareness – awareness of ourselves and of the path to our target performance.

'Culture,' says Ferran Soriano, 'is like an organism, continually growing and changing. The cultural challenge is constantly changing. It's not a static thing.' The best leaders hunt for the small signs of progress that we have identified in the Arc of Change.

Teresa Amabile and Steven Kramer explore this idea in their fascinating book *The Progress Principle*. In it, they analyse 12,000 diary entries from 238 subjects to get a picture of the subjects' inner work lives. They conclude that the common trait of highly successful subjects is that they are focused on achieving 'small wins' – those small progressions which add up, over time, to big changes.

'Building trust, developing people and driving high-performance behaviours are never-ending tasks,' agrees Guardiola. Through the deliberate employment of Stories, Speeches, Symbols and Ceremonies, you can orientate the people you are leading on the Arc of Change and keep them moving towards the Big Picture.

As UCLA basketball coach John Wooden said, 'Don't look for the big, quick improvement. Seek the small improvement one day at a time. That's the only way it happens – and when it happens, it lasts.'

Now we have learned how to track our progress towards the Big Picture, we must turn to the routines and habits which keep us moving forward.

3. RECURRING SYSTEMS AND PROCESSES

'We are what we repeatedly do. Excellence, then, is not an act, but a habit.'
Will Durrant

'All our life, so far as it has definite form, is but a mass of habits,' wrote William James, the father of modern day psychology, in 1892.[1] Most of the choices we make each day may feel like the products of well-considered decision-making, but they are not. They're recurring habits. And even though each habit means relatively little on its own, over time they come to have an enormous impact on our culture. One paper published by a Duke University researcher in 2006 found that more than 40 per cent of the actions people performed every day weren't actual decisions, but habits and processes.[2]

William James – like countless others, from Aristotle to Oprah – spent much of his life trying to understand why habits exist, but for the purposes of this section, we will understand how habits *work* – and more importantly, how they can be changed to help create a high-performing culture.

This section is divided into three parts. The first chapter focuses on how we frequently judge and perceive others' effectiveness through the wrong lens. We will see how identifying and valuing the trademark behaviours – humility, hard work and putting the team first – can mean the difference between an individual and a team being considered a failure or success.

The second chapter examines the recurring systems of the successful organization. It details how Pep Guardiola designed the daily working environment as a continuous feedback loop to ensure that the daily habits and associated behaviours could be constantly kept at the forefront for all members of the community.

The third chapter looks at keystone habits and how they can be maintained under pressurized situations. We will explore where these habits reside in our brains and how to shape the neural pathways to ensure desired behaviours become second nature.

At its core, this section illustrates that understanding how recurring systems and processes reinforce the right habits is key to creating a high-performing culture. By harnessing habits, we can understand how to transform our own organization.

3.i   FUNDAMENTAL ATTRIBUTION
ERROR

There was a sign fixed to a wall at FC Barcelona's training ground during the 1960s and 1970s: 'Turn around if you are here to offer a young player who is shorter than 1.80m.' It was a word of warning, but also an indication of football's wider philosophy. Physical attributes were king, power and presence prioritized over poise. Barcelona were merely following the trend of every other club.[1]

In 1986, fifteen-year-old Pep Guardiola celebrated after learning from club doctors that he would grow to be 1.80m tall. Ten years earlier, Barcelona manager Laureano Ruiz had planted the seeds of change, ripping down that sign. Yet the underlying principle still remained: if you couldn't hold your own in a fight, you wouldn't make it at the highest level.

Two years after Guardiola's tests, Johan Cruyff arrived at Barcelona with a dream, a vision of Total Football that would change the club forever. As long as the club held fast to this dream, physicality would never again be the deciding factor in selection.

Fast forward to 1998 and we arrive at the first-team debut of Xavi Hernández, who, at 1.68m tall, would once have been shown that sign on the wall and then shown the door. Xavi: the poster boy for the La Masia vision; the personification of Cruyff's ideology; the greatest midfielder of his generation; the backbone. From Cruyff to Guardiola to Xavi – a seam running through the modern history of Barcelona. Xavi is representative of the lifeblood of the club for which he played for nearly a quarter of a century.

When he walked out onto the Camp Nou pitch for that last time as a player, the trophies he had won were arranged in the same fashion that you might arrange coffee mugs in a cupboard. The array of silverware was astonishing: eight La Liga trophies, three Copas del Rey, six Spanish Super Cups, two European Super Cups, two Club World Cups and four European Cups. The two European Championship and one World Cup winner's medals he'd collected with Spain were presumably back at home. The captain lifted trophies after each of his last three games at his hometown club (the league title, Copa del Rey and European Cup), perhaps the grandest send off in the history of club football. On the day he made his last Camp Nou appearance, Barcelona had won eighty-four major trophies in their history; Xavi was present for twenty-five of them.

It was Hristo Stoichkov who once suggested that Barcelona's history would be judged in terms of pre- and post-Xavi. In an age of the sport when physicality has been cherished, Xavi was the standard-bearer for technique over physique. He was the very definition of the kind of player Cruyff had in mind to burnish the Big Picture, one who turned passing a football into an art form. As the man himself said: 'Physically I'm limited, but I've survived by using my head.'

Given his iconic status, it seems bizarre that Xavi could ever have been anything other than vital to Barcelona. Yet he twice came close to leaving the club, once as a teenager and once again towards the end of Frank Rijkaard's reign, when the club had begun to drift away from its purpose, as journalist Graham Hunter has described: 'In sporting terms, Barça had become flabby; training lacked intensity; several players had lost both a mental edge and the ability to press the ball with the same hungry intensity.'[2]

'Six years ago, I was extinct as a player; footballers like me were in danger of dying out,' Xavi said in an interview with the *Guardian* in 2011.[3] He had already spoken to his family about the merits of Manchester United and AC Milan, the two suitors who were most ardent in their pursuit.

The defining moment would come in summer 2008, when Guardiola was appointed as coach of Barcelona and steered the club back on its true course. As we have seen, Guardiola was appointed to be the keeper of the flame, to place the philosophy above mere pragmatism. As he had replaced his new manager in the first team a decade earlier, there was now no doubt that Xavi would stay. When viewed through the lens of the Big Picture, the man who had been deemed dispensable now became invaluable.

'Xavi is a player who has the Barcelona DNA: someone who has the taste for good football, someone who is humble and someone who has loyalty to this club,' Guardiola said. 'From the first moment I saw him play, I knew he would become the brain behind Barcelona for many years to come.'

Guardiola's first-team appointment coincided with Spain's Euro 2008 triumph, where Xavi was named Player of the Tournament. Coach Luis Aragonés had understood that rather than utilizing power, his team had to find a methodology for maximizing the talents of his team. Xavi was the orchestrator of a new Spain. Barcelona was their blueprint.

Xavi's career from 2008 to 2012 is arguably the greatest period of individual performance in the sport's history. As Sid Lowe noted in a column for *World Soccer* magazine, in each of those years Xavi won the most important trophy available: European Championship, Champions League, World Cup, Champions League, European Championship. In four seasons between the ages of twenty-eight and thirty-two, Xavi played 260 matches for club and country, a model of astonishing consistency and unprecedented collective success. A legacy had been assured.

Receive, pass, offer. Receive, pass, offer. Receive, pass, offer. Repeat *ad infinitum*. Everything he did looked simple, yet the reality is anything but. There was a precision to each and every movement. The placement of the pass allows the receiver to make space, the weight allows for the move to proceed with maximum efficiency and the hours of practice make for a touch and technique beyond anything else in world football. Former Barcelona president Sandro Rosell described tiki-taka as 'Xavi's registered trademark'. Most of his former teammates knew him as '*Màqui*', short for *La Màquina* – The Machine.

'I'm a team player.' Xavi invoked the trademark behaviours when speaking with Graham Hunter for his book *Barça*. 'Individually, I'm nothing. I play with the best and that makes me a better player. I depend on my teammates.'[4] Never as much as those teammates depended on him.

'I pass and I move, I help you, I look for you, I stop, I raise my head, I look and, above all, I open up the pitch,' Xavi says of his metronomic style. If it looks simple, it's because he's doing it right. 'Only those who have patience to do simple things perfectly ever acquire the skill to do difficult things easily,' as the boxer James R. Corbett once said.

Xavi's forefather would undoubtedly agree. 'Simple play is also the most beautiful,' was Cruyff's mantra. 'How often do you see a pass of forty metres when twenty metres is enough? A good player almost always has the problem of a lack of efficiency. He always wants to do things prettier than strictly necessary.'

Without Xavi pulling the strings in the middle alongside his friend Iniesta and later La Masia graduate Sergio Busquets, the success of FC Barcelona this century appears almost inconceivable, yet he came close to departing not once, but twice. How could anyone, let alone football men with their highly trained eyes, fail to recognize such greatness?

The answer, it seems, is partly down to our ability to recognize the power of our cultural environment.

In a famous article, Stanford psychologist Lee Ross surveyed dozens of studies in psychology and noted that people have a systematic tendency to ignore the situational forces that shape other people's behaviour. He called this deep-rooted tendency the 'Fundamental Attribution Error'. The error lies in our inclination to attribute people's behaviour to *the way they are* rather than *the culture or situation they are in*.[5]

The Fundamental Attribution Error is the reason why we love TV shows like *Supernanny* or Gordon Ramsay's *Kitchen Nightmares*, in which seemingly irredeemable kids or hapless restaurateurs are tamed by outsiders who come in with a new system of discipline. At the beginning of each episode of the former, for example, we're presented with a child who won't obey the simplest of commands, and we simply can't avoid jumping to conclusions about their character: 'That boy is a terror.' And when they're reformed, in the course of a short intervention, it blows our minds. If we could cure ourselves of the Fundamental Attribution Error, these shows would seem obvious to the point of absurdity.

As we have seen, before Guardiola was promoted to Head Coach, the culture at Barcelona had shifted and power was valued over technique, pace over precision, showboating over humility, individual skills over teamwork, spectacular over the basics. Within this culture, it is understandable that Xavi's talents were regarded as dispensable. When viewed through the Big Picture lens which Guardiola used, where humility, hard work and putting the team's needs above individual agenda were the trademark behaviours, he was recognized as essential.

It can be easy to jump to conclusions about people, but what can look like a person problem is often a cultural problem.

Now you can see why this element of our cultural framework is so critical. If you want people to change, to demonstrate the ability to behave and perform effectively and consistently under pressure, you must provide clear behavioural direction.

EXERCISE – STOP JUDGING TALENT; START OBSERVING CHARACTER

Sorry to break this to you, but you are a pretty bad judge of talent.

It's not your fault. We're all bad at judging talent because we instinctively tend to overrate the visible stuff (performance), and underrate the invisible stuff we call 'character' – namely work habits, competitiveness, ambition, and grit – which turn out to be far more important in the long run.

The Australian swimming coach, Bill Sweetenham, manages to avoid this trap when he is selecting swimmers to join his elite programme. How? Because he's figured out an efficient way to test for character.

Here's how it works: Sweetenham invites the prospect to a meeting room. The athlete walks in, Sweetenham says a brisk hello, clicks off the lights, then presses the play button to start a video of one of the athlete's worst moments. Then he turns to the prospect and asks, 'So what happened there?'

Sweetenham is not really interested in what happened, of course. He's interested in how the athlete *reacts to adversity*. How does their brain handle failure? Do they take responsibility, or make excuses? Do they blame others, or talk about what they would do differently? (When one swimmer started ripping into his coach, Sweetenham flicked on the lights and ended the interview right there.)

The idea is not just to weed out people with the wrong mind-set, but also to identify those who have the right one.

The challenge for us is to avoid being easily distracted by brilliant performance and start to pay attention to those quieter things that really matter in the long run.

3.ii   IT'S THE ENVIRONMENT, STUPID!

Most of us go through our lives unaware of how our environment shapes our behaviour.

As you go through your day, notice how many times you change your behaviour according to the environmental context you find yourself in. Notice also how people have tweaked the environment to shape your behaviour. Traffic engineers wanted you to drive in a predictable, orderly way, so they painted markings on the road and installed traffic lights and signs. Supermarket managers wanted you to spend more time in their store, so they positioned the milk you came in for all the way at the back. Your boss's boss wanted to encourage more collaboration among employees, so they approved an 'open floor layout' with no cubicles or dividers. The bank was tired of you leaving your ATM card in the machine, so the machine now forces you to remove it before you can claim your cash.[1]

Even when we are aware of our environment and welcome being in it, we become victims of its ruthless power. When I first started travelling on planes, I regarded being on a plane as the ideal environment for reading and writing. No phones, no screens, no interruptions. The constant travel wasn't an annoyance – it allowed me to be extra productive. But as the airlines' in-flight entertainment offerings gradually expanded from one film on a single screen to universal Wi-Fi and fifty on-demand channels at my seat, my productivity dropped. What had been a pocket of serenity had become a smorgasbord of distraction. And I was easily distracted. Instead of getting work done or catching up on much-needed sleep, I'd sit and watch a couple of films. Each time I walked off the plane, instead of being happy to arrive safely, ready to charge into my next job, I berated myself for the time I had wasted in-flight. I felt I'd relaxed my discipline. It took me a couple of years to realize that the on-board environment had changed – and I had changed with it.

It's not all bad. Our environment can sometimes act like an angel on our shoulder, making us a better person – like when we find ourselves at a wedding or a school reunion or an awards dinner and the joyous feeling in the room overwhelms people. Everyone is hugging and promising to stay in touch and get together again soon. Of course, the feeling often fades the moment we return to our regular lives – in other words, find ourselves in a different environment. We are altered by the change. We forget our promises; we don't stay in touch. The contrast could not be sharper. One environment elevates us, the other erases the good vibes as if they never happened.

We often think we are in sync with our environment, but actually it is frequently at odds with the behaviour we want to display. If there is one thing I am trying to address in this chapter, it is our awareness of our environment and how we can harness its power to create our own cultural dynasty.

What we will see at FC Barcelona is that behaviours shift when our environment shifts. This makes sense – our habits are essentially stitched into our environment. Research bears this out. According to one study of people making changes in their lives, 36 per cent of the successful changes were associated with a move to a new location, and only 13 per cent of unsuccessful changes involved a move.

Many smokers, for example, find it easier to quit when they

are on holiday, because, at home, every part of their environment is loaded with smoking associations. Everywhere you look, there are reminders of your habit. There's the drawer in the kitchen where you stash the lighters, the plant pot outside the back door which is full of ash, the ever-present smell of smoke in your car. When a smoker goes on holiday, the environment recedes towards neutrality. That doesn't mean it's easy to quit, but it is *easier*.[2]

In 2009, FC Barcelona moved its training ground and had the chance to stitch the essential behaviours into this new environment. Previous sessions on the training pitch next door to the Camp Nou had a fairly high-profile feel about them, partly due to the location, where fans could gather to watch the sessions taking place. The Joan Gamper Training Ground, to which the first team moved in January 2009, is strictly off-limits to press and public on a daily basis. This was such a revolutionary step that the media christened it '*La Ciudad Prohibida*' – The Forbidden City.

It's unrealistic, however, to think that most of us can shift our environment so dramatically. If you're trying to change your team's habits at work, then, yes, relocating your office would be a big help. Good luck selling that idea to your boss. There are, however, two practical ways of creating behavioural habits within your current environment: feedback loops and action triggers.

For our purposes in this chapter, let's focus on how Barcelona used the training ground environment to kick-start the feedback loop and embed their trademark behaviours – humility, hard work and teamwork.

Feedback loops

The classic template for analysing problem behaviour in children is known as ABC, for antecedent, behaviour and consequence. The antecedent is the event that prompts the behaviour. The behaviour creates a consequence. A common classroom example: a student is drawing pictures instead of working on the class assignment. The teacher asks the child to finish the task (antecedent). The child reacts by throwing a tantrum (behaviour). The teacher responds by sending the student to the head teacher's office (consequence). That's the ABC sequence. Armed with this insight, after several repeat episodes the teacher concludes that the child's behaviour is a ploy to avoid class assignments.

Feedback – both giving it and receiving it – is our first step, the antecedent in becoming smarter and more mindful about the connection between our environment and our behaviour. Feedback teaches us to see our environment as a triggering mechanism. In some cases, the feedback itself is the antecedent.

Consider, for example, all of the feedback we get when we're behind the wheel of a car, how we ignore some of it and why only some of it triggers desirable behaviour.

Say you're driving down a country road at the speed limit of 50 mph, approaching a village. You know this because half a mile outside the village a sign reads: SPEED LIMIT AHEAD 30 MPH. The sign is just a warning, not a command to slow down, so you maintain your speed. Thirty seconds or so later, you reach the village, where the sign says SPEED LIMIT 30 MPH. You might comply, but if you're like most drivers you'll maintain your speed – or slow down slightly – because you've been driving on autopilot in a 50 mph environment and it's easier to continue what you are doing than it is to stop it. Only if you see a manned police car monitoring motorists' speeds will you comply with the mandated 30 mph – because a police officer handing out speeding tickets represents an unwanted consequence to you.

Every community in the developed world has to deal with speeding drivers putting its citizens at risk. For years, drivers had ignored the speed signs that told them to slow down, especially in school zones and residential neighbourhoods. Nothing worked particularly effectively to decrease speeding, not even a greater police ticketing presence, until officials installed radar speed signs – a speed limit sign posted above a digital readout measuring 'your speed'. You've probably seen them on you're own town's streets, near a school or playground. If the radar display says you're speeding, you've probably stepped on the brake immediately.

The effectiveness of the radar displays is both deeper and more reliable than any other method. Speed limit compliance increases between 30 and 60 per cent with radar displays – and the effect lasts for several miles beyond the sign.

Radar speed signs – also called driver feedback systems – work because they harness a well-established concept in behavioural theory called a feedback loop. The radar measures a driver's actions – that is, speeding – and relays the information to the driver in real time, inducing the driver to react. It's a loop of action, information, reaction. When the reaction is measured, a new loop begins, and so on and so on. Given the immediate change in drivers' behaviour after just one glance at a radar display, it's easy to imagine the immense utility of seeing our everyday environment as a feedback loop that can change people's behaviour.[3]

The potential of the feedback loop to affect behaviour was explored in the 1960s, most notably in the work of Albert Bandura, a Stanford University psychologist and pioneer in the study of behaviour change and motivation. Drawing on several education experiments involving children, Bandura observed that giving individuals a clear goal and a means to evaluate their progress towards that goal greatly increased the likelihood that they would achieve it. He later expanded this notion into the concept of self-efficacy, which holds that the more we believe we can meet a goal, the more likely it is that we will do so.[4]

In the fifty years since Bandura's early work, feedback loops have been thoroughly researched and validated in psychology, epidemiology, military strategy, environmental studies, engineering and economics. (In typical academic fashion, each discipline tends to reinvent the methodology and rephrase the terminology, but the basic framework remains the same.)

Despite the volume of research and a proven capacity to affect human behaviour, we don't often use feedback loops in everyday life. Blame this on two factors: first, until now, the necessary catalyst – personalized data – is difficult to collect. Second, collecting data is cumbersome. Although the basic idea of self-tracking has been available to anyone willing to put in the effort, few people stick with the routine of toting around a notebook, writing down everything they consume or every flight of stairs they climb. It's just too much bother. As a result, feedback loops are often considered niche tools, for the most part rewarding for those with the money, willpower or geeky inclination to obsessively track their own behaviour, but impractical for the rest of us.

A feedback loop comprises of four stages: evidence, relevance, consequence and action. Once you recognize this, it's easy to see why the radar speed displays' exploitation of the loop works so well. Drivers get data about their speed in real time (evidence). The information gets their attention because it's coupled with the speed limit, indicating whether they are obeying or breaking the law (relevance). Aware that they are speeding, drivers fear getting a ticket or hurting someone (consequence). So they slow down (action).[5]

This is how feedback is ultimately the antecedent to trigger desirable behaviours. Once we deconstruct feedback into its four stages of evidence, relevance, consequence and action, the world never looks the same again. Suddenly we understand that our good behaviour is not random. It's logical. It follows a pattern. It makes sense. It's within our control. It's something we can repeat. It's why some obese people finally – and instantly – take charge of their eating habits when they are told they have diabetes and will have more serious ailments if they don't make a serious lifestyle change.

So feedback loops work. Why? Why does putting our own data in front of us somehow compel us to act? In part, it's because feedback taps into something at the core of the human experience, even into our biological origins. Evolution itself, after all, is a feedback loop of gene selection, albeit one so elongated as to be imperceptible to an individual. Feedback loops are how we learn, whether we call it trial and error or course correction. In so many areas of life, we succeed when we have some sense of where we stand and some evaluation of our progress. Indeed, we tend to crave this sort of information; it's something we viscerally want to know, good or bad. As Albert Bandura put it, 'People are proactive, aspiring organisms.' Feedback taps into those aspirations.

Which brings up the obvious question: *What if we could control our environment so it triggered our most desired behaviours – like an elegantly designed feedback loop?*

This was the question which Pep Guardiola addressed when embedding the behaviours which he had defined in the Big Picture. If we view the structure of a training day through the eyes of a Barcelona player, the feedback loop becomes evident.

EXERCISE – THE OODA LOOP

How do you decide where and how to build a feedback loop?

We find a useful answer from an unlikely source: a fighter pilot named John 'Forty Second' Boyd. Boyd, a Korean War pilot who went on to be head of instruction at the USAF Weapons School, was famous for his standing bet with trainees: he could, from a position of disadvantage, defeat any of them in a dogfight in forty seconds or less.[6]

Boyd's secret? The OODA Loop, developed to increase the speed and agility of fighter pilots, and since adopted by many businesses. It works like this:

Observe: *collect the data. Figure out exactly where you are and what's happening*

Orient: *analyse/synthesize the data to form an accurate picture*

Decide: *select an action from possible options*

Action: *execute the action, and return to step one*

The genius of Boyd's idea is that it shows that speed and agility are really about information processing. They're about building more and better feedback loops. The more high-quality OODA loops you make, the faster and more effective you will become.

When you tune into it, you start to see OODA feedback loops everywhere, such as in Google's quicksilver iterations of its online products or in the daily routines of successful stock traders. They're all fast, but they succeed because they are ruthless about following the OODA loop. They observe, orient, decide and act – and then start the cycle anew.

So, start by being merciless about where you are and where you want to go and then begin to put yourself and your team through the OODA loop.

Daily displays of feedback

Guardiola was normally first to the training ground every morning – usually not long after 8 a.m. Punctuality, as a representation of being mentally prepared, became strictly enforced. That work ethic is very much part of the Catalan character: saving the soul through industry, effort and honest labour and giving your all to the job. In a suitably symbolic place – the Catalan parliament – and on being awarded the National Gold Medal, the country's highest honour for a Catalan citizen, in recognition of his representation of Catalan sporting values, Guardiola said in his acceptance speech: 'If we get up early, very early, and think about it, believe me, we are an unstoppable country.'[7]

First, the team arrived in time to breakfast together. Not everyone was forced to eat together in the morning, although lunch was almost regarded as a part of the training day and thus obligatory.

Although he wanted an element of democracy within the group, with players using their own initiative, making suggestions and keeping an open mind to new ideas, Guardiola did not delay in imposing a number of strict rules in his first few days in charge: such as insisting upon Castilian and Catalan as the only languages spoken among the group, arranging a seating plan at meal times to encourage the players to mix and prevent the team forming into different cultural or national groups or cliques.

The players had to sign in by a specific hour, usually sixty minutes before training began. If training started at 11 a.m. then that was when you were expected to be on the training pitch, fully kitted; ready, physically and mentally, to put everything into the session, or you were fined.

The fines for lateness were €500 per five minutes, up to a

limit of €6,000, and whoever was late had to start training on his own. Tying up your laces on the training pitch, arriving ten seconds past eleven, any breach, no matter how small, was forbidden. Latecomers were greeted with ironic applause from absolutely everyone else involved in the session. 'If you didn't already know, you quickly learned,' says goalkeeper Victor Valdés, 'that you should never be late.'[8]

However, Guardiola's rules – and the imposition of fines for breaking them – were not introduced to keep the players under strict control, but rather to encourage a stronger sense of solidarity and responsibility. Two years later, Guardiola learned the lesson from this particular feedback loop and abolished his own system of sanctions and penalties, feeling that they had become unnecessary, with the group exercising an impressive degree of self-discipline.

Monday to Friday, the players were expected to be at home by midnight at the latest and they could expect a late-night call from Guardiola or one of his assistants. If a phone call to the house went unanswered and was not properly explained, another four-figure fine was on the way. When and where players were allowed to film commercials or work for their sponsors was tightly controlled and only one man, Guardiola, made the final decision. Use of mobile phones and headphones were both controlled and players were told that taking their place in the rota for press conferences and signing autographs for fans on away trips were obligatory.

There was also the aforementioned incentive scheme, based on a system Guardiola had developed when he was in charge of the young players of Barcelona B: if the team won four straight La Liga matches or two consecutive Champions League ties, Guardiola would pay for either a lunch or dinner for the entire squad plus staff.

Why didn't the fines pay for the dinners? Although that is

the norm for many teams, where a system of fines imposed by the boss goes towards an end-of-season party, Guardiola thought that to be self-defeating. If your fine eventually goes towards paying for an alcohol-fuelled night out, then how have you been penalized? Instead, all fines collected were sent, at the end of each season, to a charitable cause, often associated with hospitals.

These simple rules – and the associated feedback loop which reinforced them – were not for everyone. One example was Alexander Hleb, a sublime dribbler but also having the passing range and slight physique associated with Iniesta, the latter being the traits that attracted Barcelona's recruitment team. Hleb moaned about Guardiola not having faith in him as a footballer but he was, simultaneously, repeatedly late for the signing-in book, often claiming he had arrived on time but forgotten to sign in; he regularly traipsed onto the training pitch unprepared, if not physically then certainly mentally (the evidence stage of the feedback loop).

Guardiola showed understanding to this talented but immature player, a Belarusian, who needed help to adapt to life in Spain. 'Please learn Spanish,' he was told. 'It will help you to integrate within the team' (relevance). 'How can we help you learn Spanish?' he was then asked, when no tangible progress had been made.

On the pitch, he too often tried his trademark dribbling and didn't pass and move like his teammates needed him to (relevance). He was chided, coaxed and warned – then dumped at the end of the season (consequence).

EXERCISE – HOW TO GET (FEEDBACK) RICH OR DIE TRYING

Consider the life of a typical twenty-something. From the moment she was born, her world has been rich in feedback. When she presses a button, something happens. When she plays a video game, she gets a score. When she sends a text message, she hears a sound that confirms it went out. She has lived her whole life in a landscape lush with feedback.

However, once she steps into the workplace, the main – often the only – mechanism for giving her information on how she's doing on the job is the annual performance review. She goes from feast to a famine of feedback in the place she spends most of her waking hours.

This sturdy feature of organizational life is deeply flawed in at least two ways.

First, it's annual. It's hard to get better at something if you receive feedback on your performance just once a year. Think about Rafael Nadal. His job is to hit tennis balls back and forth across a court. Now imagine if Nadal played tennis for an entire season – and got feedback on his performance only once a year in a forty-five-minute meeting with his coach. Absurd, right?

Second, performance reviews are rarely authentic conversations. More often, they are meetings in which people recite predictable lines in a formulaic way and hope the experience ends very quickly.

The workplace is one of the most feedback-deprived places in modern life.

Fortunately, it needn't be that way. Let me suggest a couple of modest strategies for making the workplace a little more feedback-rich.

1. *Do it yourself*
Formal performance appraisals have their place. But we

should supplement them with evaluations we do ourselves. Here's how a DIY performance review would work: at the beginning of the month, set out your goals – your performance goals and your learning goals. Then, at the end of the month, call yourself into the office. Where are you making progress? Where are you falling behind? What tools or information do you need to do your job better?

If a conversation with yourself seems odd, try it with a few colleagues. Indeed, many top-performing teams already do this as a matter of course – often without the boss's permission, sometimes without the boss even knowing. This ethic of self-evaluation is also a hallmark of star athletes and great musicians. They set high standards for themselves and then meticulously monitor their own progress.

2. Do it through peers

I worked with one company who introduced a peer-to-peer approach, where anybody at any time can award a colleague a £25 bonus.

Instead of once-a-year acknowledgment from a boss who may not remember your heroic deeds, these modest bonuses allow colleagues to recognize good work instantly – and that, in turn, can create an environment in which feedback more regularly bursts through into office life.

A person's supervisor must sign off on each award, but ultimately the decision rests with peers, not bosses – which can make the feedback and recognition more meaningful. It puts the feedback control in the hands of the people who are closest to the activity.

3. Speedback

It's useful to judge feedback in the same way that you would judge the quality of a GPS mapping app on your phone: the best ones are real-time, detailed and crystal-clear. The problem is that most of the time – especially at work – the feedback we get is not timely or clear. So we tend to wander, and get lost.

In other words, the feedback question is really a design question: how do you tighten the OODA loop, and deliver the right signal in a timely way?

Karen May, vice president for people development at Google, has invented a method she calls 'speedback'. It works like this: partway through a training session she will tell everyone to pair off and sit knee to knee, and give them three minutes to answer one simple question: 'What advice would you give me based on the experience you've had with me here?' Participants say that it's some of the best feedback they've ever received.

3.iii   ACTION TRIGGERS

An important thing to realize is that while even small environmental tweaks can make a difference, forming a habit isn't just environmental – it's also mental. It would be very difficult, for instance, to tweak the environment in a way that would *compel* you to learn how to play the piano.

During one press conference, Guardiola was asked to define the Barcelona model. His response, in English, was simple, a mantra: 'I get the ball, I pass the ball, I get the ball, I pass the ball, I get the ball, I pass the ball, I get the ball, I pass the ball . . .' To have the mental capacity to execute this seemingly simple requirement under the harshest glare of elite competition is not an accident.

So, how do you lay the mental groundwork that enables essential behaviours to become an easily replicable habit?

Peter Gollwitzer, a psychologist at New York University, is the pioneer of work in this area. He and his colleague Veronika Brandstarter found that *implementation intentions* – action triggers – are effective in motivating action.

In one study, they tracked college students who had the option to earn extra credits in class by writing a paper about how they spent Christmas Eve. But, like all these studies, there was a catch: to earn the credit, they had to submit the paper by 26 December. Most students had the best of intentions, and planned on writing the paper, but only 33 per cent of them got round to actually doing so. Other students in the study were required to set action triggers – to note, in advance, exactly where and when they intended to write the report. For example, 'I'll write this in my dad's office on Christmas morning, before everyone else is awake.' A whopping 75 per cent of those students wrote the report.[1]

Does this mean that by simply *imagining* a time and place where you'll do something, you increase the likelihood that you'll actually do it? Yes and no. Action triggers won't get you – or anyone else – to do something you really don't want to do. An action trigger would never have convinced college students to participate in an online maths class on Christmas Day. But, as the extra-credit study demonstrates, action triggers can have a profound power to motivate people to *do the things they know they need to do.*

Gollwitzer and Brandstarter argue that the value of implementation intentions – action triggers – resides in the fact that we are *preloading* a decision. Dropping off the kids at school triggers the next action, going to the gym. There's no cycle of conscious deliberation. You simply get out of the way of your thinking.

That's why action triggers have unexpected value. Gollwitzer and Brandstarter say that when people pre-decide, they 'pass the control of their behaviour on to the environment.' Action triggers 'protect goal pursuit from tempting distractions, bad habits, or competing goals.'

EXERCISE – HOW TO PREPARE FOR THOSE KEY MOMENTS

One of my favourite ideas about high-performing cultures is taken from the US Navy SEALs. The mantra which underscores their organization is: 'When you come under pressure, you don't rise to the occasion. You descend to the level of your training.'

Life is made up of tests: the big game, the final exam, the crucial presentation. In those moments, we naturally tend to focus on the externals of our performance. Were we successful or not?

The Norwegian psychologist Willi Railo once advised: 'If a coach is hoping to influence players in the dressing room before the match, they have not done their job well enough. It is far too late. The job must be done long before you reach the dressing room.'

I think it might be more revealing to focus on the days of preparation leading up to the performance – one of the foundations of your culture. How do you know when you're ready for a big test? How do you know that you're fully prepared?

When reading the book *No Easy Day*, about the US Navy SEALs' mission to take out Osama Bin Laden, I was more impressed with their mindset than their obvious physical toughness – especially when it came to their methods of preparing for big tests.

So how did the SEALs prepare for the test of killing Bin Laden? They built a precise, full-scale mock-up of Bin Laden's compound, and they rehearsed. And rehearsed. And rehearsed. For several weeks, they ran endless variations of possible situations, from best-case scenarios down to total disaster.

'Every single contingency was practised to the point where we were tired of it,' the author, Matt Bissonnette, writes.[2]

I love that line because it gives us some insight into what real preparation for a big test truly is. You do something repeatedly – covering every single contingency – until you are tired of it.

This is not normally how we think about preparation. In normal life, we think that practice ends when we get it right a couple of times in a row. But in truth, that's when practice truly begins. The goal is not to do it right once. The goal is to do it often enough, in realistic conditions and under pressure, so that you can't get it wrong.

But how do you know when you've reached that point? Here are a few clues.

1) You can perform the action while paying attention to other, extraneous things. For instance, if it's a speech or a song, you can perform it while retaining a bit of brain space for noticing things. Call it automaticity, call it autopilot – the point is that you've built a reflex.

2) You are genuinely, deeply tired of it. You know every molecule of the material so well that if you ran through it one more time you might explode. This relationship – call it a healthy exasperation – is a good sign that you've mastered it.

3) You can vividly and accurately pre-create the big moment in your imagination – the sights, the sounds, the smells, the sensations. You don't get surprised or knocked off balance by the big test because, in a profound way, you've already experienced it.

All of which adds up to a basic truth known to the SEALs: the trick of succeeding in the biggest moments is to use practice to reduce them into a series of small, controllable moments.

Keystone habits

Our lives are filled with habits and time is limited. Knowing how to improve behaviours doesn't resolve a central question: where to begin? Is it better to create an exercise habit, or reform eating patterns? Should someone focus on procrastination? Or biting their fingernails? Or both at the same time?

The answer lies in what the author Charles Duhigg describes as 'keystone habits'.[3] Some habits, say researchers, are more important than others because they have the power to start a chain reaction, shifting other patterns as they move through our lives. Keystone habits influence how we work, eat, play, live, spend and communicate. Keystone habits start a process that, over time, transforms everything.

This, then, is the answer of where to start: focus on keystone habits, those patterns that, when they start to shift, dislodge and remake other habits.

To find them, you have to know where to look. 'Not only did Guardiola know Barcelona's house style inside out,' said Txiki Begiristian, 'he also knew how it could be improved.'[4]

Guardiola once compared Barcelona's style to a cathedral. Johan Cruyff, he said, had built this particular place of worship. The task of those who came afterwards was to renovate and update it. Guardiola was always looking for updates. Most of Cruyff's thinking was about attack. 'I didn't mind conceding three goals, as long as Barça scored five,' he once said. Guardiola, it seemed, also wanted to score five, but he minded conceding even one. While still a player, Guardiola wrote a series of columns for *El País*, Spain's leading daily newspaper. In 1995, when, aged twenty-four, he had already established himself as the axis around which Johan Cruyff's Barcelona revolved, he wrote: 'Without the ball there is no pass, without the ball there is no control, with no control the fewer opportunities you have to score.' If Barcelona is a cathedral, Guardiola has added the buttresses.

Guardiola's friend, David Trueba, offers an insight into how these foundations were laid. 'Pep does something similar to the way Bob Dylan used to compose songs,' he explains. 'He fills page after page with material and then pares it all down so that he ends up with only the key verses he wants. Pep makes thousands of notes and then reduces them to bare essentials.'[5] The crux of his game plan and strategy can was based on the implementation of two keystone habits.

EXERCISE – MAKING TIME TO THINK

I love this simple idea taken from Annika Sorenstam, the golfer.

It goes as follows. Draw an imaginary line that separates your practice space from your performance space. When you're inside the Thinking Zone, your brain is fully switched on. You're thinking, strategizing, planning. But when you step across the line into the Play Zone, you click off your mind and just play.

Essentially, she draws an imaginary line about a yard behind the ball. She deems the area behind the line as the 'thinking' zone and the area in front of the line as the 'play' zone. In the thinking zone, she receives feedback from her caddy and thinks hard about the wind, the aim, which club, which shot, visualization, etc. Then, once she has figured out what she wants to do, she crosses the line into the 'play' zone, turns her mind off and hits the shot (or 'plays' as if she were a little girl again), like she has done millions of times before.

There's plenty of brain science that supports this method (MRI scans show that the more skilled an athlete is, the less they're thinking). And, of course, we know that top performance happens when we relax and go on autopilot, letting our unconscious brain do its magic. But I like it because this Play Zone idea could be applied to lots of stuff beyond sports. Think about delivering an important presentation. We all have a zone where we build, and then a zone where we relax and show what we've built.

I also like it because it shows the real paradox at the heart of improvement. During practice, thinking and planning are your friends. During performance, however, thinking and planning are your enemies. You can't avoid this paradox; you need to build a routine that embraces both sides. You essentially have two brains, the conscious and unconscious; so the best way to improve is to give one zone to each.

Does your environment allow you to do this?

I regularly conduct management training days in which attendees have to react to pressure and perform both as a member of the team and as a leader. The day is composed of a series of games and activities, with the delegates split into teams and a different person being the leader on each activity. The person in charge is not only responsible for their team's performance, but also needs to coach their team members in the skills and tactics for a contest with the other teams.

The first activity is a simple possession game, not unlike the rondos or netball, with five players per team. The object is to complete as many passes as possible between players on the attacking side, while the defending side's job is to win the ball back. The complicating factor? The defending side can only field three players to the attacking side's five, so that when the attacking side loses possession they have to take two players off – an added challenge for the respective leaders.

Without exception, the start of the game is always absolute chaos. Everyone charges around after the ball, people scream for it to be passed to them, the ball is dropped, passes go astray – it's like watching a game in a school playground played by hyperactive kids. The players, excited and pumped on adrenalin, have usually lost track of the score by now and any other information not relevant to the one thing they're doing: chasing blindly after the ball.

After about sixty to seventy seconds of pure pandemonium,

the game is halted. In a simple five-versus-three game like this, the simplest and most effective tactic for the offensive team is to have one player in the middle and one in each of the corners, making it impossible for the defending team to mark everyone, in turn meaning there is always someone to pass to. Once the players absorb this concept, the game seems to slow down and the players find themselves with more space in which to operate, and consequently more time to make decisions, as long as they are disciplined with their positions on the court.

The next task is an extension of basically the same game but with one important adjustment: no verbal contact is permitted – only eye contact. This, thankfully, makes for a quieter game, but it also leads to a dramatic increase in the players' awareness of the position and spacing of their own team members. By the end of the day, the teams have improved no end from the unrestrained chaos of the start to showing a massive increase in awareness, communication, empathy and control – and eventually posture and composure.

With a bit of understanding and a series of specific practices, every player has left the rushed, time-cramped style and is now able to make less hurried and better decisions. In just one day the people on the training course have become markedly better at making effective decisions under pressure. They appear to have 'more time on the ball' and 'see things a lot earlier'.

The point I emphasize to these leaders is that no one is born with this innate skill. It requires hours and hours of deliberate practice.

FC Barcelona's two keystone habits

The five-second rule

The action trigger which Guardiola introduced was that the team must attempt to get the ball back within five seconds of losing it. 'This,' explains Victor Valdés, 'was the key to our success.' Everything else – from fitness through to team spirit and game strategy – flows from it.

Barcelona start pressing (hunting for the ball) the instant they lose possession. That is the perfect time to press, because the opposing player who has just won the ball is vulnerable. He has had to take his eyes off the game to make his tackle or interception, and he has expended energy. That means he is unsighted, and probably tired. He usually needs two or three seconds to regain his vision of the field. So, Barcelona try to dispossess him before he can give the ball to a better-placed teammate.

Furthermore, if the opponent who won the ball back is a defender, and Barcelona can instantly win it back again, then the way to goal is often clear. The Barcelona player who lost the ball leads the hunt to regain it. But he never hunts alone. His teammates near the ball join him. If only one or two Barça players are pressing, it's too easy for the opponent to pass around them. 'If we don't play this way,' warned Guardiola repeatedly, 'then, ciao, we're cooked.'[6]

If Barça don't win the ball back within five seconds of losing it, they revert to Plan B – another action trigger habit – retreat and build a compact, ten-man wall.

Peter Gollwitzer's work has shown that creating an action trigger such as this simple rule is most useful in the most difficult circumstances – the occasions when we come under intense periods of pressure. One study analysed people's success in accomplishing 'easy' goals or 'hard' goals. With easy goals, the use of action triggers – and the associated habits which follow – increased success only slightly, from 78 per cent to 84 per cent. But with hard goals, action triggers almost tripled the chance of success – goal completion skyrocketed from 22 per cent to 62 per cent.[7] 'Executing your habits in these key moments is what distinguishes the good from the great performer,' suggests Jim Loehr, the renowned sports psychologist. Doing it in the pursuit of the hardest goal in European football, winning the Champions League final, is, therefore, critical.

Gollwitzer says that, in essence, what action triggers do is create an 'instant habit'. Habits are behavioural autopilot, and that's exactly what action triggers are setting up. Even though they are not perfect, it's hard to imagine an easier way to make an immediate change more likely. A recent meta-study that analysed 8,155 participants across eighty-five studies found that the typical person who set an action trigger to respond in a certain manner did better than 74 per cent of people on the same task who didn't set one.

Keystone habits represent a rare point of intersection between the aspirations of self-help and the reality of science. And you can't get any more practical. The next time your team resolves to act in a new way, challenge team members to take it further. Have them specify where and when they're going to put the plan into motion. Get them to set an action trigger to precipitate the change. Then set another one for yourself to monitor it.

EXERCISE – A WINNING HABIT

Keystone habits are really all about culture – specifically, how to build a winning one.

When I work with sports coaches, I encourage them to pay attention to the state of the dressing room. For many coaches, players' lockers are considered their private domains. The result is often that the dressing room looks like a laundry bomb has gone off. When I worked with the rugby league coach Tony Smith, he chose to issue an edict: the dressing room mattered. Players were issued a diagram of precisely how their lockers should be kept.

This seems like a small thing – a tiny drop of change in a larger ocean of changes. But on a deeper level, these kinds of changes work because they are *keystone habits*: the kind of habits that create structures to let productive behaviours flourish. As we have witnessed, the keystone habit is often quite humble. After all, the way in which a player keeps his club suit should have little bearing on the team's on-field performance. But it does. Because it changes the atmosphere. It sends a clear signal – *be organized* – that echoes into other behaviours.

Keystone habits are a core part of winning cultures. In his wonderful book *The Power of Habit*, Charles Duhigg tells how Alcoa CEO Paul O'Neill used the keystone habit of worker safety to remake the organization's fortunes, and how weight-loss programmes succeed far more often if they embrace the keystone habit of journaling. The message: turnarounds are not about willpower or desire; they're about designing an environment that supports the habits you want to create.[8]

What do the best keystone habits have in common?

1) They deal with preparation/organization.

2) They are daily routines.

3) They are fantastically detailed. Here's how UCLA basketball coach John Wooden used to teach his players how to put their socks on:

Now pull it up in the back, pull it up real good, real strong. Now run your hand around the little toe area . . . make sure there are no wrinkles and then pull it back up. Check the heel area. We don't want any sign of a wrinkle about it . . . The wrinkle will ensure you get blisters, and those blisters are going to make you lose playing time . . .[9]

It's a small detail. But it succeeds because it's the right detail – a keystone habit whose signal echoes through the mind of an entire team.

How can you create a habit that supports the change you're trying to make? There are two things to think about:

1. The habit needs to advance the mission.

2. The habit needs to be relatively easy to embrace. If it's too hard, then it creates its own independent change problem. For instance, if you're trying to exercise more and you decide to 'create a habit' of going to the gym, you're really only retaining the core problem. It may be more productive to try to start building an easier habit, like laying out your gym clothes before you go to bed or asking a friend who already works out to pick you up on the way to the gym.

The second of Guardiola's keystone habits is:

Possession is nine-tenths of the game

Keeping the ball has been Barcelona's key tactic since Cruyff's day. Some teams don't worry too much about possession. They know you can have oodles of possession and lose. But Barcelona aim to have 65 or 70 per cent of possession in every game.

The logic of retaining possession is twofold. First, while you have the ball, the other team can't score. A team like Guardiola's Barcelona, short on big, physical ball winners, defends first by keeping possession. Second, if Barça have the ball, the other team has to chase it, and that is exhausting. When the opponents win it back, they are often so tired that they surrender it again immediately. Possession gets Barcelona into a virtuous cycle.

In November 2011, José Mourinho, Real Madrid's coach and Barcelona's nemesis, tried to exploit this devotion to passing. In the Bernabéu, Madrid's forwards chased down goalkeeper Victor Valdés from kick-off, knowing he wouldn't boot the ball aimlessly clear. The keeper miscued a pass, and Karim Benzema scored after twenty-three seconds. Guardiola could be observed on the touchline, encouraging Valdés to retain the relentless focus on keeping possession – to stick to the habit of playing the ball short. Barcelona won 1–3. 'Courage,' explains Valdés, 'is one of the most important qualities for a player at Barcelona. Pep reminded me to stay courageous and continue doing what I had been taught since I joined the club as a young boy.'[10]

Investing time in developing this habit was crucial because it is a touchstone for the whole of the Big Picture. If those charged with the responsibility of making this dream a reality can master it, success will follow.

The Rondo

Call it piggy-in-the-middle, 3 v 1 or any other variation where a numerically superior group of players has the ball and a smaller group of players tries to win the ball back. At Barcelona, this drill is done with precise and frenetic one-touch passes, creating dizzying pinball-like combinations and working those in the middle to exhaustion.

But there's more to the rondo than organizing some players in a circle, putting some unfortunate souls in the middle and torturing them with a teasing game of keep-away. The rondo reinvented modern football.

In Stan Baker's book *Our Competition is the World,* Johan Cruyff, the man who first introduced the principle to La Masia, described the rondo – and its purpose – succinctly: 'Technique is not being able to juggle the ball 1,000 times. Anyone can do that by practising. Technique is passing the ball with one touch, with the right speed, at the correct foot of your teammate.

'Everything that goes on in a match, except shooting, you can do in a rondo. The competitive aspect, fighting to make space, what to do when in possession and what to do when you haven't got the ball, how to play "one touch" soccer, how to counteract the tight marking and how to win the ball back.'[11]

This seemingly simple game contains the defining features of FC Barcelona, combining the essential habits with the culturally critical trademark behaviours in order to realize the Big Picture. It is the single clearest manifestation of the Cruyff/Guardiola philosophy.

What makes the rondo so useful is the close proximity it's played in, which forces players to exhibit all the qualities required to succeed on a full-sized pitch. Players can't hide by stretching the space to allow for more time on the ball. In a rondo, players touch the ball far more often than in a normal game – six times more often per minute, according to a Liverpool University study. Players must continuously identify and make decisions with respect to the shifting environment. That is, they are subject to instant decision-making in close quarters based on what others do. It places players inside an environment where they must make and correct errors, constantly generating solutions to problems. Players touching the ball 600 per cent more often will learn far faster, without realizing it, than they would in the vast, bouncy expanse of the outdoor game. At FC Barcelona, it's estimated that a player who has developed through La Masia would have invested between 1,500 and 1,800 hours playing the game of rondo. 'To be able to touch the ball perfectly once,' Cruyff maintained, 'you need to have touched it a hundred thousand times in training.' Technical ability is paramount, as is the ability to communicate, compete and anticipate while remaining composed offensively and defensively. The demands the rondo places on players are match-realistic.

If you could wear a pair of magic glasses that revealed how this apparently simple exercise weaves the invisible forces of culture, history, genes, practice, coaching and belief together to form that elemental material we call 'talent' – you would find that science has discovered a way to see talent as a substance as tangible as muscle and bone.

Think of a neuron as resembling an uprooted tree. The roots of the tree, called dendrites, are long and thin; they collect the signals from other neurons. At the opposite end of each neuron is the axon, which is longer and thicker, and branches out at the top to pass signals on to other neurons. Between the axon of one neuron and the dendrite of the next, there's a gap called the synapse. This is a gap that electrical impulses can't cross, and so, when a neuron fires, it releases neurotransmitters – chemical messengers that float across the gap to pass the message on to the next neuron and trigger it to fire.

When one neuron causes another one to fire, or when two neurons fire in close succession, the connection between them becomes strengthened due to chemical changes at the synapses. It's a simple rule: neurons that fire together wire together.[12]

EXERCISE – CATCH!

Whenever I want to illustrate the power of these neural pathways, I use a simple exercise with a tennis ball.

Find a ball and throw it to someone, then ask them to throw it back to you. Do it again, a little faster this time. Do this a few times; throwing it back and forth until you are both doing it comfortably and easily. Now, go to throw the ball, but hold on to it instead, making your partner think you are going to throw it. What happens?

The chances are they will move their hands and try to catch it, even though you have kept hold of it.

You see, once those neurons come together, they stay linked forever by the chemical reaction that happens. Every time you repeat the same action or thought the chemical link gets thicker and the pathway gets wider. The more you repeat the same thought or action, the wider it gets. Think of it like going from a narrow lane, to a road, to a dual carriageway and eventually to a motorway, allowing the chemicals to travel really quickly. Eventually, this means that your reactions improve; you do things quicker and almost without any conscious effort.

This idea is an old one. It was first suggested by Sigmund Freud, but it is now known as Hebb's Law, after being outlined in Donald Hebb's 1949 book *The Organization of Behaviour*.[13] Its precise chemical workings weren't pinned down until the 1960s, when neuropsychiatrist Eric Kandel began to study a giant marine slug called *Aplysia californica*. These sea slugs are unique because they have only around 20,000 neurons (the human brain has around 100 billion), and those they do have are unusually large and translucent, which allows them to be easily studied. By isolating a single neuron circuit within the sea slug, Kandel was able to identify the changes that happen at the synapses when memories are made.

As discussed, when two neurons fire together their connection is strengthened. A gene is activated which changes the structure of the neurons on both side of the synapse: the first one changes so that it will release more neurotransmitters in the future; the second one develops more receptors for those neurotransmitters to bind to. One study by Kandel and his colleagues found that the number of receptors in a single neuron could more than double during this process.

This is the basic mechanism of learning and memory. When you experience something or perform an action, your neurons fire in sequence, each one triggering those around it. The very act of them firing together strengthens the connections between them, as neurotransmitters are released, receptors are grown and new synaptic connections are built. That's how cortical maps – areas of brain function that respond to stimuli – change shape. This helps to illustrate the importance to Barcelona of immersing players into the club ethos from a young age. The boys in La Masia spend much of their childhood playing passing games. 'Football,' Cruyff once said, 'is choreography.' That's why so many of Guardiola's Barcelona side was home-grown, and why the club still has more academy graduates in its first team than almost any other major European club. Barcelona are not only training young players physically and embedding the culture of the club in their DNA, they are quite literally changing the shapes of their brains.

But that's not the only change.

Even after you have mastered a skill, practising it can be beneficial. It makes the brain more efficient. Think of employees in a job they've been doing for years – they know the demands of the task well, so they are very good at it, and they're also able to complete their work to the same standard as before but without having to put in as much effort. This is because of the neurons in their brain.

When you learn a new skill, your cortical map for the area of the body you're using expands, but eventually you need fewer neurons and less energy to do the same job because you learn to use your muscles more effectively. You can observe the effects of this increased neural efficiency in the best sportspeople.

In 2014, researchers in Japan got the chance to examine how much more efficient all that practice had made Neymar's brain. They scanned him in an fMRI machine while he rotated his right ankle clockwise or anti-clockwise every few seconds. Compared to three other professional footballers, two top swimmers and an amateur footballer who did the same task, they found the brain activity during this task was smaller in the footballers than in the swimmers, smaller in the professional footballers than the amateurs, and smallest of all in Neymar's brain.

The researchers believe this unique pattern of brain activity comes from Neymar's years of practice. His brain has changed. The connections between neurons have been strengthened. The area of the brain that controls his feet has grown bigger, but has also grown more efficient.[14]

We might call this 'muscle memory' in layman's terms, and this increased neural efficiency is just one part of it. The other aspect involves speeding things up, with the help of a fatty substance called myelin – the brain's white matter.

A neuron is like an electrical wire, and insulating a wire means the current within will flow faster and more efficiently. Myelin is the body's electrical insulation, wrapping around neurons like insulation around a copper wire. It keeps the signals in, so they can travel faster with less signal loss. 'Myelin quietly transforms narrow alleys into broad, lightning-fast superhighways,' writes Daniel Coyle in *The Talent Code*. 'Neural traffic that once trundled along at two miles an hour can, with myelin's help, accelerate to two hundred miles an hour.'[15]

As we've seen, a crucial thing that separates athletes from the rest of us is their ability to pick up perceptual cues ahead of time, and to make decisions quickly and accurately. Speed is of the essence, and myelin is the essence of speed.

When a neuron fires, not only does it strengthen the connection to the neurons around it, it also attracts the attention of cells called oligodendrocytes, which resemble Space Invaders in brain images, glowing an eerie green. They build myelin, squeezing out a layer of coating that wraps itself precisely around the neuron in an ongoing process that can take relative aeons in the brain's super-fast timescales.

'It is one of the most intricate and exquisite cell-to-cell processes there is,' says Dr Douglas Fields in *The Talent Code*. 'And it's slow. Each one of these wraps can go around the nerve fibre forty or fifty times, and it can take days or weeks. Imagine doing that to an entire neuron, then an entire circuit with thousands of nerves. It would be like insulating a transatlantic cable.'[16]

No wonder, then, it takes experts many years of intense training to develop their skills. Not only do they have to create the neural pathways – the long-term memories of the knowledge they need to perform – they also need to build up their bandwith, the myelin coating around the neurons which will grant them speed and efficiency. 'Skill is a cellular insulation that wraps neural circuits and that grows in response to certain signals,' writes Coyle, repeatedly.

Myelin controls the impulse speed, and impulse speed is crucial. The better we can control it, the better we can control the timing of our thoughts and movements, whether we're running, reading, singing or, perhaps more to the point, taking part in a rondo.

EXERCISE – THE MAD MEN METHOD

One simple way to improve our working lives is to use the Mad Men Method. This method involves asking yourself a simple question: what are you doing right now that your grandkids will find ridiculous fifty years from now?

For example, one of the reasons for the success of the television programme *Mad Men*, which follows the characters in the New York advertising industry in the 1960s, is the opportunity to look back to the early Sixties and see societal habits that seem, in retrospect, comically short-sighted – habits like sexism, the way people ate, smoked, drank, drove (usually all at the same time).

So what are you doing today that will have your grandkids chuckling in 2068?

Here's my answer: brainology.

I think our grandchildren will look back and say, back in 2018, when leaders wanted their people to learn how to change, they didn't bother teaching them the most important part: how the learning machine actually works. What the heck were those people thinking?

Right now, leaders in our society focus their attention on teaching the material, getting through the curriculum. This is the equivalent of trying to train athletes without informing them that muscles exist. It's like teaching nutrition without mentioning vegetables or vitamins. We feverishly cram our classrooms with whiz-bang technology, but fail to teach the kids how their own internal circuitry is built to operate.

It's all completely understandable, of course. Our parenting and teaching practices evolved in an industrial age, when we presumed potential was innate. Brains were fixed. It's another assumption we should have moved past – as we have with smoking being healthy and three-martini lunches being normal

– but haven't. In fact, you could argue that teaching a child how their brain works is not just an educational strategy – it's closer to a human right.

Here's a suggestion: start to teach brain education to your staff. Why not devote a chunk of time, especially before asking them to change, to teaching how the brain grows when it learns. Show how repetition builds speed and fluency. Help your people to understand and experience the biological truth that struggle makes you smarter, that the brain grows when challenged.

Even small exposures can have a big impact. Carol Dweck, professor of psychology at Stanford University, conducted an experiment where she divided 700 low-achieving children into two groups. Both were given an eight-week workshop on study skills, and one group received a fifty-minute session that described how the brain grows when it's challenged. (The other group's session was about generic science.) In a few months, the group that had learned about the brain had improved their grades and study habits to the point where teachers could accurately identify which student had been in which group.

It's not rocket science. In fact, it's easy, because it pays massive dividends. Plus, it gives our grandkids one less thing to laugh at us about.

In Simon Kuper's book *The Football Men,* Pep Guardiola stated: 'Without the ball we are a horrible team. So we need the ball.'[17] In context, Guardiola was referring to Barça's smaller physical size and superior technical ability against often physically dominant opposition. The ability to keep the ball and resist playing panicked football in possession has long been valued in individual players. However, when the collective nous of a team is built upon using possession to the same devastating effect, the game transcends the conventional and the Big Picture comes into focus.

Perhaps the most famous Barcelona rondo was seen at Wembley before the 2011 Champions League final. In that match, Barcelona played Manchester United off the pitch in a blistering display of incisive one-touch passing combinations that forced United to chase shadows. As Barcelona's warm-up footage spread around social media, the rondo offered a glimpse of what would happen next.

Barcelona imposed themselves with total authority. Passing of such tempo and precision is a 'death by a thousand cuts'-style of football torture for the teams subjected to its hypnotic and frustrating effects. Xavi recalls, 'Rooney came up to me before the end of the game. It must have been around the eighty-minute mark, something like that. And he said to me: "That's enough. You've won. You can stop playing the ball around now."'[18] Eric Abidal laughs. 'The United players were really furious. We had turned Wembley into a huge rondo and there was nothing they could do about it.' The statistics back up his assertion: Barcelona had nineteen attempts on goal to United's four, had 67 per cent of the possession and completed 667 passes to United's 301. They won 3–1 and lifted their fourth European Cup.

In his post-match comments, a shell-shocked Sir Alex Ferguson candidly stated, '[We were] well beaten, there's no other way to address the situation. They do mesmerize you with their passing.' The legendary Scot went on to say, 'They're the best in Europe, no question about that. In my time as a manager, I would say they're the best team we've faced. Everyone acknowledges that and I accept that. It's not easy when you've been well beaten like that to think another way. No one has given us a hiding like that. It's a great moment for them. They deserve it because they play the right way and enjoy their football.'[19]

What some overlook is the process involved in something like the rondo, which seems simple. Great players aren't born with a ball at their feet, but the Barcelona culture demands they take pride in their technique. In that environment, mistakes are accepted, processed and then corrected, but not at the expense of quality.

The rondo – along with the focus on creating the right environment and other carefully selected repetitive practices – beautifully epitomizes Leonardo da Vinci's words, 'Simplicity is the ultimate sophistication.'

EXERCISE – HOW TO MEASURE YOUR KEYSTONE HABITS

Once you have identified the keystone habits, how do you measure them?

If you distilled all the new science about keystone habits into three words of advice, they would be 'practise them better'.

The most basic truth is that if you practise the keystone habits better, you'll develop your ability to deliver on them.

For most of us, that's precisely where we bump into a common problem: *how*? Specifically, which practice method to choose? What's the best way to spend the limited time we've got?

I like to use a simple gauge for measuring keystone habits: REPS.

R stands for Repeating.

E stands for Engagement.

P stands for Purposefulness.

S stands for Strong immediate feedback.

The idea behind the gauge is simple: you should choose

habits that contain these key elements, and avoid methods that don't.

REPEATING: Does the habit you have identified have a repetitive nature?

Scenario: a teacher trying to teach multiplication tables to thirty students.

Teacher A selects a single student to write the tables on the board.

Teacher B creates a 'game show' format where a maths question is posed verbally to the entire class, then calls on a single student to answer.

Result: Teacher B chose the better option because it creates thirty reaches in the same amount of time. In Classroom A, only one student had to work – everybody else could lean back and observe. In Classroom B, however, *every single member of the class* has to stretch in case their name is called.

ENGAGEMENT: Is the habit immersive? Does it command your attention? Does it use emotion to propel you towards a goal?

Scenario: a violin student trying to perfect a short, tough passage in a song.

Student A plays the passage twenty times.

Student B tries to play the passage perfectly – with zero mistakes – five times in a row. If they make any mistake, the count goes back to zero and they start again.

Result: Student B made the better choice, because the method is more engaging. Playing a passage twenty times in a row is boring, a chore where you're simply counting down until you're done. But playing five perfectly, where any mistake sends you back to zero, is intensively engaging. It's a juicy little game.

PURPOSEFULNESS: Does the task directly connect to the skill you want to build?

Scenario: a basketball team keeps losing games because they're missing late free-throws.

Team A practises free-throws at the end of a practice, with each player shooting fifty free-throws.

Team B practices free-throws during a game so each player has to shoot them while exhausted and under pressure.

Result: Team B made the better choice, because their practice connects to the skill you want to build – the ability to make free-throws under pressure, while exhausted. (No player ever gets to shoot fifty straight in a game.)

STRONG IMMEDIATE FEEDBACK: In other words, the individual always knows how they're doing – where they're making mistakes, where they're doing well – because the practice is telling them in real time. They don't need anybody to explain that they need to do X or Y, because it's clear as a bell.

Scenario: a student trying to improve her GCSE grade.

Student A spends a Saturday taking a mock version of the entire test, receiving results back one week later.

Student B spends a Saturday taking a mini-version of each section, self-grading and reviewing each test in detail as soon as it's completed.

Result: Student B made the better choice, because the feedback is direct and immediate. Learning immediately where she went wrong (and where she went right) will tend to stick, while learning about it in a week will have little effect.

The idea of this gauge is simple: practices that contain all four of these core elements (REPS) are the ones you want to choose, because those are the ones that will produce the most progress in the shortest amount of time. Audit your practices and get rid of the methods that have fewer REPS and replace them with methods that have lots.

The other takeaway here is that small, strategic changes in

habits can produce huge benefits in delivery. Spending time planning your keystone habits is one of the most effective investments you can make in developing your culture.

3.v   RECURRING SYSTEMS AND
PROCESSES SUMMARY

Human beings are creatures of habit. But these habits don't just develop by themselves. There's a complex series of impulses and triggers at work behind the scenes, in the human brain, that underpin how every human being responds to a certain set of circumstances.

Throughout his life, William James wrote about habits and their central role in creating happiness and success. He eventually devoted an entire chapter in his masterpiece *The Principles of Psychology* to the topic. Water, he said, is the most apt analogy for how a habit works. Water 'hollows out for itself a channel, which grows broader and deeper, and after having ceased to flow, it resumes when it flows again, the path traced by itself before.'[20]

Here, I've shown that by creating a culture where the right people are placed in an environment that offers a constant measure of the correct trademark behaviours and the keystone habits, FC Barcelona ensure that their culture becomes ingrained and helps to move them towards the Big Picture, to become 'more than a club'.

This is the real power of habits; the insight that your habits are what you choose them to be. Once that choice is made – and becomes automatic – it's not only real but it starts to seem inevitable. The thing, as William James wrote, that bears us 'irresistibly towards our destiny, whatever the latter may be.'

In your own organization, this focus on recurring systems and processes can in fact be altered to suit whatever the chosen destiny is. Once you know how to redirect that path, you have the power to shape a culture.

It is now time to look at the people who deliver the results: the cultural architects.

4. CULTURAL ARCHITECTS AND ORGANIZATIONAL HEROES

'Never doubt that a small group of thoughtful,
committed citizens can change the world.
Indeed, it is the only thing that ever has.'
Margaret Mead

Harvard Business School professor Frances Frei suggests that, 'Culture is what happens when the leader isn't in the room, which is of course most of the time.'[1]

Sir Ernest Shackleton, one of the greatest adventurers of all time, knew this. In his diaries, he wrote of his understanding that maintaining unity among his men was critical. A mutiny could leave everyone dead.

He emphasizes the role of what we'll call Cultural Architects, the 'leaders without authority'. They were the informal leaders, champions and advocates who provided essential motivation and engagement to others on a daily basis. When their ship, the *Endurance*, became stuck in Antarctic ice, it was these men who led games, involving racing dogs, and organized variety shows which were designed to promote camaraderie, hope and fortitude.

Shackleton came up with a creative solution for dealing with the whiny, complaining types – what I'll term the Cultural Assassins. He assigned them to sleep in his own tent. When people separated into groups to work on chores, he grouped the complainers with him. Through his presence, he minimized their negative influence and allowed his Cultural Architects to maintain morale during the nine long, dark months they were stuck. They were later cited as an important reason why all twenty-two of his crew survived.[2]

In this section, we will see how navigating a constantly changing landscape – while maintaining the engagement of others – requires a more flexible, adaptable approach to leadership. Forward-thinking leaders have recognized this and are using the powerful influence of the Cultural Architect to support them and to direct, influence and inspire others in the workplace. The presence of these architects offers enormous benefits, including the effective management of the destructive Cultural Assassins.

We will also look at how to select and develop the right individuals to perform the Architect's role before finally observing how to maximize the positive impact they can have. All leaders agree that success on their journey is achieved when they experience high levels of people engagement throughout the organization. Engagement is an important stage on the journey. It demonstrates buy-in and commitment to the ambitious plans for the organization. But it isn't easy to achieve.

4.i THE INFLUENCE AND POWER OF PEERS

Think of the last time you were in a situation where you weren't totally sure how to behave. Maybe it was your first time in another country, or maybe it was a party where you didn't know many of the guests. What did you do to try and fit in?

You watched other people, of course.

In ambiguous situations, we all look to others for cues about how to behave. Maybe you've had the experience of scanning the table frantically at a fancy dinner, trying to figure out which fork is for dessert. When the environment is unfamiliar, we sprout social antennae that are acutely sensitive. It is the same when we enter a new culture. In the fancy dinner scenario, our antennae work great because *someone* at the table knows what to do, and we can just copy that person.

As the esteemed psychologist Solomon Asch found, the power of group conformity is incredibly strong, and it depends on unanimity for its power. Asch ran a famous experiment where an unsuspecting participant was placed in a room full of actors briefed to give the wrong answer. A single actor, however, was obliged to give the right answer.[1]

This lone dissenting voice was enough to break the spell, as it 'gave permission' to the real participant to break ranks with the other members of the group. In almost all cases, when a dissenter spoke up, the participant flew in the face of the group and gave the correct response. The really interesting part, though, is that the dissenting actor didn't even need to give the *right* answer to inspire the participant to speak up with the correct response; all it took to break the sway was for someone to give an answer that was *different* from the majority.

To prove how powerful the dissenter – even an incompetent one – really is, a clever experiment was conducted. In this variation, administered by psychologist Vernon Allen, a participant was once again placed in a group made up of actors and asked to answer simple questions. But in this version, each participant was told that before the start of the study he would have to fill out a self-assessment survey alone in a small office. After five minutes, a researcher knocked on the door and told the participant that due to a shortage of rooms, he would have to share the space with another subject, who was, in reality, a paid actor.

The most striking thing about the actor was the glasses he wore. As Allen details in his study, the glasses were custom-made by a local optometrist and fitted with 'extremely thick lenses that distorted the wearer's eyes, and gave the impression of severely limited visual ability.'

As if that weren't enough, to really drive home the point of the actor's visual impairment, the actor and a researcher engaged in a pre-scripted conversation. 'Excuse me,' the actor asked, 'but does this test require long-distance vision?' When it was confirmed that it did, the actor apologized and explained, 'I have very limited eyesight and can only see close-up objects.' The researcher asked the actor to read a sign on the wall. After straining and squinting to make out the words, the actor failed.

The desperate researcher explained that he needed five people for the study to be valid. He invited the actor to participate, stating, 'Just sit in, anyway, as long as you are here. Since you won't be able to read the questions, answer any way you want; randomly, maybe. I won't record your answers.'

But the actor, thick glasses and all, still enabled participants to escape from the sway of the group. Ninety-seven per cent of participants conformed to the group when there was no dissenter present, but only 64 per cent conformed when the visually impaired participant was among them giving a different – but equally wrong – answer. Obviously, we wouldn't expect a clearly incompetent dissenter to turn around as many participants as would a competent dissenter, but it's important to note that the presence of a dissenter – any dissenter, no matter how incompetent – still made it possible for a large segment of participants to deviate from the majority and give the right answer.

We all talk about the power of *peer pressure*, but 'pressure' may be overstating the case. Peer *perception* is plenty. In this entire book, you may not find a single statement that is so rigorously supported by empirical research as this one: you are doing things because you see your peers doing them. It's not only body-pierced teens who follow the crowd. It's *you*, too. Behaviour is contagious. Drinking is contagious. A study showed that when college males were paired with a dormitory roommate who drank frequently in high school, they saw their grade point average (GPA) go down a quarter point on average. There's an endless list of other behaviours that are contagious, as well: marriage, shaking hands to greet someone, fashion choices.[2]

Which is why we need at least one person to recognize our conundrum and come to guide us around. In other words, we need the presence of Cultural Architects.

Cultural Architects

'Cultural architects are people who are able to change the mindset of others,' the psychologist Willi Railo said. 'They are able to break barriers, they have visions. They are self-confident and able to transfer self-confidence to other players. At least three, and not more than five, such figures in a squad are needed by a coach to extend the "shared mental model" that a team needs for success.'[3]

'These are the dressing room leaders,' says Carlo Ancelotti, the hugely successful Italian coach. 'They will emerge through their technical or social skills, but they will emerge. You have to find and use them.'[4]

When Prime Minister Tony Blair was experiencing problems within his cabinet, particularly from Gordon Brown, his Chancellor, he sought advice from Sir Alex Ferguson about how to handle the matter. 'Sack the cunt,' was the blunt response from the Scot.[5] This was a repeat of the advice he once gave Guardiola at a UEFA coaches' meeting, when Guardiola asked him one question: if you get to a situation where the balance seems broken, what do you do? Do *you* go or do you change players? Ferguson gave Guardiola the answer he perhaps didn't want to hear: you change players.[6]

Ferguson was offering hard-won advice from his own career. He had witnessed the effect that Eric Cantona, the man once referred to as 'Bravura Cantona, the conductor of United cantata', in an *Independent* newspaper headline, had upon the culture of the Manchester United empire.

If Ferguson's teams were built around the twin behaviours of hard work and a willingness to risk all for victory, two examples of Cantona's technical and social influence resonate. At the end of his very first United training session, Cantona asked his manager if he could have the assistance of two players.

'What for?' Ferguson asked.

'To practise,' he replied.

'That took me aback,' admitted Ferguson. 'It was not exactly a standard request but I was naturally delighted to accede to Eric's wishes.'

Meanwhile, the rest of the playing staff had gone indoors, but soon realized that Cantona had not come back in. They began to explore why. 'At the end of training the next day, several of them hung around to join in the practice with Eric, and it soon became an integral part of my regime,' Ferguson explained. 'Nothing he did in matches meant more than the way he opened my eyes to the indispensability of hard work and continuous practice.'[7]

The second example led Roy Keane, himself a distinguished leader, to observe, 'Cantona led by his example and presence more than anything else – his charisma.'

Keane recounts one incident when the players conducted a draw to determine who would win a pool of money from endorsement deals. 'We decided to put all the cheques into a hat, and the last cheque out, whoever's name was on it he got to keep all of the cheques.'

The younger players, who then included David Beckham and Gary Neville, were allowed to opt out. 'They were new on the scene and didn't have the money to spare.' However, two young players, Paul Scholes and Nicky Butt, insisted on being included.

Eric Cantona's was the last name out, winning him approximately £16,000.

'Eric, you lucky bastard,' was Keane's response.

The next day, Cantona presented Scholes and Butt with £8,000 each. 'He said,' Keane explains, 'the two of them had had the balls to go into it when they couldn't really afford it.' Cantona rewarded their willingness to take a risk.

'What a gesture,' Keane marvels. 'Nobody else would have done it.'[8]

Carlo Ancelotti concurs with Ferguson:

> Leaders can only really lead if people believe in them. It doesn't matter why they believe in them. It could be their personality or it could be their example. It can be both. This is how I like to think of the leaders, as either personality leaders or technical leaders. A personality leader uses his strength of character to lead. He is always a talker in the team, speaking to his teammates a lot, often shouting across the pitch, helping everyone out. He should be positive and fearless and he will always step forward when the occasion demands it.
>
> A technical leader will not speak as much, but lead by example. Such players are always very professional, someone for all the youngsters to aspire to be like. The technical leader is the player who has the most knowledge on the pitch. They train hard and play hard and behave correctly off the pitch too, in the spirit of the culture of the club. I have found it effective to have a combination of these types of leader, while being aware that the qualities are not mutually exclusive – a player can be a strong personality and set a great example.[9]

So this is the first step to creating a winning dressing room. How do you decide who your Cultural Architects are?

'You don't,' said Willi Railo. 'They will find you. But you do have to create the right conditions for them to emerge.'

If not, according to Railo, your organization becomes fertile ground for Cultural Assassins – those who 'are negative, who tell you why something can't be done rather than how it can be done'.

Cultural Assassins

Ignoring this very point has far-reaching consequences when building a winning culture. This was the case within the FC Barcelona dressing room during the 2007–08 season. Samuel Eto'o railed against the continued protection of Ronaldinho's status as dressing room leader, despite his excesses.

Over the two years when the Brazilian's physical decline began and his party lifestyle increased, his once overwhelmingly positive influence began to become less benign. The players within the Barcelona squad suffered ten divorces or separations in those seasons of descent. Eto'o preferred to keep his distance from that group and his enmity with Ronaldinho gradually divided the squad and club. The two stars continually made gibes at each other in the media, until Eto'o exploded at one famous press conference. The Cameroonian, not renowned for his diplomatic graces, denounced Frank Rijkaard – 'He's a bad person' – in part for his continued protection of the Brazilian.

He then turned his ire on Ronaldinho. 'What you have to remember is I have always trained even when injured and with a few knocks,' Eto'o said. 'If a teammate says that you have to think about the group, I agree. You do have to think about the group. But I always think about the group first, and then about the money.'

To remove any trace of doubt about the team's dynamic, he summarized, 'This is a war between two groups.' The team, in such a disharmonious state, went into a downward spiral towards the end of the season, resulting in their failure to win any titles or cups.

Messi signals

Of equal concern to Guardiola when he took charge were the lessons being imparted to the next generation of players growing up within this febrile environment. This was the situation faced by sixteen-year-old Lionel Messi in 2005, after 'he knocked down the door to the dressing room through his sheer talent,' according to Frank Rijkaard, the head coach.

'He is not normal,' said César Luis Menotti, a tactician revered in Argentina for his spell with the national team, in Álex de la Iglesia's 2014 documentary *Messi*. The documentary brings together many legends of the game – Menotti, Jorge Valdano and Johan Cruyff among others – to share stories about Messi and discuss how great they found him to be. Ronaldinho understood it earlier than most. When collecting his Ballon d'Or award in 2006, he told both the football establishment and the world's media that the then teenager was a very special talent indeed: 'This award says I'm the best player in the world, but I'm not even the best player at Barcelona.'

Messi's origin story is well known: he had been born into a middle-class, 'stable and ordinary family' in Rosario and had begun playing in the youth ranks of his local football club, Newell's Old Boys, one of the nation's top sides.

There was a problem, though, an ocean separating potential and realization. When Messi was nine, he stopped growing. Doctors discovered a hormone deficiency and put him on a regimen of daily injections, which he gave himself, carrying around a little cooler when he went to play with friends.

'Will I grow?' a teary Messi asked.

'You will be taller than Maradona,' his doctor, Diego Schwartzstein, told him. 'I don't know if you will be better, but you will be taller.'

Newell's Old Boys agreed to help pay for the drugs, but, as

costs mounted, they eventually stopped. Frustrated, Leo's father, Jorge, found someone who would pay: Barça. So, when Leo was thirteen, he and Jorge moved to Spain. Before Messi left, he visited his doctor's office to say goodbye. Dr Schwartz-stein wished him luck and Messi handed him his Newell's jersey, tiny, with the number nine on the back. He autographed it, then rode with his father to Buenos Aires airport, trading his old comfortable life for an unknown new one.

His mother stayed behind with his siblings, dividing the family, and Messi, always shy, struggled. When he cried, which was often, he hid. He didn't want his father to see. His whole family revolved around his future; Barça even employed Jorge while Leo trained at La Masia. He went to class, reluctantly, but really he was a professional athlete at the age of thirteen.[10]

'Leo was still just a teenager,' comments Joan Laporta, 'who was playing with Ronaldinho, the best player in the world. Just imagine that. They promote you to the first team and the best player in the world realizes that *you*, the new boy, are actually the best player in the world. You, promoted at sixteen. He was a teenager spellbound, of course he was, by Ronnie's way of life.'

When he was initially asked to join the Argentinean national youth team set-up, the invitation was addressed to 'Leonel Mecci'. Once he joined the Argentina set-up, many failed to appreciate the quiet boy's nature. He once went to a team-building barbecue and never said a word, not even to ask for meat. Some thought he was really Spanish. In Barcelona, Messi inspired the same reaction. People noticed he didn't speak Catalan and protected his Rosarino accent. He bought meat from an Argentine butcher and ate in Argentine restaur-ants. In many ways, he was a boy without a country.

Ronaldinho accepted the young boy as one of his group, along with fellow Brazilians Deco and Thiago Motta. Leo and

Ronaldinho would enjoy playing with a little ball, the size of a tennis ball. If Ronaldinho managed to come up with a new way to hit the ball or play with it, he would look at Messi, smiling. 'He would make a face that would say, "Did you see that? I have a new challenge,"' Messi remembered in the *Sin Cassette* programme. 'I would practise and a couple of days later I would try to do that touch or move to perfection.'

Laporta heralds this inclusive attitude. 'Ronnie welcomed him instead of isolating him. We are all human and can make mistakes, but I think the way he welcomed Leo on the pitch was very positive, and on top of that Ronnie integrated him into his group of friends. Leo was a boy at the time, with twenty-seven- or twenty-eight-year-old men. I believe that real life experiences are incredibly important, to know what suits you and what doesn't, and Leo learned a lot from Ronnie, and he definitely learned in every sense of the word.'

However, as Ronaldinho began to physically decline and indulge his less professional instincts, he was not always a good example to Leo off the field. 'There came a day when Ronaldinho, he of the eternal smile, the player who had given Barcelona the self-esteem they had lost after five dark seasons, allowed himself to be consumed by long nights of partying, with the corresponding hangovers that were slept off on a massage bed in the changing room gym,' explained the highly regarded Catalan journalist Lluís Canut in *Els Secrets del Barça*.[11] During matches, if he felt worn out but thought he had done enough, he would tell Rijkaard that he had a muscular injury so the coach would substitute him. The message being given to the rest of the squad – and in particular to the boy genius – was a dangerous one.

Returning from one of the Brazilian's parties, Messi had an accident with a van in Barcelona. Having crashed, he faced the indignant owner who, fortunately, was a fan and was happy to reach an agreement. There were other stories of incidents in Barcelona's nightclubs. The 'Ronaldinho effect', which had once rejuvenated the club, was now having more serious consequences, especially for the next generation.

On one occasion, a group of fans was waiting for the players to emerge from the Camp Nou car park. Ronaldinho sped past them. Next came Messi, with his father Jorge beside him. Messi accelerated to follow his teammate but his father made him turn the car around and roll his window down to oblige the people who wanted autographs. He was showing him, reminding him, that there was another way to be a star.

'He has to go, he is influencing this boy, he is seeing how a football star behaves. He must never fall into that trap,' explained one key board executive.[12] Guardiola, it seemed, agreed; the Brazilian was sold to AC Milan just two months after he took charge of the Barcelona first team. The groundwork was laid for a new generation of Cultural Architects to emerge.

Cultural Architects – How to select them

'In Spain, the tradition is the group identifies the leaders they wish to represent them to management,' says journalist Guillem Balagué. 'The group will often hold a ballot to elect the leaders – the Cultural Architects – they choose to lead them,' recounts Txiki Begiristain.[13]

Gerard Piqué explains the rationale: 'When we vote for the captains, in the players' vote, it's because we see something in them we like and we want to go on and be the same person.' One of the leaders, Andrés Iniesta, was chosen for this very reason. 'Andrés knows that he is important within the dressing room and that gives you a certain power. The question is how you use that power. Andrés always uses it for good,' he reasons. 'You need to find a balance and at Barcelona, we have done that. We have a brilliant group, we get on well and I think that shows on the pitch.'[14]

EXERCISE – WOPAS

I promised one leading sports team I was working with that they would change and improve their performance as long as they were prepared to be honest about each other's behaviour as elite players.

Unlike the technical assessment of skills and abilities they had been repeatedly subjected to as players, they had rarely discussed the best behaviours. So we sat in a circle and openly and honestly agreed upon the three behaviours that consistently brought them the best results.

We then adapted an idea which Jeff Bezos, the CEO of Amazon, implemented with his customer service staff. He set up WOCAS (What Our Customers Are Saying) reports, which went straight to him, along with 'customer verbatim' – the actual emails sent in by customers – on the behaviours which they felt were most important.

In our sports team, our approach was to create a WOPAS (What Our Peers Are Saying) report, with everyone on the team assessing each other's behaviour after every game.

There was a particular example that highlighted the power of this simple system. The team captain had driven his team mercilessly during one pre-season training exercise. In his mind, he had done what was required of him because they had fully completed the training exercise on time. And using the traditional assessment guidelines, the boxes would have been ticked off and that would have been the end of it.

But when we sat down afterwards to look at how he might improve his behaviour and performance, he received some very strident feedback from the group, who were in reality using a far more comprehensive set of performance criteria than any technical checklist had ever assessed.

Their feedback suggested that his leadership style was in fact deeply flawed; he'd given no thought whatsoever to the quality of performance, how tired they were by the end of it or how that affected their capacity to train effectively the next day. As obvious as his behavioural shortcomings were once they had been raised, they certainly weren't obvious until the team had pointed them out.

The feedback from the group on the WOPAS exercise was extraordinarily positive; their responses unequivocally supported my belief that regular peer feedback on our behaviour amounts to a very powerful learning tool.

Who better to create a winning environment than the people who are responsible for winning?

Ultimatum game

One obvious concern about a peer vote for Cultural Architects is the possibility that the group will vote for someone who doesn't possess the cultural behaviours you desire. The solution, however, is to rely on our own innate sense of fair play. Let me explain.

Such a vote engages in a process which is similar to the 'ultimatum game', which is the most well-known experiment in behavioural economics.[15]

The rules of the game are simple. Two people are paired up and given £10 to divide between them. According to this rule one person (the proposer) decides, on his own, what the ratio of the split should be (50:50, 70:30, or whatever). He then makes a take-it-or-leave-it offer to the other person (the responder). The responder can either accept the offer, in which case both players pocket their share of the cash, or reject it, in which case both players walk away empty-handed.

Now, if both players are rational, the proposer will keep £9 for himself and offer the responder £1, and the responder will take it. After all, whatever the offer, the responder should accept, since if he accepts, he will get some money and if he rejects, he gets none. A rational proposer will realize this and make a low offer.

In practice though, this very rarely happens. Instead, low offers – anything below £2 – are routinely rejected. Think about what this actually means. People would rather have nothing than let the other person walk away with too much of the money. They will give up free money to punish what they perceive as greedy or selfish behaviour.

The interesting thing is that the proposer anticipates this – presumably because they know that they would act the same way if they were in the responder's shoes. As a result, the proposers don't make many low offers in the first place. The most common offer in the ultimatum game is, in fact, £5.

What makes this test even more interesting is what happens when the rules are changed. In the original version of the game, only luck determines who gets to be the responder and the proposer. So people feel that the split should be fairly equal. But people's behaviour in the game changes quite dramatically when the rules are changed. For instance, when the researchers decide that the proposers earn the position through performing better in an exam, proposers offer significantly less money, which rarely gets rejected. If people think that a proposer merits his position, he deserves to keep more of the money.

Put simply, what this test demonstrates is that most people want a reasonable relationship between what we achieve and what we deserve. In short, we are naturally inclined to play fair. If there are outstanding – both technically and socially – candidates within your environment, social justice will often ensure they are acknowledged.

In a dressing room, you have to find the leaders – technical and social – that regularly demonstrate the behaviours you want to promote. Guardiola, the player, had once remarked, 'We always have to respect the guidelines – the trademark behaviours – set by the coaches, but it is brilliant for a team that a player can get involved and take on a role on the pitch.'

EXERCISE – SELECTION CRITERIA

What are the most important things you need from Cultural Architects?

I posed this question to twenty elite coaches. The responses centred around three criteria: talent, attitude and the ability to be a model of the 'trademark behaviours'.

Apply this same criteria to your team and see who begins to emerge.

Player	Talent (grade: A, B, C)	Attitude (grade: A, B, C)	Behaviours (grade: A, B, C)
1.			
2.			
3.			

4.ii   DEVELOPING CULTURAL ARCHITECTS

When Guardiola inherited his squad, he purged the destructive influences and encouraged players who had come up through the ranks from the youth teams to take on the lion's share of responsibility. These players had become the standard bearers of the values of the institution: Puyol, Xavi, Iniesta and Valdés. Messi, who had been at risk of being led astray by the Brazilian group and would be the star of the rebuilt team, fitted that same profile.

Former Olympic high jumper Martí Perarnau, a journalist and leading analyst of the Barcelona youth system, describes how Cultural Architects – technically and socially adept leaders – were developed within the walls of La Masia.

In Perarnau's fascinating book *The Path of Champions*, he describes how the changes Cruyff demanded at the academy meant La Masia began regularly producing the players he wanted, as well as providing the kids with a sound education. 'The player who comes through La Masia has something different from the rest, it's a plus that only comes from having competed in a Barcelona shirt from the time you were a child,' says Guardiola.[1] He is not simply referring to footballing ability, but about human qualities. The players are taught to behave with humility and civility. The theory being that not only is it pleasant to be unassuming, but also if you are humble, you are capable of learning – and the capacity to learn is the capacity to improve.

This confidence which Guardiola had in the group of dressing-room leaders he fostered was well founded.

Identity questions

James March, a professor of political science at Stanford University, says that when people make choices, they tend to rely on one of two basic models of decision-making: the consequences model or the identity model.[2]

The consequences model is familiar to students of economics. It assumes that when we have a decision to make, we weigh up the costs and benefits of our options and make the choice that maximizes our satisfaction. It is a rational, analytical approach. This is the approach which had taken hold of the dressing room, from Eto'o's admittance that 'I think of the money' to Ronaldinho's decision to come straight to the training ground from the night club.

In contrast, when using the identity model of decision-making, we essentially ask ourselves three questions:

Who am I?

What kind of situation is this?

What would someone like me do in this situation?

Notice what is missing: any calculation of costs and benefits. The identity model is the way most people vote, which contradicts any notion of the self-interested voter. It helps to shed light on why a millionaire would vote against a politician who'd cut their taxes or why an elite footballer would challenge dysfunctional but indulgent behaviours within a training environment.

Generally, when the word identity is used, we are talking about a trend of some kind – such as racial, ethnic or regional identity. But that is a relatively narrow use of the term. We are not just born with an identity; we adopt identities throughout our lives. We aspire to be good mothers or fathers, devout Catholics or Muslims, patriotic citizens and so on.

Or consider a professional identity, such as a musician. Veteran rock stars have a lot to teach us about this, as some of them follow the identity model quite brilliantly. Sir Paul McCartney is someone who saw the Beatles as a means rather than an end to his identity; he saw his work in the 1960s as something on which he could build. After starting a new band, Wings, he continued to work with a wide range of other musicians. He also topped the classical music charts, as well as continuing to have hits with 'conventional' rock albums, and he still fills stadia today just as well as he ever did – 50 years at the top of the most competitive market in the world.

Being a musician is an identity you seek out and one that others, such as your mentors, consciously cultivate in you. As you grow and develop in that identity, it becomes an increasingly important part of your self-image and triggers the kind of decision-making that March describes.

Imagine you are Paul McCartney. An opportunity to write a classical composition presents itself. From a consequence point of view, the decision to accept would be difficult – you have never done it before and it may not be as successful as your other work. It's outside your comfort zone. You may alienate your fan base and face ridicule from critics. But from an identity point of view, the decision to accept would be a no-brainer. You'd wonder, 'What would a musician like me do in this situation?'

As we have already seen, much of what is unique about FC Barcelona's culture can be traced back to La Masia. The principles of the identity model can be seen in how they identify leadership qualities. With the group of Cultural Architects who took on the reins of power in Guardiola's dressing room, the club could be confident that they would observe unhelpful or dysfunctional behaviours and ask, 'What would a La Masia graduate do?'

Guardiola, himself a Cultural Architect as both a player and coach, summed up these principles for his B-team players when he delivered his introductory speech at the Mini Estadi: 'I like to win. I like to train, but above all, I want to teach people to compete representing universal values: values based on respect and education. Giving everything while competing with dignity is a victory, whatever the scoreline suggests.'[3]

'This emotional attachment gives a unique power,' observes Manuel Estiarte. 'They transmit a special dedication to the club to the other players. They set the bar in terms of professionalism and the serious attitudes they have. Don't underestimate the power of this engine which drives them on.'[4]

EXERCISE: IDENTIFYING TALENT

All over the world, in everything from academics to sports to music, millions of pounds and thousands of hours are being spent on singling out high-potential performers early on. And the plain truth is, most of these talent-ID programmes are little better than rolling dice.

Take the National Football League (NFL), for instance, which represents the zenith of talent-identification science. At the pre-draft NFL 'combine', teams exhaustively test players in every physical and mental capacity known to science: strength, agility, explosiveness, intelligence. They look at miles of game film. They analyse every piece of available data. And each year, they manage to get it absolutely wrong. In fact, out of the forty top-rated combine performers over the past four years, only half are still *in the league*, never mind star performers.

A lot of smart people have been thinking about why this happens, and they've decided the problem is not that the measures are wrong – the problem is that measuring performance is the wrong way to approach talent identification.

According to much of this new work, what matters is not current performance, but rather *growth potential* – the complex, multi-faceted qualities that help someone learn and keep on learning, to work past inevitable plateaus; to adapt and be resourceful and keep improving.

This can't be measured with a stopwatch or a tape measure. It's more subtle and complex. Which means that instead of looking at performance, you look for signs, subtle indicators. In other words, you have to close your eyes, ignore the dazzle of current performance and instead try to detect the presence of a few key characteristics.

So what are the factors? Here are two:

One is *early ownership*. As psychologist Marjie Elferink-Gemser's work shows, one trend among successful athletes begins when they're thirteen or so, and develop a sense of ownership of their training.[5] For the ones who succeed, this age is when they decide that it's not enough to simply be an obedient cog in the development machine – they begin to go further, reaching beyond the programme, deciding for themselves what their workouts will be, augmenting and customizing and addressing their weaknesses on their own.

Another factor in success is *grit*. This quality, investigated by the pioneering work of Angela Duckworth, is a combination of stubbornness, resourcefulness, creativity and adaptability that helps someone make the tough climb towards a long-term goal.[6]

Duckworth gave her grit test to 1,200 first-year West Point military academy cadets before they began a brutal summer training course called the 'Beast Barracks'. It turned out that this test was eerily accurate at predicting whether or not a cadet would succeed, far more accurate than West Point's exhaustive battery of NFL-combine-esque measures, which included IQ tests, psychological profiling, examining grade point averages and testing physical fitness. Duckworth's grit test has been applied to other settings – including academic ones – with similar levels of success.

A decent rule of thumb is to spend twice as long reviewing your team's development as you do setting targets. If you are going to get their goals set at the right level to maximize their motivation, learning and confidence, then you need to give them time to assess their efforts and growth. Here are some of the questions I encourage coaches to ask.

— *How well did you do what you said you would do? Did you put your goals into action?*
— *How successful were you at achieving your goal?*
— *What worked well in helping you to achieve?*
— *What did not work so well and detracted from your success?*
— *What main reasons would you give for your success?*
— *What changes would you make to the goals you set based on the result?*
— *How will you make sure that you get the same or better level of success with your next target?*

By fostering a power base among home-grown players, Guardiola had overseen the transition from a consequences model of decision-making to an identity model, and in doing so sent out a clear signal of intent, mapping the way forward for years to come. He had also achieved something that hadn't been seen at Barcelona for a long time: the club was in the hands of those who understood it and truly cared for it. It also meant that Guardiola was giving the home-grown players and the academy set-up a boost: a vote of confidence. Now they had to repay his trust and faith in them through their performances, hard work and commitment.

Pedro was moved to the first team alongside Sergio Busquets, another footballer who had shown intelligence, focus and a fundamental understanding of his role in the youth ranks. For Guardiola, it also helped that he didn't have a ridiculous haircut or tattoos. 'They are like a throwback,' observes Javier Mascherano, the Argentine defender or midfielder. 'No tattoos, earrings, nothing like that. It can feel like they are from a different age. They love football, love what we do and that's it. They would rather avoid all the stuff that comes with football and just play.'[7]

Guardiola believed that Busquets would prove to have the character to continue in Xavi and Puyol's footsteps as captain of the team. 'It was more than a generational shift, it's the passing down of a footballing philosophy,' said Xavi. 'They represent the Barcelona DNA. They carry the weight of responsibility for Barcelona.'

Cultural Architects need to be nurtured – and as a coach, it is your job to provide the environment for that nurturing. This is the cultural component which can take the longest time to percolate, but it is also the part which offers the longest and deepest impact. When we assess Guardiola's legacy, long after he left the club, it is clear that his Cultural Architects have remained true to the principles which he and La Masia taught them.[8]

Before the 2015 Champions League final, three years after

Guardiola had left the club, Andrés Iniesta was struggling in training. 'He had constant niggles and discomfort that just wouldn't go away,' Xavi said. 'If Andrés had not been fit to start the final, I would have played. It was my final game. Instead, I told the manager, "This guy doesn't need to train; he has to play in the final and that's that."' Humility, leadership and a team ethic – Guardiola's commitment culture borne out by his Cultural Architects.

4.iii GROUP NORMS

Imagine you have been invited to sign for one of two teams. Before you decide, you manage to obtain footage of the dressing room for each team, where you can observe the behaviours during a team meeting.

Team A is composed of elite players who have been expensively acquired from other teams, where they had demonstrated exceptional ability and a certain 'star' quality. When you watch a video of them working together, you see respectful professionals who take turns speaking and are polite and courteous. At some point, when a question arises, the coach – clearly the subject expert – speaks at length while everyone else listens. No one interrupts. When another person veers off topic, a colleague gently reminds him of the agenda and steers the conversation back on track. The team is efficient. The team meeting ends exactly when scheduled.

Team B is different. It's evenly divided among elite players and young professionals at the foothills of their career. Some are players who have won everything in the game; others, as yet, have little in the way of professional achievements. On a video, you see teammates jumping in and out of discussions haphazardly. Some ramble at length; others are curt. They interrupt one another so much, sometimes it's hard to follow the discussion. When a team member abruptly changes the topic or loses sight of the point, the rest of the group follow them off the agenda. At the end of the meeting, the meeting doesn't actually end. Everyone sits around and gossips.

Which group would you rather join?

Before you decide, imagine you are given one final piece of information. When both teams were formed, each member was asked to complete what is known as the 'Reading the Mind in the Eyes' test. This is a study where they were shown thirty-six photos of people's eyes and asked to choose which word, among four offered, best described the emotion that person was feeling.

The test, you are told, measures people's empathy. Team A's members ticked the right emotion, on average, 49 per cent of the time. Team B: 58 per cent.

Does that change your mind?

In 2008, a group of psychologists from Carnegie Mellon and MIT wondered if they could figure out which kinds of teams were superior. 'As research, management and many other kinds of tasks are increasingly accomplished by groups – both those working face-to-face and "virtually" – it is becoming even more important to understand the determinants of group performance,' the researchers wrote in the journal *Science* in 2010. 'Over the last century, psychologists made significant progress in defining and systematically measuring intelligence in individuals. We have used the statistical approach they developed for individual intelligence to systematically measure the intelligence of groups.'[1]

Put differently, the researchers wanted to know if there is a collective intelligence that emerges within a team that is distinct from the intelligence of an individual member.

To accomplish this, the researchers recruited 699 people, divided them into 152 teams, and gave each group a series of assignments that required different types of cooperation. One assignment involved having ten minutes to brainstorm possible uses for a brick and getting a point for each unique idea. Another entailed planning a shopping trip as if they were housemates sharing a single car and each housemate had a different shopping list – the only way to maximize the team score was for each member to sacrifice an item on their list in exchange for something that pleased the whole group. Next, the teams had to arrive at a ruling on a disciplinary case in which a college basketball player had allegedly bribed his teacher. Some people had to represent the college management, others the teacher. Points were awarded for reaching a verdict that fully recognized the concerns of each side.

Each of the tasks required full team participation; each demanded different types of collaboration. As the researchers observed groups going about the tasks, they saw various dynamics emerge. What was interesting, however, was that teams that did well on one assignment also seemed to do well on the others. Conversely, teams that failed at one thing seemed to fail at everything.

Some might have hypothesized that the 'good teams' were successful because their members were smarter – the group intelligence might be nothing more than the sum of the intelligence of the individuals making up the teams. But researchers had tested IQ levels beforehand and cumulative individual intelligence didn't match the team performance. Ten smart people in a room didn't make them any faster.

Others might have argued that the good teams had more decisive leaders. But the results showed that this wasn't the case either.

The researchers eventually concluded that the good teams had succeeded not because of the innate qualities of team members, but because of how they treated one another. Put another way, the most successful teams had group norms which caused everyone to mesh particularly well.

'We find converging evidence of a general collective intelligence factor that explains the group's performance on a wide variety of tasks,' the researchers wrote in their *Science* article. 'This kind of collective intelligence is a property of the group itself, not just the individuals in it.'[2]

There were two behaviours that all good teams did share. In 2011, FC Barcelona players Lionel Messi and David Villa inadvertently offered a public demonstration – and subsequent explanation – of these same two behaviours when they engaged in a frank exchange of views during a match between Barcelona and Granada. After Villa had failed to pass the ball to Messi when the latter was in a scoring position, the television broadcaster *Canal+* shared the footage of the players' 'discussion' of the incident:

Messi: Play it in front of me, in front! Play it there!

Villa: But you can't control it! Fucking hell, man. I had one and I gave it to you.

Messi: Over there, for fuck's sake [pointing to the space where he should have received the ball]

The first behaviour the researchers identified was that all of the members of the good teams spoke in roughly the same proportion, a phenomenon referred to as 'equality in distribution of conversational turn-taking'. In some groups, conversation ebbed from assignment to assignment, but by the end of the day, everyone had spoken roughly the same amount. In the Barcelona example, the player generally regarded as the best player in the world was not granted special status that rendered him above criticism.

The second behaviour was that the good teams tested as having 'high average social sensitivity' – another way of saying that these groups were skilled at intuiting how members felt based on their tone of voice, how people held themselves and the expressions on their faces.

When Messi was asked to comment on the disagreement, he appeared bemused by the public reaction. 'I have said that you should not look for problems where none exist, look somewhere else,' Messi told *El País*. 'There is nothing here. It's a dressing room that functions above and beyond sport, spectacularly well. We've been together a long time and we get on very well together at a human level. No one knows how much fun we have. After so many years that isn't easy.'[3]

Juan Cruz Leguizamón, one of Messi's oldest friends, confirms Messi's willingness to ensure equality within a group. '[Messi's childhood friends] are conscious of the fact that we have the best player in the world in front of us, but there is a certain confidence in the feeling we are all equal. We speak about the lives of everyone. We mess around. There are jokes,' he pauses, a slow grin enveloping his face, 'about his ears, for instance.'[4]

'We were like brothers, we were all equal,' explained Victor Valdés, when asked to describe the team spirit at Camp Nou. 'We loved spending time in each other's company. We would go to eat together away from the training ground. It was a very special group.'[5]

This was reinforced by Manuel Estiarte, Guardiola's assistant:

> I have seen a lot of things in life and have had a long career in sport. In three years, there has not been a single argument in the dressing room. You could see that as a slightly negative thing. With twenty-two people together like that, the most natural thing would be for there to be the odd falling out. One day one player tells the other to 'fuck off' and the next day apologizes. That would be totally normal. From time to time, that happens in every club in the world. Here, there has not been a single incident where you have

to worry about a personality clash or religious arguments or tensions between different age groups.[6]

As alluded to at the start of this chapter, one of the most effective ways to gauge social sensitivity is to show someone photos of people's eyes and ask them to describe what the person is thinking or feeling. This is a test of 'how well the participant can put themselves into the mind of another person, and "tune in" to their mental state,' wrote the creator of the test, Simon Baron-Cohen of Cambridge University.[7]

'In the dressing room, I sit in one corner,' Messi offers, 'and Andrés Iniesta sits in another. We connect; with just a look we understand each other. We don't need more than that.'

EXERCISE – THE EYES TEST

If you ever want to understand your colleagues, see if they'll play a little game.

It only takes thirty seconds.

Ask one of them to extend their right forefinger and draw a capital E on their forehead.

Do they draw the letter so that it faces them – that is, backwards to a person looking at them? Or do they draw the letter so that the viewer can read it? Neither way is right or wrong, but the direction of that letter might tell you something about the disposition of that person.

This seemingly innocent parlour trick is actually a method social scientists have used for more than a decade to measure perspective-taking – the ability to step outside one's own experience and see the world from someone else's viewpoint.

People who write the E so that it's backwards to themselves but legible to others have taken the other's perspective. Those who draw the E so that it would be readable to themselves but backwards to others haven't considered the other person's point of view.

This finding might reveal something about your culture. In the pursuit of being action-orientated and tough-minded, have you sacrificed the fundamental human quality of empathy?

If you're a leader, simply treat everybody with respect. And if one of your team asks you to draw a letter on your forehead, you now know what to do.

There is strong evidence that group norms play a critical role in shaping the emotional experiences of participating in a team. Research from psychologists at Yale, Harvard, Berkeley, the University of Oregon and elsewhere indicate that norms determine whether we feel safe, threatened, enervated or excited, and motivated or discouraged by our teammates. Group norms, the research suggests, are the answer to improving a team's performance. You have to manage the *how* of teams, not the *who*.

Coming back to the question at the start of the chapter of which team to join, if you are given a choice between the serious-minded, professional Team A, or the free-flowing, more informal Team B, you should always opt for Team B.

Team A is smart and filled with effective colleagues. As individuals, they will all be successful. But as a team, they still tend to act like individuals. There is little to suggest that, as a group, they become *collectively* intelligent, because there is little evidence that everyone has an equal voice and that members are sensitive to teammates' emotions and needs.

In contrast, Team B is messier. People speak over one another, they go on tangents, they socialize instead of remaining focused on the agenda. Everyone speaks as much as they need to, though. They feel equally heard and are attuned to one another's body language and expressions. They try to anticipate how each other will react. Team B may not contain as many individual stars, but when the group unites, the sum is much greater than any of its parts.[8]

EXERCISE – GIVE ME A BREAK

I like to demonstrate the power of team bonds by asking a player to snap eleven pencils bound together: breaking the pencils is very difficult, and the player usually fails. Then I produce four pencils bound together, then three and finally two. Eventually, the player snaps the pencils – usually two – and the team cheers!

The point is clearly demonstrated, especially with younger players, that a whole team bound together is difficult to break. One or two, isolated from the rest, are vulnerable.

Phil Jackson, the hugely successful basketball coach, articulates it like this: 'Basketball is a great mystery. You can do everything right. But if the players don't have a sense of oneness as a group, your efforts won't pay off. The bond that unites a team can be so fragile, so elusive.'

Dressing room politics

The power of the Cultural Architect plays out in many different ways. But before we see how, it's important to understand the full power of the psychological dynamics underlying this force.

To do so, we turn to a family therapist. The Boston-based David Kantor led what may very well have been the first incarnation of reality TV. In an effort to study how schizophrenia manifests in family systems, Kantor set up cameras in various rooms of people's houses, then pored over hours of footage of these ordinary folks' lives. Although Kantor's research didn't tell him much about schizophrenia, he did detect a pattern that emerged again and again within every group dynamic, regardless of whether schizophrenia was a factor.[9]

In analysing the tapes of the families he studied, Kantor found that family members traded-off playing the same four distinct roles. As we shall see, three of these roles were considered especially important within the confines of the Barcelona dressing room. The fourth type – the *detached*: those who are disengaged – are not as critical when actively changing the culture.

The first role was that of the *initiator*: the person who has the ideas, likes to start projects and advocates new ways of moving forward.

At FC Barcelona, this role was defined as the visionary. Ferran Soriano said, 'Enthusiasm and courage are two of the visionary's characteristics. Their strength is contagious and they exude a positive excitement that impregnates the group.'[10]

Think of someone like Xavi. He was the ultimate playmaker, who on several occasions achieved 100 per cent passing accuracy during games when he had the ball more than 100 times. He once said: 'I must have at least a hundred touches of the ball each match. If I had to go back to the dressing room with only fifty, I would be ready to kill somebody.'

He wanted the ball all the time: 'The one who has the ball, is the master of the game,' he said, and 'Think quickly, look for spaces, that's what I do. All day. Always looking. Space, space, space.'

When you're in the same room with a visionary type, it's hard not to get excited about whatever new project or idea they have in mind. You can always count on initiators to come up with new ideas; they aren't necessarily the life of the party, but they will definitely be the ones who suggest having a party in the first place.

If initiators are represented by Xavi, or sometimes more flamboyant players like Ronaldinho or Lionel Messi, their opposite – *blockers* – are best represented by Carles Puyol. 'We call these characters Dr No,' says Soriano. 'As the name clearly states, this is the person in the organization who often tries to scupper the visionary's plans, maybe even telling him what he is proposing is impossible. He is at the opposite end of the scale to the visionary and he is just as necessary, as he contributes prudence, perspective and cold analysis. He is the one who brings a dose of reality to all the discussions. He is also the planner and controller.'[11]

This was powerfully illustrated in 2011, as the ball nestled in the net and the scoreboard indicated the fifth goal. The beleaguered Rayo Vallecano players trudged wearily back into position – too numbed by the real prospect of relegation to berate each other for the mistakes which preceded the goal – as Thiago began his snake-hipped dance routine in celebration and was joined by his team mate Dani Alves. Carles Puyol trotted over to the pair and put a stop to it, directing them back towards the centre circle.

It wasn't the samba rhythm of the dancing which offended the defender, a big fan of metal music, namely Napalm Death, but the lack of humility. His long-time defensive partner Gerard Piqué smiled in recognition of the message. 'There was a match where we were winning by four or five and there was only a few minutes left. One of the opposition was injured and a stretcher was coming on and I just went to see how he was. The next thing I knew Puyi was roaring at me to concentrate. He was on me like a hawk, telling me to leave them to it, get back in position and concentrate. He never stops.'[12]

Following the Vallecano game, Guardiola issued a contrite apology: 'That's not the attitude of Barça players. It won't happen again.' Thierry Henry, the enormously gifted French striker who played for Barcelona between 2007 and 2010, explains Guardiola's attitude: 'He'd say, "If we have to win 11–0, win 11–0. Be ruthless."[13] Showboating, however, makes him angry. He said it shows the opposition a lack of respect.' It had been the team's captain – and Dr No – however, who had led by example, as he had done throughout his fifteen years' service in the first team.

Of course, it's easy to think of blockers as pure curmudgeons. But as Soriano suggests above, they play a vital role in maintaining balance within a group.

'Puyol could do that and be effective because the other members of the team respect him,' Soriano further explains. 'Football clubs are excitement factories and as such they are full of visionaries, people inside and outside the club with fabulous, amazing and extraordinary ideas for making the club victorious. The risk of taking decisions on an emotional basis, especially after unexpected or inappropriate defeats, for example, is very high and in a football club, every decision costs a lot of money.'[14]

Most of the tension in the group lies between the initiator and the blocker. Initiators are all about making new things happen. They have a wealth of fresh ideas. They might be wildly optimistic and have a tendency to rush to action, but their creativity, energy and drive can be instrumental when it comes to innovation. In contrast, blockers question the merit or wisdom of new decisions. Instead of merrily going along for the ride, they raise points about the potential harmful consequences that might follow.

A blocker functions as the brakes that prevent the group from going down a potentially disastrous path. Even if the blocker's opinion is wrong, at least it adds a perspective to the debate – giving others an opportunity to look at things in a different light.

There is no question that dissenters in a group setting do make the process messier, and blockers are not always given much of a voice. This is easy to understand, as the desire to present a unified front is important. But, the end result is actually improved by dissent. The majority have to revise their opinion in response to points raised by the dissenters. Blocking may not be pleasant – for anyone involved – but it is a necessary component of healthy group dynamics.

The aviation industry is a brilliant example of the importance of having blockers in a successful team. In the aftermath of the 1977 plane crash at Tenerife airport, which killed 583 people – the deadliest accident in aviation history – agencies scrutinized cockpit recordings from every plane crash and near miss over the years. Seventy per cent were determined to be the result of human error, and the majority of them were to do with team dynamics. It was NASA's research into plane crashes that ultimately helped to revolutionize aeronautical procedures. A new model for cockpit interaction was born – Crew Resource Management (CRM) – which teaches pilots, among other skills, how to be effective blockers.[15]

The tradition within the airline industry was that the captain was almighty, in charge of everything. When a decision was made by the captain, no one would overrule him. CRM changed these dynamics. Pilots are now trained to communicate effectively and accept feedback, and crew members are taught to speak up when they see that their superior officer is about to make a mistake.

For example, when co-pilots spot a departure from the safety procedures, they are trained to challenge the captain. The challenge takes the form of three steps. The first is to *state the facts*, for example, 'Our approach speed is off.' If that's ineffective, the next step is to *challenge*. Research shows that generally the best way to challenge is to use the captain's first name and add a quantifier to the fact. 'Mike, are you going to make it on this approach? Check your altitude.' That will get the captain's attention and bring them out of their tunnel vision. If these two procedures fail, the third step is to *take action*. If someone were flying an unstable approach – that is, approaching the runway a little too high or fast and unable to make a safe landing – you would get on the radio and the radio tower would cancel the landing clearance.

More often than not, the first two steps are enough to get the captain's attention; there is rarely need for the first officer to take action. The training emphasizes the need for the blocker to speak up and for the person in charge to listen and communicate effectively.

The freedom to give feedback and voice concerns – and the willingness of those in charge to tolerate dissent – is just as important in a dressing room, a boardroom, or anywhere else where a costly mistake can be averted by being open to dissent from blockers in the group. Accordingly, it's not just pilots who have benefited from CRM training. The medical community is also responding to human-error failures by adapting aviation's approach to crew coordination.

Whatever the situation, be it the cockpit or the dressing room, a dissenting voice can seem, well, annoying. And yet, as frustrating as it can be to encounter blockers, their opinions are absolutely essential. It's natural to want to dismiss a blocker's nay-saying, but as we have seen, a dissenting voice – even an incompetent one – can often act as the dam that holds back a flood of irrational behaviour.

'At each moment and in each circumstance affecting an organization you have to ask yourself what combination of visionaries, Dr Nos and backbones the management team needs and which of them has to be the leader,' counsels Soriano. In Kantor's research, when initiators and blockers locked horns, the *supporter* steps in, taking one side or another – these are the people Soriano calls backbones:

There is a tendency to think that the visionary has to be the leader, but that isn't so. There are circumstances and times when order and control are more important. That's when the leader should be Dr No. Sometimes, when everybody can see very clearly what needs to be done, and it is time to get down to the nitty-gritty, put the pedal to the floor and get it done, the leader should be the backbone.

When the visionary and Dr No have finished arguing about the idea, the backbone takes their decision and puts it into practice. It becomes his task. The characteristics that best define them are drive and perseverance; they have the sacrificial spirit and are tireless workers. The backbone gives balance to the rest of the group and also provides an overview of the situation because he sees, perhaps better than anyone, what is required to achieve the objectives. He looks at the job entrusted to him in a positive way, finds the best method of achieving the required result, and puts it into practice.[16]

Iniesta, who scored the only goal in the 2010 World Cup final, is not just the backbone of the team but also its beating heart. Iniesta embodies the club's trademark behaviours, possessing an innate humility; happy to let his more extravert teammates enjoy the spotlight. He gleefully recounts the time when, not long after the World Cup, he was leaning against a bar and was approached by an attractive woman. 'Excuse me,' she began. 'Yes?' Iniesta replied, expecting the next line to be the usual request for an autograph or a photo. Instead, she said: 'I'd like an orange Fanta, please.'[17]

Equally illuminating is his insight into how he reads the game:

Every pass is important. A bad pass loses possession and puts the team under pressure. Short passes build momentum and if you have the ball then the opponents can't do anything. Know the time to make a killer pass. If you need a goal, search for the space to make the pass. If you're protecting a lead, keep possession and play safer. Because we have played together for a long time to a certain system, everyone knows where to move. That makes my job easier, knowing where Xavi or Leo [Messi] will be.

If you think before your opponent where the ball is going to go then you have an advantage. If you stay with the ball at your feet and think about what to do, you are going to lose the ball. The best players are the quickest thinkers. Where is my teammate going to run to? Will he stay onside? Which one has space? Which one is looking for the ball? How do they like the ball – to their feet or in front? You can be the best passer in the world, but without your teammates being in the right position, it's no good.[18]

In the same way that in the business world there might be people who know how to fulfil more than one of these three roles at any given time as demanded by the circumstances, you can also find players that have the characteristics of more than one type. When it comes to putting the team together and deciding the tactics and line-up, the coach must decide what the balance of visionaries, Dr Nos and backbones the team needs for a specific game – depending on the opposition and circumstances. During the match, there can be changes in the dynamics, introducing larger doses of visionaries, Dr Nos and backbones to change or maintain the result.

It's easy to see why people and organizations are naturally

attracted to initiators. They bring in fresh energy and new ideas, and for them the sky is always the limit. It's equally easy to see why those same people and organizations would want to steer clear of blockers. It is critical, however, to strike a balance between the input of initiators and blockers and to ensure there are enough supporters to prevent there being an impasse.

EXERCISE – QUESTIONS FOR THE VISIONARY, DR NO AND BACKBONE

If you want to accelerate the process of creating a high-performing culture, I find that allocating people one of the identified roles can offer an innovative and practical approach to problem solving.

Asking people to see the world through the eyes of a visionary, Dr No or backbone can be invaluable. To help them along the way, I have provided some useful questions for each role.

VISIONARY generates broad brush solutions, creating new ideas and approaches to achieve the desired outcome, with an attitude of 'anything is possible'. The visionary draws on qualities of innovation and possibility to answer questions like:

What do I want to do?

Why do I want to do it? What is the purpose?

What are the benefits?

How will I know when I have them? What will the evidence of these benefits be?

When can I expect to get them?

Where do I want this idea to get me in the future?

Who do I want to be or be like in order to make this idea a reality?

BACKBONE defines in detail the steps to achieving the solution generated by the visionary, acting as if it is achievable. The backbone draws on qualities of invention and flexibility to answer questions like:

When will the overall goal be completed?

Who will be involved? (Assigns responsibility and secures commitment from the people who will be carrying out the plan.)

How specifically will the idea be implemented? What will be the first steps?

How will ongoing feedback tell me if I am moving towards or away from the goal?

How will I know when the goal is achieved?

DR NO evaluates the acceptability of the plan developed, considering what problems might occur, the fit with available resources, the consequences for others, and the situations in which the plan would be appropriate or inappropriate. Dr No draws on qualities of acceptability to answer questions like:

Who will this new idea affect and who will make or break the effectiveness of the idea?

What are their needs and payoffs?

Why might someone object to this plan or idea?

What positive gains are there in the present way(s) of doing things?

How can I keep those things when I implement the new idea?

When and where would I not want to implement this plan or idea?

What is currently needed or missing from the plan?

What is a 'How' question I could ask in relation to what is needed or missing?

4.iv   CULTURAL ARCHITECTS SUMMARY

A culture – whether it be a government, a business or a football club – is only as good as the people who inhabit it. The Cultural Architect is an important leadership role in the organization, helping other leaders to navigate the Arc of Change and realize the Big Picture.

Cultural Architects informally act as the eyes and ears of the organization, offering feedback to each other and to the senior managers on how the organization can meet the challenges ahead. They are instrumental in building trust, improving lines of communication and enlisting the support of others. The level of engagement enjoyed on the journey is directly linked to the number of Cultural Architects in the organization. Remember, the role of the cultural leader on the Arc of Change is not to generate more followers, but to create more leaders.

5. AUTHENTIC LEADERSHIP

'The most powerful leadership tool we all have is our own example.'
John Wooden

A Premier League coach once asked me, 'How do you manage a team of millionaires?' If you think about it, it's a really good question. The really interesting word here is 'manage'. You see the problem with management is that, whether it is in business or football, it's all about control. And it is difficult to use control to drive a high-performing culture.

Johan Cruyff provided his own answer to this particular question: 'In order to be a coach of Barcelona, it is more important knowing how to lead a group of players than knowing how to correct a mistake made on the field. You have to have influence over the group, to be able to seduce, convince and understand them.'

Cruyff's description of a head coach at a top football club can be applied to the job of a chief executive within a corporation. They don't make the products, they don't do the advertising or the marketing and they don't cook the food at lunchtime. If a problem crops up in any of those areas, however, then they are ultimately responsible.

Which begs the obvious question: in what areas then can a leader maximize their positive influence on a team and its culture?

To create a high-performing culture, the difference between commitment and compliance is significant. It is more about leadership than control. Perhaps if we view the culturally aware coach as a leader and not a manager, we can discern that their role is to forgo self-interest and actively sell the Big Picture vision, to devise strategies to optimize individual talent and inspire and motivate performance. We can then start to see the tangible differences in the way an authentic leader builds a culture.

In this chapter, we will look at the importance of cultural compatibility and the consistency and transparency required from an authentic leader, traits which enable them to resolve multiple issues and ensure they protect and sustain the culture for longer than their own tenure.

5.i   CULTURAL COMPATABILITY

In his book *My People, My Football*, Pep Guardiola recounts, 'Charly Rexach always said that in order to be a trainer you have to think 30 per cent about football and the rest about everything surrounding the team: about the environment.'[1]

Giovanni Trapattoni, the great Italian coach, believes that 'a good coach can make a team 5 per cent better, but a bad coach can make a team 30 per cent worse.' Arsenal's longest serving manager, Arsène Wenger, half-concurs: 'At most a coach might make 5 per cent of difference, improving the performance or making it worse. But that is it.' However, he adds the caveat, 'a good coach still plays a very important part. They are ones who put the team together and create the right climate for them to perform.'

In *Soccernomics*, the economist Stefan Szymanski and the journalist Simon Kuper took this received wisdom and rigorously analysed it. They wrote that money determines somewhere between 80 and 90 per cent of the performance of football clubs. That leaves 10 or 20 per cent for other factors, one of which may or may not be the manager. Bas ter Weel, a Dutch economist who also studied the effect of managers on their football teams, compared their influence to that of prime ministers on the economy: probably no other single individual has more influence, but it's still marginal.[2]

In a recent *Harvard Business Review* article, Boris Groysberg and Abhijit Naik referenced some compelling research carried out in the 1990s by Jeff Borland and Jenny Lye about the importance of a leader who understands the importance of culture in Australian Rules Football.[3]

Borland and Lye studied data on Australian football coaches between 1931 and 1994. They found that well-matched coaches – coaches that had a good cultural fit with the teams they lead – did indeed affect team performance. In other words, a winning record was dependent on the degree of match between coach and team. The research provided two important takeaways, which we can see reflected both in Guardiola's four-year tenure at Barcelona and far beyond Aussie Rules Football.

First, Borland and Lye found that a coach's years of experience might not be as powerful a factor as people might think in explaining a team's winning percentage. This finding implies that experience, defined purely in terms of duration, sometimes might be overrated when it comes to choosing coaches.

Guardiola's single year's coaching experience with Barcelona's B team before his own big break is testimony that a cultural fit can be found even when the coach/employee is inexperienced. There are several other such examples among coaches in the NFL, including Bill Walsh, who went straight from coaching college football at Stanford to coaching the San Francisco 49ers and leading them to three Super Bowl victories.

Second, the research concluded that the cultural fit of a leader – in extracting the most of this 10 per cent impact – really does matter; it is not a *nice to have* add-on, but essential to peak performance. Groysberg and Naik point out the irony that, 'the processes used to determine a good fit are deemed successful after the fact – a classic case of survivor bias.'

Ferran Soriano's initial decision to approach the recruitment of the head coach in the same way that any other major corporation would set about hiring a senior executive – by utilizing a methodical and analytical selection process which placed culture at the front and centre of any decision – was a way of addressing this. It was not a case of hoping to get lucky.

EXERCISE – CULTURAL FIT

I've worked with both leaders and those recruiting them to help them identify a good cultural fit. The questions below should be asked of any potential leader, either by those recruiting them or by the leader themselves.

1. *What environment do you thrive in the most and what drives your passion?*
This question helps frame the conversation in terms of what the candidate wants rather than what you want. It's open-ended, so they have to think about their response. The answer to this question may give you insight into whether this candidate prefers to work alone and uninterrupted or perhaps does best in a team.

There's really no wrong answer. You just need to assess whether your company is an environment they will thrive in.

2. *If you were starting a company from scratch, what would you want your company's culture to be?*
This is a great opportunity to dig into what they think company culture is. Do they want pizza and beer or do they care most about a good work–life balance?

You should be thinking about whether their answer matches your company's actual culture.

3. *What does your ideal work day look like?*
We all have different ideal days. I prefer silence while I work

but others like to play music. You need to know whether you are a good match to provide the candidate's ideal day.

4. *What are your personal values and how are they aligned with the company's values?*

Here you can make sure the candidate understands what your company's values are. They also have to explain how their values fit yours.

5. *Describe your perfect job, company and work environment. Whatever factors are most important to you.*

This is similar to asking about the candidate's ideal work day, but a little more specific. It should give you some insights into what they value most in a job. It's great to always follow up and ask for specific examples.

6. *In your opinion, what is leadership?*

I like this question because it can give you insight into what the candidate's past experiences with being led are. Since the question is framed in a very general way, you will get a more honest answer than if you ask them directly about their previous boss.

7. *What is your leadership style?*

This is a great follow-up to the previous question. Once they describe their style, you can ask them to provide specific examples from their life where they demonstrated these leadership qualities.

Josep Guardiola – cultural leader

Josep Guardiola Sala, whose father was a bricklayer, was born in 1971 in the small Catalan town of Santpedor, seventy-three kilometres north of Barcelona. When he was thirteen he left home to take up residence at La Masia.

When he arrived at his first Barcelona training session, a member of the club's staff asked the coach who had recruited him what the big deal was with the new boy. 'He's got no shot, he can't dribble, he's not physically strong. All he has is a very large head.'

'That's it,' the coach replied. 'The secret is in his head.'[4]

This provides, in part, an answer to the question of how a man who began his big-league coaching career aged thirty-seven achieved so much, so soon. He spent twenty-four years, from the day he arrived at the club, preparing himself for the job.

Johan Cruyff, a fundamental part of Barcelona and Guardiola's Big Picture, as we have seen, plucked him from the club's youth ranks for the first team. In Pep's hungry eyes and tautly alert bearing, Cruyff saw an avid learner. The Dutch master never had a more attentive pupil – Cruyff's core message remains Guardiola's today.

To keep the ball, to defend by denying it to your opponents and to create more opportunities than them to score, you need skill, self-possession and intelligence. Cruyff saw enough of the first quality in Guardiola, and an abundance of the second and third.

He played at number four, just in front of the defence, the link man with the attack. Eusebio Sacristán, a former Barcelona player who was on the pitch on the day of Guardiola's first-team debut, remembers that Pep was far from being a complete player but that his footballing brain compensated for any skill deficiencies: 'He had no pace, he couldn't run with the ball, he wasn't strong in the tackle yet he became the axis around which Cruyff's team revolved. His brain worked so fast he could make those around him play at the speed of light.'[5]

Guardiola became Cruyff's chief artificer on the pitch. Guardiola processed every game in his mind, every training session, every lesson Cruyff imparted. Evaristo Murtra, then a club director and owner of a large textile business, was the man who pushed for Guardiola to be named coach of the Barcelona B team. 'It was a horrible assignment,' said Murtra. 'The team had just gone down to the third division and the task he was set was to promote them immediately back to the second.' He took the job on, transformed a demoralized team and, as required, won them promotion.

Despite his impeccable cultural credentials, polls showed that public opinion in Barcelona was overwhelmingly sceptical of Guardiola when he was promoted to head coach. They had no knowledge of the piece of paper, detailing the cultural characteristics on which they would appoint the club's next coach, written up by the club's board. *El País* relegated their report on Guardiola's accession to the thirteenth page of their sports section.

Indeed, incredulity was Guardiola's own initial reaction to being offered the role. When he met Joan Laporta in the Michelin-starred Drolma restaurant in the centre of Barcelona, the president told him that if Frank Rijkaard left, he would be the next coach of Barcelona.

'You wouldn't have the balls to do that!' blurted Guardiola, who later admitted that the wine may have contributed to his reaction.[6]

Juan Carlos Unzué, the team's goalkeeping coach for three of the four years when Guardiola was creating a commitment culture, watched the spectacle up close: 'In terms of tactics, in terms of motivation, in terms of every single facet required in a coach, Guardiola is outstanding, in a class of his own.'

As we have seen, the players he led were no ordinary group, either – not an easy bunch to win over. Most of them had won the European Cup under Rijkaard and several had just triumphed in the European Championship with Spain, and the squad had won a host of other trophies between them. Lots of very rich young men with very big global reputations. Guardiola subordinated them to his – and by default, the club's – will because they came to see that acting on his instructions was the recipe for victory. 'The main quality which Guardiola offers,' observes Victor Valdés, 'is that he knows how to win.' And, as Unzué said, there was another thing: 'Practically all the players confessed it to me that Pep had made them better.' Not excluding Lionel Messi, who is on record as acknowledging he would not be the player he has become without Guardiola's help.

Messi played on the right wing during that first season, in which the team won everything and for which he won his first Ballon d'Or. But Guardiola never ceased to believe there was room for improvement. Halfway through the 2009–10 season, Messi suffered a rare loss of form. For three games in a row he went missing in action. The third, in February 2010, was a first-leg Champions League game away to Stuttgart. The game ended in a disappointing 1–1 draw, with Messi more ineffectual than ever. 'The standard reaction of a coach would have been to blame the player and give him a wake-up call by dropping him for the next match,' recalled Murtra. 'Instead, Pep thought: *It's my fault. It's me who's failing to get the best out of him.* Pep thought hard about where he was going wrong. Then it came to him. He saw he was wasting Messi's talent playing him out wide, he spoke to him and said, "From now on you're going to play up front, in the middle."' Guardiola also said, as Messi would later recall, 'Now you're going to score three or four goals a game.'[7]

'Messi had always been regarded, unquestioningly, as a winger,' says Unzué. 'But Pep suddenly saw that he had to be positioned where he would receive more of the ball and have the greatest possible impact.' He was right. Three weeks later, in the return game against Stuttgart, Barcelona won 4–0 and Messi scored two goals, setting up another. He didn't score three or four goals every game, but he came close. His scoring rate soared, and has yet to drop off. In his first season with Guardiola, Messi scored a hugely impressive thirty-eight times; in his fourth, he scored a barely believable seventy-three. In 2009–10, Barcelona won the Spanish league for the second season running, lighting up the world, to the disgust of Real Madrid, who responded by hiring José Mourinho as head coach.

Six months later, now in Guardiola's third season, Barcelona humiliated Mourinho's Madrid 5–0 in an exhibition of 'choral' football, as they call it in Spain, never before seen. It was a perfect manifestation of Cruyff and Guardiola's Big Picture. For all future encounters with Barcelona, Mourinho battened down the hatches, paying his rivals the compliment of 'parking the bus', as small teams do against big ones. Real Madrid played a backs-to-the-wall defensive game and Mourinho deployed every trick he knew on and off the field to put his rivals off their stride, not least by seeking to sully their reputation and engaging in the kind of rhetorical mud-slinging at which he excels. It didn't work in his first season at Madrid, 2010–11, as Barcelona won the league for the third year in a row, plus the European Cup again, but it did work the season after that, Guardiola's last. Real Madrid were crowned champions of Spain, and towards the end of the season Barcelona began to lose their edge. The team remained, to the end, a mirror of their coach. Guardiola had dedicated every waking moment for four years to devising new tactics, new ways to motivate his players, new responses to new challenges. His batteries were drained. 'He always said success wears you down and in his case he was right,' said Evaristo Murtra. 'He needed a rest.' For his own good and, as he saw it, that of the team, which he felt he could no longer improve, he quit.

Cruyff, who regularly shared long meals with Guardiola, warned his protégé, 'Don't stay longer than you should.' He confided that if he could relive his own experiences, he would have left the club two years earlier. Soon after this advice had been passed along, Guardiola applied it to his own situation. 'In order to be a great institution for four years,' he said, 'you must have a lot of courage. The players get tired of you and you get tired of the players; the press gets tired of you and you get tired of the press, seeing the same faces, the same questions, the same things. In the end, you must know when the time comes and say, "Look, it's time for me to leave."'

But it was not in a spirit of mourning or defeat, no matter Real Madrid's triumph, that the Barcelona faithful crowded into the Camp Nou one balmy evening in May 2012 to bid him farewell. The message that night was a joyous 'Gràcies, Pep!' – 'Thank you, Pep!' All present now knew what the novice coach had delivered: the Big Picture made real; the admiration of the world won. As Sir Bobby Charlton, a legendary figure in English football, had said a few months earlier, it didn't matter if Real were ahead on points: 'Barcelona have it all. They have the values. They have an idea: an idea that having possession of the ball gives you an advantage. They are unique and the world should learn from them.'

'I took over a legacy,' Guardiola said of his time as the keeper of the flame, 'and the greatest pride I can feel comes from seeing that everything continues the same as when I was there, or better.'

The culture continues.

5.ii AUTHENTIC LEADERSHIP

If there was one way of summarizing the role of a leader in establishing a high-performing culture, it would be this: set an authentic example.

'There is not a single coach, nor player, that can guarantee success,' Guardiola once wrote. 'Nor are there magic formulae. It's not possible to please everyone and there is no point in trying to be what other people think you should be. For me, it's important to be who I am, not just to be different but to be as authentic as I can be.'

Maybe this advice sounds too common-sense: define and enshrine your core behaviours and priorities, then lead by example. It's not exactly a radical stance. But there are two reasons why it is uncommon to find people who have actually acted on this seemingly basic advice.

First, people rarely establish their priorities until they're forced to. Furthermore, it's easy to imagine how other organizational leaders, facing a values conflict, might escape without pinning down their own behavioural priorities. In an autocratic cultural model, a more egotistical leader might have said, 'Here's what I have decided', settling the issue without articulating anything about priorities. In a bureaucratic culture, a more wishy-washy leader might have resolved the issue politically, supporting whichever faction they needed to curry favour with that quarter. In short, while behavioural priorities are vital for making good decisions, they are also totally voluntary. Authentic leaders articulate their priorities.

Second, establishing priorities is not the same as binding yourself to them. In one series of interviews led by William F. Pounds of MIT, managers were asked to share the important problems they were facing in their organizations. Most managers mentioned five to eight problems. Later in the interview, they were asked to describe their activities from the previous week. Pounds shared the punchline that 'no manager reported any activity which could be directly associated with the problems they had described.'[1] They had done no work on their core priorities. Urgencies had cancelled out priorities. Authentic leaders, however, will work hard to ensure that urgencies – the most vivid and immediate circumstances – rarely replace priorities. They maintain this through consistency and transparency in their approach to all aspects of leadership.

Leading by example – honouring the trademark behaviours

It is estimated that we have to make up to 10,000 trivial decisions every single day. Most of our day-to-day decisions – which route to take to work, which sandwich to buy for lunch – are pretty effortless. But the tough calls can take a toll. 'Great leaders,' suggests the Italian coach Fabio Capello, 'will learn to make fewer mistakes than most.'[2]

How can you ensure that your decisions accurately reflect your core priorities? And, going a step further, how can you take the offensive against the less-important tasks that threaten to distract you from them?

Once you have realized the trademark behaviours, you must do something important: you must enshrine them, making them known to everybody in the organization, so that they can influence dozens or even hundreds of future decisions.

Of course, this is supposed to be the whole point of organizational mission statements and values. Unfortunately, the top executives of most organizations have chosen to retreat behind vague endorsements of values like 'diversity', 'trust', 'integrity', and so on. Only in the most extreme cases are these values sufficient enough to tip a decision. No one could resolve an issue like how to deal with a difficult problem by simply asking which option showed most 'integrity'.

That's why it's so important to enshrine and then role-model the identified behaviours, not just cheerlead for generic values. 'In the end, the jobs we do can be reduced to mere moments in time,' Guardiola says. 'That's true whatever your profession. It's those moments that make sense of the work I do.'[3]

Even the guy working the cash register at an ice-cream stall will routinely encounter conflicts among behavioural priorities. If a customer drops his ice cream, should he offer a free replacement? Is it more important to ensure that the customer is satisfied or that the owner is profitable? Without clear behavioural guidelines, the decision will be made idiosyncratically, depending on the employee's mood at that moment. While we can tolerate some randomness when it comes to fumbled ice creams, alignment is critical in many other situations.

That's why Guardiola's diligence in offering guidelines to inform his own – and others' – decisions is critical to developing a winning culture.

This is one of the classic tensions of leadership: you want to encourage people to use their judgement, but you also need your team members' judgements to be correct and consistent. So Guardiola's simple principles could serve as guardrails for handling these dilemmas. He sought, as he put it, 'guardrails that are wide enough to empower but narrow enough to guide.' So, as we have seen in the Big Picture section, he clearly articulated a list of guiding principles: the trademark behaviours.

Show humility; Work hard; Put the team first

These guidelines enshrined the priorities for the group. They ensured that different people would make similar decisions in similar circumstances and do so quickly. When we identify and enshrine our priorities, our decisions are more consistent and less agonizing.

'The players put you to the test each day,' Guardiola says, 'that's why it is important to be convinced about what you want and how you want to put it across.'[4]

When he signed a marketing agreement with Sabadell Bank, committing to a number of lectures and personal interviews as part of the deal – while still refusing to grant personal interviews to the media – he was initially labelled as a money-grabber by some critics. However, he was soon vindicated when it emerged that he had shared out all the money he received from the bank between his staff as a way of acknowledging their dedication to selflessly putting the team first.

Again, at the start of one season, when Audi presented a car to each first-team player as well as the coach, Guardiola refused to accept his: if there were no cars for his technical staff, then he would not take one either. When he learned that Angel Mur, the club's massage therapist for thirty-three years but by then retired, did not have tickets for the 2009 Champions League final, Mur was invited as a special guest of the manager. In 2011, when he agreed to sign a new contract, he only did so once new, extended terms for all his backroom staff had been approved.[5]

Our calendars are the ultimate scoreboard for our own priorities. If forensic analysts confiscated your calendar and email records and web browsing history for the past six months, what would they conclude your core priorities are? I worry that mine would include drinking coffee, reading about Manchester United and carefully deleting junk email on an hourly basis.

Parents experience this too: quality time with your kids gets pushed out by last-minute errands and meal preparations. The problem is that urgencies – the most vivid and immediate circumstances – will always hog the spotlight.

To spend more time on our core priorities necessarily means spending less time on other things. That's why Jim Collins, the author of *Good to Great*, suggests that we create a 'stop-doing list'. When he was a graduate student, a professor told Collins that he wasn't leading a disciplined life, merely a busy one.

She asked him how he would change his behaviour if he received two life-changing phone calls. In the first call, he'd learn he had inherited $20 million, no strings attached. The second call would inform him that, due to a rare and incurable disease, he had only ten years left to live. In this situation, she asked him, what would you stop doing? Thus was born Collins's 'stop-doing list' – which he compiles once a year. Collins wrote in 2003:

> A great piece of art is composed not just of what is in the final piece, but equally important, what is not. It is the discipline to discard what does not fit – to cut out what might have already cost days or even years of effort – that distinguishes the truly exceptional artist and marks the ideal piece of work, be it a symphony, a novel, a painting, a company or, most important of all, a life.[6]

The key insight is that we spend too much time on addition

and not nearly enough on subtraction. Yet it's only taking away what doesn't matter that allows us to reveal what does matter.

It's tempting but naive to pretend that we can make time for everything by multitasking or by working more efficiently. But let's face it, there's not that much slack in your schedule. An hour spent on one thing is an hour not spent on another. So, if you have made a commitment to spend more time with the kids or to exercise more, then part of that resolution must be to decide what you're going to stop doing. Make it concrete: look back over your schedule for the past week and ask yourself, 'What, specifically, would I have given up to carve out the extra three or four hours that I needed?'

In return for victories and hard work, Guardiola instituted a new and at the time controversial policy. Once the preparation had been done, Guardiola wanted his players as far away from tension and pressure as possible. So, for home matches, he did away with the much-hated *concentración*, the widespread, traditional idea that the team needs to be taken away from their homes and put into a hotel the night before every game so they can concentrate. Equally, he would always attempt to fly to games on the day itself, thus avoiding the boredom and frustration of endless travel, and wasting time in hotel restaurants and airports. Across a season, it was estimated that this saved hundreds of hours travelling, thus minimizing the frustration and boredom felt by both staff and players.[7]

In organizations, especially, the stop-doing list may require some initial investment of time – ten hours spent now to save thirty hours spent later. Every day, all of us struggle to stay off List B and stick with List A. It's not easy. Peter Bregman, a productivity guru and blogger for the *Harvard Business Review*, recommends a simple trick for dodging this fate. He advises us to set a timer that goes off once every hour, and when it beeps, we should ask ourselves, 'Am I doing what I most need to be doing right now?'[8]

Guardiola asks himself a similar question: 'I strive to live with passion and not to be desensitized to life. Things matter to me. You've got to live like that. Otherwise, what's the point? I regularly ask myself, am I as authentic as I can be?'[9]

EXERCISE – THE STOP-DOING LIST

The two most influential management gurus of the past thirty years are Tom Peters and Jim Collins. In 1982, Peters taught the corporate world how to go *In Search of Excellence*.[10] Nineteen years later, Collins showed leaders how to move from *Good to Great*. Walk into any large organization just about anywhere in the world and there's a 50–50 chance you'll see either Peters's book (which he co-authored with Robert H. Waterman, Jr.) or Collins's on the bookshelves.

And even if you don't glimpse actual dog-eared copies of *In Search of Excellence* or *Good to Great*, you'll detect their philosophies in corporate practices and hear their lingo in office conversations. Wow projects. Management by walking around. Pushing the flywheel. Level 5 leadership.

In my opinion, these books both suggest that the secret to high performance for individuals is deciding what not to do. That's why when I began writing this book, I used the stop-doing list technique. I posted my list on the wall next to my desk, where it's always in view, and revised it when circumstances demanded. Let me share with you what's been on the list:

— Stop answering email during peak morning writing hours
— Stop accepting meetings or conference calls initiated by others that you wouldn't have initiated yourself

— Stop going to bed later than 11 p.m.

Have I eradicated all unproductive behaviour and become a self-disciplined, self-actualizing productivity machine? Not exactly. But I have improved. However, without consciously making that list — and then being forced to confront it at my desk — I doubt I would have been able to make those improvements.

I urge you to give the method a try and make a list of your own.

5.iii   CONSISTENCY

Throughout the book, we've discussed ways of nudging and inspiring groups to improve performance and embrace change. In such an environment as FC Barcelona, packed densely with high egos, there is a bit of 'collateral damage' for those who weren't selected to play or even worse, deemed surplus to requirements – anger, hurt feelings, or loss of confidence in the new direction. How can you militate against this? Consistency and transparency are key.

Eric Abidal laughs about his initial reaction to Guardiola. 'I didn't know the boss or how he worked,' he remembers. 'The first month was difficult, because I'm a father, I'm thirty years old, and you don't speak the same way to a young player who has just started in professional football as you would to a veteran. And he was doing exactly that! He made us change who we sat with at meal times and he made me speak Castilian with my fellow Frenchman, Thierry Henry, when we were in the group. I went to speak with the president, Laporta, to tell him that I wouldn't tolerate it, that I wanted to leave, but he told me to calm down, that it was his way of doing things and that everything would go well. Now, I still laugh when I think about it.'[1]

Guardiola countered this scepticism by sharing the process. 'As a professional footballer, they look for that figure that tells them, "Hey, come this way . . ." This is what we coaches have to do. We have to transmit that trust and security in all the decisions we have to make. That trust, security and sincerity are fundamental pillars for a good coach. The players have to believe in the manager's message. He must always speak to the players fearlessly, sincerely and tell them what he thinks. Without deceiving them.'[2]

There are a few additional ideas to ensure that you can lead change with the consistency required.

Group thinking

Guardiola argues that there are two types of coaches: those who think problems solve themselves and those who solve problems. He welcomes the chance to find solutions to problems. To do so, he has gathered a committee of advisers, people from whom he says he can 'steal ideas, ideas are shared, they go from one person to another.'

One study, which compared forty-one Nobel laureate scientists with a sample of similarly experienced scientists, found that a major difference between the two groups was that the Nobel laureates canvassed a wider range of opinions than the regular scientists. They were open to a wider variety of ideas when it came to actively solving problems.[3]

This requires some advance planning, as research indicates that we tend to look for feedback from people with similar outlooks to ourselves. For centuries, the Catholic church made use of a 'devil's advocate' in deciding who would be named a saint. The devil's advocate was known inside the church as *promoter fidei* – the 'promoter of the faith' – and his role was to build a case *against* sainthood.

John Paul II eliminated the office in 1983, ending 400 years of tradition. Since then, tellingly, saints have been canonized at a rate about twenty times faster than in the early part of the twentieth century.[4]

How many of us have ever consciously sought out people we knew would disagree with us? One of the real dangers of not gathering a wide range of feedback is that small groups of similar minds could easily only tell you what they think you want to hear.

Guardiola's group

Despite his status in Barcelona, where Guardiola is widely revered because, by birth and by inclination, he is one of their own, to view his successful approach to leadership simply as a product of one institution is unsatisfactory. His influences are far more varied. He consistently sought the counsel of four people to help him reach his big decisions: Juan Manuel Lillo, Manuel Estiarte, Marcelo Bielsa and Johan Cruyff. He knew they would challenge him and contradict his thinking, when necessary. 'It is important,' he said, 'to spend time with people who speak so much sense.'

As his playing days were drawing to a close, Guardiola made his way to Culiacán, a dangerous city in the heartland of territory controlled by Mexico's most powerful drug-trafficking organization, the Sinaloa cartel, led then by Joaquín Guzmán Loera, better known as El Chapo. He did this so he could play for, and pick the brain of, Juan Manuel Lillo, a much-travelled Spanish coach he had always admired. 'If it was in Barcelona that his ideas were formed, it was in Mexico where they were refined,' suggests Rory Smith, the *New York Times* writer.

'The story of how I met Pep is true,' Lillo said in an interview. 'He had played against my teams before, and then, after a game in 1998 between his Barcelona and my Real Oviedo, my assistant delegate knocked on the door of my office and said Pep would like to introduce himself. Would I see him? How could I say no to a player I liked so much? He said he liked my way of playing, and we talked. We always stayed in touch after that.'

After his time as a player at Barcelona came to an end, followed by a spell in Italy, Guardiola moved to Qatar for what many assumed would be the final, lucrative coda to his playing career. During his time in Qatar, he would spend pre-season training with Lillo's teams, maintaining his fitness. The two became so close that Lillo now describes him as 'one of the most important people in my life, like a son to me.'5

'He had always said that the three coaches he liked the most were me, Bielsa and Arsène Wenger,' Lillo, now an assistant at Sevilla, said. Late in 2005, with his friend working in Mexico, Guardiola saw what was probably his last chance to experience playing under one of the three men.

That year, Lillo had taken charge of Dorados de Sinaloa, an unremarkable team at the wrong end of Mexico's first division, Liga MX. The club was not a rich one: there were occasional struggles to pay the players, and Lillo had to train his players at a water park. However, when Lillo asked Guardiola to sign a short-term contract, he accepted, the lure of playing for his friend enough to overcome any doubts.

The adventure ended unhappily – Dorados were relegated, and Guardiola, plagued by injury, made only ten appearances – but the impression he made was a strong one. 'I look at my career and see that there was me before I played with Guardiola and me afterward,' said Marco Mendoza, a Mexican midfielder who played on that team. 'Just by playing with him, watching him, listening to him, he made me better. There was so much to learn from him.'

It was not just the players who were furthering their

education. Guardiola would carry a black book with him in training, detailing all of Lillo's exercises extensively, and staying behind when sessions were finished to pick his mentor's brain. Guardiola would turn to Lillo at any time of day and ask, 'How do you solve this type of situation?' 'If I do this, what will happen?'

According to Martí Perarnau, hardly a day goes by without Guardiola starting a sentence with, 'As Juanma used to say . . .'[6] Lillo, however, modestly scotches the notion that he could take any credit for the coach Guardiola has become, but it is telling that Guardiola has described Lillo as his 'maestro' and 'the best coach I ever had'.

The midfielder was asked to study opponents for his boss, and would even take teammates aside in sessions to explain to them certain technical and tactical ideas. Lillo and Guardiola spoke daily while they were together in Culiacán, the coach said, exchanging and forming ideas. It was a practice which continued beyond their Mexican adventure.

Lillo was so impressed that when Guardiola wasn't in the matchday squad, he would invite him onto the bench instead of making him sit in the stands. It wasn't uncommon to see Pep barking out orders from the touchline while Lillo remained seated. That brief foray in Mexico meant Guardiola wouldn't finish his coaching badges until July 2006, but his coaching career had effectively already started.

Lillo later admitted: 'I knew he was going to be a great coach. Pep's the opposite of the rest: everyone else has been a player, then later they gradually become coaches. Not with him. He was playing while he was waiting to become a coach!'

Guardiola recognized the value advisers can offer. He employed a number of assistants at Barcelona, but one of them stands out above the rest because of his own legendary sporting status. Manuel Estiarte was not a footballer in his playing days

– his sport was water polo. Having played in six Olympic Games, Estiarte was so good he earned the nickname 'The Maradona of water polo', winning Olympic Gold and World Cup titles, to name only two of his many individual and team honours.

At the Camp Nou, Estiarte was appointed as Guardiola's right-hand man, someone who commanded respect and trust among the squad for his sporting past, and as such was a valuable figure for the coach when he wanted to learn how his team's mindset was, or needed a sounding board when he had a new idea.

'Manuel is essential for Pep,' Pere Guardiola, Pep's brother, explained to me.[7] 'They have been close friends for a long time. Pep trusts his judgement and knows that he has his best interests at heart at all times. He will tell him what he needs to hear not what he wants to hear.'

The third influence was Marcelo Bielsa. When Guardiola was initially offered the job as Barça B coach, he said, 'You have to respect the fact that this is a process, a learning curve. The first steps are vital and there are no second chances once you step up.'

He travelled to Argentina to deepen his knowledge. 'It is a country where the taxi drivers know as much about the finer details of football as the coaches,' laughs Pere Guardiola. There, he met Ricardo La Volpe, Marcelo Bielsa and César Luis Menotti. Menotti later said, 'Pep didn't come here looking for us to tell him how it was done. He knew that.' He also met a fans' group who had set up a blog to discuss the creative side of football. They presented him with a biography of Bielsa, *Lo Suficientemente Loco – The Sufficiently Mad* – by Ariel Senosian.[8]

With his friend David Trueba, Guardiola drove the 309 kilometres from Buenos Aires to Rosario to meet Bielsa himself. The meeting between the two football men took place in the

Argentinean's *charka*, or villa, and lasted eleven intense – yet productive – hours. There were heated discussions, revision of techniques, detailed analyses of positional play which, at one point, included Trueba man-marking a chair. The two coaches shared their obsessions, manias and passion for the game – emerging from the *charka* declaring their admiration for each other.

Legend has it that Bielsa asked Guardiola: 'Do you really like blood that much?' He was testing him to determine whether he was prepared to make the endlessly tough decisions a leader encounters. Guardiola presumably decided that he did.

His final ally was Cruyff. Since his coaching debut, Guardiola has never tired of repeating that Cruyff was the inspiration for his approach, and this sense of continuity has been a good thing for the club. 'We are a little bit like disciples of the essence that Cruyff brought here,' said Guardiola.

Guardiola always addressed Cruyff in the '*usted*' form – the formal 'you' in Spanish, a very rare and old-fashioned habit. 'It is a case of the pupil showing respect and humility towards his former coach and master,' explained Pere.

Cruyff also recognized the strength of seeking support from a wide range of people and deferring to others' greater expertise. 'If you have a toothache,' Cruyff once explained in his enigmatic style, 'you go to the dentist, because he understands teeth.'

'So many leaders think they have to control those below them, while in fact it should be precisely the reverse. They should allow themselves to be guided by those that know better. Their inflated egos urge them to lay down the law when they just don't have the knowledge to do so,' explained the Dutch master, who knew that it takes a combination of humility and strength to understand that, in order to be the best, it is necessary to surround yourself with other experts:

You can immediately identify such people when you ask them a question, whatever the field. Either you get an answer from someone who places himself in your shoes, or you get an answer from someone who tries to convince you he's right, and that his solution is the only solution. When I ask a question, I just want to know what I need to know, because ultimately information is more important that intelligence. I don't need chapter and verse; as long as I get the right answers from the right people, then I'm a step ahead of someone who might have more understanding but less information. That's why as a coach, I assembled as big a team as possible to be responsible for all elements of training and preparation.[9]

The reason for such a diverse cast of advisers is obvious. If a leader hatches an ambitious new plan and pushes it through, against opposition, he's taking a risk. What if his diagnosis of the problems – and the solution – are plain wrong? On the other hand, if he bargains with his advisers and staff, he may come out with a watered-down plan, but it might be watered-down only in the sense that the parts that were least likely to work have been washed away.

Pep went to see Cruyff soon after his stumbling start to the season as B-team coach. 'I've got a problem,' he told his mentor. 'I've got these two guys who I don't know if I can control, they don't listen to what I say and that affects how everybody else receives my messages. And the problem is, they are two of the leaders in the dressing room and the best players. I will lose without them on board.' Cruyff's response was blunt: 'Get rid of them. You might lose one or two games, but then you will start winning and by then you would have turfed those two sons of bitches out of the team.'

Despite his own initial reticence to be so ruthless, Pep got

AUTHENTIC LEADERSHIP   265

rid of the pair, establishing his power in the dressing room and sending a clear signal to the rest.

EXERCISE – THE TENTH MAN RULE

In the 1973 Yom Kippur War (also known as the Arab–Israeli War), so spectacular was the exposure of Israel's intelligence failure that it revolutionized Israel's approach to decision-making.

Egypt and Syria led the Arab states in an attack which caught Israel off-guard, despite Israel's Directorate of Military Intelligence (Aman) being almost completely cognizant of Arab invasion plans months in advance. Aman had made a series of assumptions – about difficulties in Egypt and Syria's alliance and military procurement, among other things – on which they based their analysis of all subsequent intelligence. The result was that they were confident the Arabs weren't serious about going to war, even when they were in possession of the Arab war plans. Aman remained confident that the probability of war was low right until the moment Israel was attacked. The episode is deemed a low point in military Intelligence history.

After an investigation into what went wrong, Aman established a control unit within their departments, the purpose of which was to play devil's advocate in any analysis of military intelligence. Max Brooks, the author of the zombie apocalypse book *World War Z*, predicts that Israel would survive the apocalypse because of this strategy, which he calls the 'tenth man rule': if ten people are in a room, and nine agree on how to interpret and respond to a situation, the tenth man must disagree. His duty is to find the strongest possible argument against the consensus the rest of the group has reached.[10]

When it comes to planning, you want to have every aspect

covered as best you can. The 'tenth man rule' always has someone play the part of contrarian, no matter how solid your plan looks, to make it even more effective.

No plan is perfect, but that doesn't mean you shouldn't try to plug as many holes as you can. The 'tenth man rule' works the same way as companies hiring people to find weaknesses in their systems and security.

You can use the 'tenth man rule' in any planning situation; you don't actually need ten people. Planning a holiday? Assign someone the job of 'tenth man'. Getting ready to make a big life decision? Ask someone you trust to be your personal 'tenth man' and poke holes in it. Effective planning comes down to strategy and reiteration. Keep finding and plugging holes until your plan is rock solid.

5.iv   TRANSPARENCY

Of course, even the level of consistency I've outlined can't make everyone happy. Some decisions will leave a group of people worse off, which is the necessary cost of doing something great for many others or for the organization itself.

If those people who lose out consider the decision-making process fair, it can make a huge difference in the way they react.

Researchers call this sense of fairness 'procedural justice': that is, the procedures used to make a decision were just. This is distinct from 'distributive justice', which is concerned with whether the spoils of a decision were divided up fairly. An extensive body of research confirms that procedural justice is critical in explaining how people feel about a decision. It's not just the outcome that matters; it's the process.[1]

The elements of procedural justice are straightforward: give people a chance to be heard, to present their case. Listen – really listen – to what people say. Use accurate information to make the decision, and give people a chance to challenge the information if it's incorrect. Apply these principles consistently across situations. Avoid bias and self-interest. Explain why the decision was made and be candid about the relevant risks or concerns.

Despite the announcement Guardiola had made at his introductory press conference, explaining his rationale for dispensing with the services of Deco, Ronaldinho and Eto'o, only two of the players moved on. Eto'o refused to take the rejection lying down and worked brutally hard to convince the new coach to change his mind. 'That summer,' recounts Graham Hunter, 'Eto'o kept his mouth shut, trained like a dervish and crucially, led the team in work rate.'[2]

Guardiola observed these behaviours and discussed his thinking with the cultural architects and his team's captains, Puyol, Xavi and Valdés, before he sat down with the Cameroonian striker. 'I like your work rate. If you play and train like you have been, then you stay. I have spoken with the team's captains and they agree that there must be no more disruptive behaviour. No more warnings, one strike and you are out.'

Eto'o agreed and the decision proved inspirational. He scored thirty-six goals in Guardiola's first season, including the crucial opening strike in the 2009 Champions League final against Manchester United.

Surely there is no real debate about whether this is the right way to make a decision – unless *you* want to argue in favour of inconsistent, disrespectful decisions? There may be times when we value our own idea more than a fair process and times when we choose expediency over procedural justice but these should be the exceptions rather than the rule, and should be explained and justified afterwards to protect the culture.

The procedural justice research shows that people can care deeply about process. We all want to believe that a decision-making process that affects us is fair, that it is taking into account all the right information. Even if the outcome goes against us, our confidence in the process is critical. By acknowledging potential flaws in the decision, a leader encourages his team to put their faith in a process rather than a single decision. Individual decisions will frequently be wrong, but the right process will be a staunch ally in any situation.

It was this very process which reassured his players, despite the lack of early success in Guardiola's senior coaching career. After Guardiola failed to win in his first two games, Andrés Iniesta, the usually reserved 'backbone' of the team who had started the matches as a substitute, approached his leader's office, gently knocked on the door, and said: 'Don't worry *mister*. We'll win it all. We're on the right path. Carry on like this, okay? Please don't change anything. You should know we're with you until the death.'[3]

Guardiola explains, 'He spoke out because he could see that there was a method we were following. We had explained why we did things the way we did and he recognized the process.'

In the following game, Barcelona scored six against Sporting Gijon and never looked back.

EXERCISE – PRIORITY PLANNING

'If you wish to know your past life, look to your present circumstances. If you wish to know your future life, look to your present actions.' – Buddhist saying

There are two factors which determine how a leader spends their time. There are the things that are classed as urgent ('I must do it and I must do it now!') and there are things that are classed as important: actions which contribute towards moving to the Big Picture destination.

I often ask leaders to allocate their time and activities into four main categories, which are:

1. Firefighting (activities which are urgent and important)

2. Fire prevention (activities which are important)

3. False alarms (activities which are urgent)

4. Fire escapes (activities which are neither urgent nor important)

Let's look at each area in detail, as this will help you to plan your time better and help you achieve your identified goals.

1. Firefighting

These are the times when you are reacting to the world around you, like when the phone is always ringing or when your boss is angry and demanding action or when the kids are crying.

If this sounds familiar and you think that you are spending a lot of your time in this area, it is likely to be because you are not prioritizing effectively.

By the way, if you read the above and thought that this is your preferred style of operating, just ask yourself: how many fires are you actually responding to and how many fires are you actually responsible for starting? Some of the best firefighters are also the best arsonists, as they enjoy the feeling of always being active and available to help. The question is whether you are putting your energies into the right areas, which contribute to your own goals.

2. Fire prevention

The more time you spend in this area will mean the less time you will have to spend fighting fires and dealing with urgent and important issues. This is because you are planning, training, innovating and heading problems off before they become raging infernos. These issues don't depend on you getting involved and tackling them. You have to act first, to anticipate and solve them.

A great example of this is given in Sir Clive Woodward's book *Winning!* He writes about the last seconds of England's 2003 Rugby World Cup win and studies every pass, every move and every thought his players took in those crucial, dying seconds of the final. He was able to identify every area of innovation, practice and planning upon which he and his coaching team had focused over the previous six years, in anticipation of that very moment when Jonny Wilkinson kicked the winning points.

He didn't wait until he was in the heat of the moment and decide to leave anything to chance. Instead, he had deliberately spent a large amount of his time in the 'fire prevention' box and had accounted for every possible eventuality, including the requirement of a last second winner.

One example of fire prevention was Clive Woodward's introduction of a training method which he called T-CUP (Thinking Correctly Under Pressure).[4] This is a technique that is taught to the elite soldiers of the SAS. Woodward had noticed that when the team had lost their previous three Grand Slam deciders, the players had lost all composure and control when they were chasing the game, and they had reverted to a style which wasn't their normal approach and which played straight into the hands of their opponents.

T-CUP training involved putting his players in pressurized situations and then teaching them how to handle their own emotions and not to panic. In convincing his players of the benefits of this coaching, he delivered a perfect example of prioritization.

He explained this by starting from the players' goal, which was to win the World Cup. If they lost control, they would lose their discipline. If they lost their discipline, they would lose penalties. If they lost penalties, they would lose points. If they lost points, they would lose games. If they lost games, they would lose the World Cup. When he explained it in these terms, the players all understood why they had to prioritize.

3. *False alarms*
This box is a deception, and although it feels like firefighting,

it isn't. Events here feel as though they are urgent because of the noises of emergency and panic which people make. On closer inspection, you will find that it's usually a matter that is urgent to them alone.

4. Fire escapes

This is the area where you find yourself doing anything, such as tidying your desk or other easy distractions and excuses, rather than doing what really needs to be done.

Follow these simple steps to help you prioritize:

1. Think about the 5 most important tasks you need to achieve.
2. Now grade them 1–10 on how happy you are with the amount of time you spend on them (1 = not happy; 10 = very happy).
3. Now think about what you would like the ratings to be. Grade them 1–10 on what you wish the time spent was.

This should give you a good indication on where you are spending most of your time. Is it in the areas and percentages you want?

5.v   AUTHENTIC LEADERSHIP SUMMARY

We usually think about leadership as the art of doing big, important stuff: creating a vision, making decisions, inspiring people. In other words, *leading*.

However, all too often, our behaviour as leaders on a day-to-day basis does not accurately honour our core values – or those of the group around us. The most effective way a leader can communicate the kind of culture they want to preside over is through their own example.

Ray Kroc, the founder of McDonald's, was famous for his adherence to hygiene and efficiency, two pillars of his fast-food empire. 'Every night you'd see him coming down the street, walking close to the gutter, picking up every McDonald's wrapper and cup along the way,' former McDonald's CEO Fred Turner told author Alan Deutschman. 'He'd come into the store with both hands full of cups and wrappers. I saw Ray spend one Saturday morning with a toothbrush cleaning out holes in the mop wringer. No one else really paid attention to the damned mop wringer, because everyone knew it was just a mop bucket. But Kroc saw all the crud building up in the holes, and he wanted to clean them so the wringer would work better.'[1]

As we have seen with Guardiola's own example, such authentic behaviour illustrates a striking pattern. Why should accomplished leaders of highly successful groups spend their valuable time on these matters?

Cultural leadership determines that these same small, humble moments are when the leader connects with those in their organization. These moments are vital because they contain several signals: *I am not above you; we have standards; you should do this kind of thing too; we are about things that are bigger than ourselves.*

The main reason these authentic behaviours are so powerful are because they send a larger signal that every group needs to be sent over and over: *we are all in this together.*

The point of authentic cultural leadership is not to do great things, but rather to create an environment where the whole group can do great things together.

6. THE X SPOT

'If you want to go fast, go alone.
If you want to go far, go together.'
African Proverb

6.i   THE X FACTOR

Date: Saturday, 28 May 2011
Time: 6.30 p.m.
Location: Wembley Stadium, London

Just over an hour before kick-off in the Champions League final, the players were gathered in the dressing room waiting for the head coach to arrive. Guardiola came into the dressing room with his jacket off, rolled up his sleeves and began talking. It was, lamented David Villa, the team's star striker, a pity there was no video recording of his performance that day. 'It would make a very useful educational tool for aspiring young coaches in how to deliver the perfect team talk.'[1]

'He told us from the beginning of his coaching career, "I won't go in the dressing room until I am needed,"' recounts Xavi. 'It's like a classroom without the teacher. And when the teacher comes in, there's silence and it's time to work.'[2]

The coach looked into his players' eyes, speaking clearly and quickly with intent. Pacing around, gesturing furiously, spontaneously, he would occasionally move up close and address one of his pupils directly, to drive home a particular point.

Mountaineers caution that one of the most dangerous points when scaling a peak is the moment you can see the summit. When the goal is tantalizingly close, it is easy to relax or rush and in either case the chances of mistakes increase.

Guardiola was attempting to navigate this same dangerous territory by helping his team identify the X spot.

For the members of the FC Barcelona squad, it had been a long, arduous journey towards the summit. They had fought together through sixty-two games that season and 191 games since they began to work together. Guardiola knew his players intimately. He intended that tonight would be the climax of everything that he had been taught by Cruyff, the legacy that he had been so resolutely building on. This was his cathedral: the crystallization of everything that FC Barcelona stood for.

6.ii   THE X SPOT

There are few better ways to witness the power of human potential than to watch a runner cross the finish line of a marathon. It's incredible to see the months and years of physical training, determination and self-discipline culminating in that one moment of pure achievement. What is fascinating about those final moments of a marathon is that you very rarely see a runner slow down as they approach the line. Despite the exhaustion they must be feeling by that point, marathon runners actually *speed up* and sprint with the full force of their remaining energy across the finish line. How?

When runners are 26.1 miles into a 26.2-mile race, a special brain event occurs right at the spot – called the X spot – where runners turn the corner and see the finish line. According to Dr Lewis Maharam, board chairman of the International Marathon Medical Directors Association, this is the moment when the brain releases a flood of endorphins and other chemicals that gives the body the required energy to accelerate through that final leg of the race.[3] If you are a runner, or any kind of athlete, you have probably experienced some form of this. When your brain sees that success is now not only *possible* but now *probable*, the reaction is physically powerful – so powerful, in fact, that a very small number of marathon runners can't handle it.

Incredibly, in the entire 26.2-mile race, the X spot is the

most likely place for a cardiac arrest to occur. This is why many international marathons, brilliantly, place medics right at the X spot. In some rare cases, fatigued bodies can't handle the incredible surge of neurochemical accelerants dumped into their bodies. Of course, the discovery of the X spot is not about stopping the rare heart attack. The X spot reveals one of the most important attributes of our brains. At the precise moment the goal comes into view and your brain realizes that attaining your goal is not only possible but probable, it releases a potent stream of chemicals that help you speed up.

Similarly, in the Wembley dressing room, Guardiola knew the players of FC Barcelona were keen to run harder and faster than ever. With the reward of a second Champions League in three years right under their noses, their brains were beginning to sanction the release of greater energy. It was important to harness this to increase vigour, speed, mental clarity and toughness.

'I know we are going to be champions. I have no doubt about it at all,' Guardiola declared. 'I told you that you would take me to the final and that if you did that, I was going to make you win. If we do things how we are supposed to, then we will be the superior team.'

He didn't deliver the simple instructions that Cruyff had given his team in the old Wembley dressing room before the 1992 final – 'go out and enjoy yourself'. Guardiola's message – clearly marking the X spot – was, 'Yes, we have to enjoy this match, but we have to suffer for it too.'

He detailed the game plan with precision. 'His greatest strength is his ability to recognize the key point to win a game and then explain it in terms we can easily understand and action,' said goalkeeper Victor Valdés.[4] His players – led by the Cultural Architects who had been shaped and developed within the club's traditions – understood the way to victory: the keystone habits, the relentless application of their own strengths, the manner in which they would defeat Manchester United.

Javier Mascherano said, 'Son of a bitch, he nailed it! That speech at Wembley was one that made the greatest impression on me. While he was talking, it wasn't as if he was referring to a game we were about to take part in, it was as if we were actually playing the game right there. He was up and down, side to side in front of the board, gesticulating; and if you shut your eyes and listened to him, you were already out there in the middle of the action. Everything that he said would happen, happened as he said it would. During the match, I was thinking, I've seen this already, I've already heard all about it – because Pep has already told me about it . . .'[5]

No matter what your goal is – winning the Champions League or creating a commitment culture – your brain behaves in the exact same way. As soon as your brain registers that you are going to achieve your goal, it releases the same chemicals that give you the extra boost to accelerate. *The closer you perceive success to be, in other words, the faster you move towards it.*

The intention of this book has been to help you understand how to create your own winning culture. We have identified the foundation stones – from drawing a vivid Big Picture to guiding people across the Arc of Change; identifying the Recurring Practices which facilitate your success, drawing upon the critical support of your Cultural Architects and leading them by your own example and Authentic Leadership. The stories and exercises have been shared – as X spot exercises – to shift you from making this possible to probable.

After the game – 'a hiding delivered by the greatest team I've ever faced,' according to the vanquished coach, Sir Alex Ferguson[6] – the doubters' argument, which rested on the notion that Guardiola was lucky at Barcelona to have stumbled upon a spectacularly talented set of players, had finally been silenced. The core of the team he had inherited, who had done nothing for two years before his arrival, had pulled off an astonishing feat. Guardiola achieved what every leader at every level knows to be the true measure of success: he extracted the very best from what he had and, almost beyond imagination, he made his players even better.

At the moment of his greatest triumph, he continued to personify and continue the relentless pursuit of excellence. Guardiola escaped from the celebrations and in a quiet corner of the Wembley dressing room, asked Manuel Estiarte, his trusted confidant, 'How could we do this again but even better?'

And therein lies the final lesson of creating a commitment culture – the simple idea that it is a journey to undertake rather than a destination to arrive at. As FC Barcelona found, choosing this particular pathway left an indelible mark on their sport and its history. Nothing will ever be the same again. The same possibility applies for you.

Acknowledgements

I have spent a large part of my life immersed within high-performing cultures and I would like to extend my sincerest appreciation and gratitude to the following people who have helped guide, illuminate and educate me in the ways of such environments.

Thank you Geraldine for your rich love, deep wisdom, gentle humour, enthusiastic support, bottomless patience and generous friendship. I love you more than I can adequately express in words.

George and Rose, this book – along with everything I do – is for you. Thank you for blessing me with your love, laughter, curiosity, kindness, understanding and all-round brilliance. This book and the lessons within show how you can combine essential decency, humility and hard work and still flourish at whatever you choose to do. Keep shining brightly. I love you both.

Thank you to my brilliantly supportive parents, Brian and Rosemarie, and to my dear brothers, Anthony and Chris. Your great example, encouragement, interest and unfailing friendship are a source of endless comfort and support.

I owe a huge debt of gratitude to Blaise Tapp for continuing to offer his considerable talents to help my ideas onto the page.

Bernard Niven, please accept my appreciation for generously sharing your insights, talent and support.

Thank you also to my brilliant editor, Robin Harvie. Your faith, trust and support is greatly appreciated. Equally, thank you to all at Pan Macmillan for your support of the initial idea and subsequent book.

Deep gratitude is also due to David Luxton, my incredibly talented literary agent.

Guillem Balagué. Thank you for making the time to meet up and share your insights and thoughts in such a generous manner. It proved to be a real catalyst.

Ferran Soriano and Txiki Begiristain. I continue to be immensely grateful for your time, candour and fascinating insights into culture you helped to shape so spectacularly. Thank you also to Abi Leckenby for your unfailing discretion and patience.

I owe a debt of gratitude to Victor Valdes for being prepared to meet and discuss the players' insights into being part of a commitment culture and for his kind introduction to colleagues who were equally illuminating with such incisive observations.

It was a deep pleasure to enjoy the company of Pere Guardiola and hear about how the shaping of a culture starts at such an early age.

Pep Guardiola, for agreeing to kindly read the manuscript of this book but, above all, for the courage, conviction and passion to shape a commitment culture.

I want to issue my appreciation to Sid Lowe, Graham Hunter and Andy Mitten, whose work has proven relentlessly illuminating, inspiring and fascinating for igniting my interest in Spanish culture, society and sport.

To all of the great players, coaches and leaders with whom I have had the immense good fortune to work and learn from. Experience is a great teacher and you have all given so freely.

Finally, to you, the reader. I do appreciate that in this age of constant distraction and proliferation of choice it is a significant commitment of time, faith and trust to buy and read this book. I don't take this investment lightly. I hope it has been as rewarding to read as it has been to research and write.

Notes

Introduction

1 Damian Hughes, interview with Ferran Soriano.
2 John Carlin, *Financial Times*, 12 March 2012.
3 'The Fifty Most Powerful People in Football', *Daily Telegraph*, 10 May 2016.
4 Edgar Schein, *Organizational Culture and Leadership* (John Wiley & Sons, 2010).
5 Paul J. Zak, *Trust Factor: The Science of Creating High-Performance Companies* (AMACOM, 2017), pp. 5–8; Laszlo Bock, *Work Rules! Insights from Inside Google That Will Transform the Way You Live and Lead* (Twelve, 2015).
6 James N. Baron and Michael T. Hannan, 'The Economic Sociology of Organizational Entrepreneurship: Lessons from the Stanford Project on Emerging Companies', in *The Economic Sociology of Capitalism*, ed. Victor Nee and Richard Swedberg (Russell Sage, 2002), pp. 168–203; James N. Baron and Michael T. Hannan, 'Organisational Blueprints for Success in High-Tech Start-Ups: Lessons from the Stanford Project on Emerging Companies', *IEEE Engineering Management Review* 31, 1 (IEEE, 2003), p. 16; James N. Baron, M. Diane Burton and Michael T. Hannan, 'The Road Taken: Origins and Evolution of Employment Systems in Emerging Companies', *Industrial and Corporate Change* 5, 2 (1996), pp. 239–75; James N. Baron, Michael T. Hannan and M. Diane Burton, 'Building the Iron Cage: Determinants of Managerial Intensity in the Early Years of Organizations', *American Sociological Review* 64, 4 (1999), pp. 527–47; James N. Baron and Michael T. Hannan, 'Organizational Blueprints for Success in High-Tech Start-Ups: Lessons from the Stanford Project on Emerging Companies', *California Management Review* 44, 3 (2002), pp. 8–36.
7 Zak, *Trust Factor*.

8 Sid Lowe, *Fear and Loathing in La Liga* (Yellow Jersey, 2014), p. 249.
9 Ibid.
10 Steve McManaman, *Four Years With Real Madrid* (Simon & Schuster, 2005).
11 Lowe, *Fear and Loathing*, p. 250.
12 Carlo Ancelotti, *Quiet Leadership: Winning Hearts, Minds and Matches* (Portfolio, 2017), p. 25.
13 Ibid., p. 27.
14 'Brendan Rogers says Liverpool must decide if they want a business model or a winning model', *Daily Mirror*, 7 February 2016.
15 Raphael Honigstein, *Das Reboot: How German Football Reinvented Itself and Conquered the World* (Yellow Jersey, 2015), pp. 177–8.
16 'Jürgen Klopp Rallies Neutrals', *Guardian*, 3 November 2013.
17 Damian Hughes, interview with Txiki Begiristain.
18 'Barcelona humble Manchester United', *Independent*, 26 May 2011.

Introducing a Commitment Culture: BARCA

1 Chris Brady and David Bolchover, *The 90-Minute Manager* (Prentice Hall, 2016), p. 18.
2 Damian Hughes, *Liquid Leadership* (Capstone, 2007), p. 29.
3 Dr Martin Luther King, *Where Do We Go from Here: Chaos or Community?* (Beacon Press, 2010).
4 Damian Hughes, *How to Think Like Sir Alex Ferguson* (Aurum, 2013), p. 151.
5 'Football's Greatest Conductor', *Guardian*, 11 February 2011.
6 Sven-Göran Eriksson and Willi Railo, *Sven-Göran Eriksson: On Management* (Carlton Books, 2002), p. 145.
7 Zlatan Ibrahimovic, *I am Zlatan* (Penguin, 2013), p. 1.

Before Commitment: The Power of Choice

1 'Football isn't a science', *Guardian*, 9 November 2012.
2 Ibid.
3 Lauren A. Leotti, Sheena S. Iyengar and Kevin N. Ochsner, 'Born to Choose: The Origins and Value of the Need for Control', *Trends in Cognitive Sciences* 14, 10 (2010), pp. 457–63.
4 Lauren A. Leotti and Mauricio R. Delgado, 'The Inherent Reward of Choice', *Psychological Science* 22 (2011), pp. 1310–18; Lauren A. Leotti and Mauricio R. Delgado, 'The Value of Exercising Control Over Monetary Gains and Losses', *Psychological Science* 25, 2 (2014), pp. 596–604.
5 'Football isn't a science'.

6 Simon Sinek, *Start With Why* (Penguin, 2011).
7 Vern Gambetta, *The Gambetta Method: Common Sense Training for Athletic Performance* (Gambetta Sports Training Systems, 2002).

1. Big Picture

1.i – The Power of Asking 'Why?'

1 Wolf Singer, 'Neuronal Synchrony: A Versatile Code for the Definition of Relations?' *Neuron* 24, 1 (1999), pp. 49–65, 111–25.
2 V. S. Ramachandran and S. Blakeslee, *Phantoms in the Brain: Probing the Mysteries of the Human Mind* (William Morrow and Company, 1998).
3 V. E. Frankl, *Man's Search for Meaning* (Simon & Schuster, 1997).
4 A. Maslow, 'A Theory of Human Motivation', *Psychological Review*, 50, pp. 370–96; A. Maslow, *Motivation and Personality* (Harper, 1954).
5 Jim Collins, *Good to Great* (Random House Business Books, 2001).
6 Sid Lowe, *Fear and Loathing in La Liga* (Yellow Jersey, 2014), p. 12.
7 J. K. Liker, *The Toyota Way – 14 Management Principles from the World's Greatest Manufacturer* (McGraw-Hill, 2003).
8 D. Silverberg, 'Sir Richard Branson's Virgin Territory', digitaljournal.com, 22 April 2005.
9 Charles Handy, *The Empty Raincoat: Making Sense of the Future* (Random House Business, 1995).
10 http://www.keytothekingdombook.com/wordpress/2012/08/the-forgotten-tale-of-walt-disneys-three-little-pigs/
11 Barry Gibbons, *If You Want to Make God Really Laugh Show Him Your Business Plan* (Capstone, 1999).
12 Theodore Levitt, 'Marketing Myopia' (1960; Harvard Business School Press, 1 June 2008).
13 Damian Hughes, interview with Ferran Soriano.
14 Taiichi Ohno, *Toyota Production System: Beyond Large-Scale Production* (Productivity Press, 1988).
15 Lowe, *Fear and Loathing*, pp. 9–12.
16 Adam Grant, *Give and Take: Why Helping Others Drives Our Success* (W&N, 2014).

1.ii: The What

1 J. C. Collins and J. I. Porras, *Built to Last: Successful Habits of Visionary Companies* (HarperCollins, 1994); James C. Collins and Jerry L. Porras, 'Building Your Company's Vision', *Harvard Business Review* 74, 5 (1996), pp. 65–77.

2 Hughes, *Liquid Leadership*, p. 41.

3 Ashley Merryman and Po Bronson, *Top Dog: The Science of Winning and Losing* (Ebury Press, 2014).

4 Rosamund Stone Zander and Benjamin Zander, *The Art of Possibility: Transforming Professional and Personal Life* (Penguin Books, 2002).

5 Hughes, *Liquid Leadership*, p. 67.

6 Damian Hughes, interview with Ferran Soriano and Txiki Begiristain.

7 Johan Cruyff, *My Turn: The Autobiography* (Macmillan, 2016), p. 128.

8 Graham Hunter, *Barça: The Making of the Greatest Team in the World* (BackPage Press, 2012), p. 43.

9 'Louis van Gaal's men do play like Manchester United', *Daily Mail*, 12 April 2016.

10 Guillem Balagué, *Pep Guardiola: Another Way of Winning: The Biography* (Orion, 2016), p. 48.

11 'Pep Guardiola: "I would not be here without Johan Cruyff. He was unique"', *Guardian*, 7 October 2016.

12 Ibid.

13 Cruyff, *My Turn*, p. 236.

14 Hughes, interview with Soriano and Begiristain.

15 Balagué, *Pep Guardiola*, p. 48.

16 'Pep Guardiola: "I would not be here"'.

17 Cruyff, *My Turn*, p. 34.

18 'Pep Guardiola: "I would not be here"'.

19 Balagué, *Pep Guardiola*, p. 132.

20 Hughes, interview with Soriano and Begiristain.

1.iii: The How

1 Ibrahimovic, *I am Zlatan*, p. 276.

2 Fred Lee, *If Disney Ran Your Hospital: 9 1/2 Things You Would Do Differently* (Second River Healthcare Press, 2004), p. 56.

3 Ibid., p. 58.

4 Ibid.

5 Barry Schwartz, *The Paradox of Choice: Why More Is Less* (Harper Perennial, 2005), p. 2.

6 Lluís Canut, *Els Secrets del Barça* (Columna, 2010).

7 Michael Beer, Russell A. Eisenstat and Bert Spector, *The Critical Path to Corporate Renewal* (Harvard Business School Press, 1990), p. 85.

8 Ibrahimovic, *I am Zlatan*, p. 280.

9 Ibid., p. 3.

10 Balagué, *Pep Guardiola*, pp. 172–3.

11 Ibrahimovic, *I am Zlatan*, p. 5.

12 Hughes, interview with Soriano and Begiristain.
13 Ibid.

2. Arc of Change: Cultural Signposts

2.i – Stories

1 Nando Parrado, *Miracle in the Andes: 72 Days on the Mountain and My Long Trek Home* (Orion, 2007).
2 Damian Hughes, interview with Victor Valdes.
3 Joseph Campbell, *The Hero with a Thousand Faces (Collected Works of Joseph Campbell)* (New World Library, 2012).
4 Hughes, *Liquid Leadership*, p. 66.
5 Stephen J. Dubner and Steven D. Levitt, *Think Like a Freak: Secrets of the Rogue Economist* (Penguin, 2015), pp. 195–8.
6 'Americans Know Big Macs Better Than Ten Commandments', Reuters. com, 12 October 2007; 'Motive Marketing: Ten Commandments Survey', Kelton Research, September 2007.
7 Balagué, *Pep Guardiola*, p. 178; Guillem Balagué, *Messi* (Orion, 2014); Hunter, *Barça*.
8 Pixar Story Rules, *Pixar Touch Blog*, 15 May 2011; Damian Hughes, *The Five STEPS to a Winning Mindset* (Macmillan, 2016), p. 268; Ed Catmull, *Creativity, Inc.: Overcoming the Unseen Forces that Stand in the Way of True Inspiration* (Bantam Press, 2014).

2.ii – Rituals and Ceremonies

1 John Carlin, *Financial Times*, 12 March 2012.
2 Kevin Roberts, *Lovemarks: The Future Beyond Brands* (Power House Books, revised edition, 2006).
3 Hughes, interview with Valdes.
4 Ruud Guillit, *How to Watch Football* (Viking, 2016), p. 24.
5 Emile Durkheim and Karen Fields, *The Elementary Forms of Religious Life* (Simon & Schuster, 1995).
6 Richard Sosis and Candace Alcorta, 'Signaling, Solidarity, and the Sacred: The Evolution of Religious Behavior', *Evolutionary Anthropology* 12, 6 (2003), pp. 264–74.
7 Balagué, *Pep Guardiola*, pp. 112–13; Hunter, *Barça*, p. 350.
8 Balagué, *Pep Guardiola*, pp. 112–13.
9 Pat Riley, *The Winner Within: A life plan for team players* (Putnam's Sons, 1993).

2.iii: Speeches

1 Violan Miguel Angel, *Pep Guardiola: The Philosophy that Changed the Game* (Meyer & Meyer Sport, 2014), p. 76.
2 'State of the Nation address', *Pittsburgh Post Gazette*, 20 March 2008.
3 Andrés Iniesta, *The Artist: Being Iniesta* (Headline, 2016), p. 123.
4 Hughes, *How to Think*, p. 155.
5 Paco Aguilar interview, http://www.bundesliga.com/en/news/Bundesliga/0000256824.jsp
6 Balagué, *Pep Guardiola*, p. 146; Hunter, *Barça*, p. 310.

3. Recurring Systems and Processes

1 William James, *The Principles of Psychology* (vol. I and II) (Dover Publications, new edition, 2000).
2 David T. Neal, Wendy Wood and Jeffrey M. Quinn, 'Habits – a Repeat Performance', *Current Directions in Psychological Science* 15, 4 (2006), pp. 198–202; D. Knoch, P. Brugger and M. Regard, 'Suppressing Versus Releasing a Habit: Frequency-Dependent Effects of Prefrontal Transcranial Magnetic Stimulation', *Cerebral Cortex* 15, 7 (2005), pp. 885–7.

3.i – Fundamental Attribution Error

1 http://www.football365.com/news/portrait-of-an-icon-xavi
2 Hunter, *Barça*, p. 72.
3 'Football's Greatest Conductor'.
4 Hunter, *Barça*, pp. 262–87.
5 Lee Ross and Richard E. Nisbett, *The Person and the Situation* (Pinter & Martin, 2011), p. 176.

3.ii – It's the Environment, Stupid!!

1 Marshall Goldsmith, *Triggers: Sparking Positive Change and Making it Last* (Profile Books, 2016), p. 25.
2 Neal, Wood and Quinn, 'Habits – a Repeat Performance', pp. 198–202; Ann. M. Graybiel, 'Habits, Rituals, and the Evaluative Brain', *Annual Review of Neuroscience* 31 (2008), pp. 359–87; D. P. Salmon and N. Butters, 'Neurobiology of Skill and Habit Learning', *Current Opinion in Neurobiology* 5, 2 (1995), pp. 184–90; Ann. M. Graybiel, 'The Basal Ganglia and Chunking of Action Repertoires', *Neurobiology of Learning and Memory* 70, 1–2 (1998), pp. 119–36.

3 Thomas Goetz, *Wired*, 19 June 2011, https://www.wired.com/2011/06/ ff_feedbackloop/; Thomas Goetz, *The Decision Tree: How to Make Better Choices and Take Control of Your Health* (Rodale Books, 2011).

4 Albert Bandura, *Self Efficacy: The Exercise of Control* (Worth Publishers, 1997).

5 Ibid.

6 R. Coram, *Boyd: The Fighter Pilot Who Changed the Art of War* (Back Bay Book, 2004).

7 Hunter, *Barça*, pp. 70–2.

8 Hughes, interview with Valdes.

3.iii – Action Triggers

1 P. Gollwitzer, 'Implementation Intentions: Strong Effects of Simple Plans', *American Psychologist* 54 (1999), pp. 493–503.

2 Mark Owen and Kevin Maurer, *No Easy Day: The Only First-hand Account of the Navy Seal Mission that Killed Osama bin Laden* (Penguin, 2013).

3 Charles Duhigg, *The Power of Habit: Why We Do What We Do and How to Change* (Random House Books, 2013).

4 Hughes, interview with Begiristain.

5 Martí Perarnau, *Pep Confidential: Inside Guardiola's First Season at Bayern Munich* (Arena Sport, 2014), p. 76.

6 John Carlin, *Financial Times*, 12 March 2012; Simon Kuper, *The Blizzard*, Issue 15.

7 Peter M. Gollwitzer, Sarah Milne, Paschal Sheeran and Thomas L. Webb, 'Implementation Intentions and Health Behaviour', in M. Conner and P. Norman (eds.), *Predicting Health Behaviour: Research and Practice with Social Cognition Models* (2nd edition, Open University Press, 2005).

8 Duhigg, *The Power of Habit*, pp. 97–101.

9 John Wooden and Steve Jamison, *The Wisdom of Wooden: My Century On and Off the Court* (McGraw-Hill Contemporary, 2010), p. 88.

10 Hughes, interview with Valdes.

11 Stan Baker, *Our Competition is the World* (Lulu Publishing, 2012).

12 Daniel Coyle, *The Talent Code: Greatness isn't born. It's grown* (Arrow, 2010), p. 27; Gary E. McPherson and James M. Renwick, 'Interest and Choice: Student-Selected Repertoire and its Effect on Practising Behaviour', *British Journal of Music Education* 19 (2002), pp. 173–88; A. D. Baddeley and D. J. A. Longman, 'The Influence of Length and Frequency of Training Session on the Rate of Learning to Type', *Ergonomics* 21 (1978), pp. 627–35.

13 Donald Hebb, *The Organisation of Behaviour* (John Wiley & Sons, 1949).

14 Amit Katwala, *The Athletic Brain* (Simon & Schuster, 2016), p. 60; E. Naito and S. Hirose, 'Efficient Foot Motor Control by Neymar's Brain', *Frontiers in Human Neuroscience* 8, 544 (2014), pp. 1–6.

15 Coyle, *The Talent Code*, p. 41; J. Pujol et al., 'Myelination of Language-Related Areas in the Developing Brain', *Neurology* 66, 3 (2006), pp. 339–43; E. M. Miller, 'Intelligence and Brain Myelination: A Hypothesis', *Personality and Individual Differences* 17 (1994), pp. 803–32.

16 R. Douglas Fields, 'White Matter Matters', *Scientific American* 298 (2008), pp. 54–61; R. Douglas Fields, 'Myelination: An Overlooked Mechanism of Synaptic Plasticity?' *Neuroscientist* 11, 6 (2005), pp. 528–31.

17 Simon Kuper, *The Football Men: Up Close with the Giants of the Modern Game* (Simon & Schuster, 2012), p. 125.

18 Iniesta, *The Artist*, p. 221.

19 'Lionel Messi Lights up Wembley as Barcelona humble Manchester', *Daily Telegraph*, 30 May 2011.

20 James, *The Principles of Psychology*.

4. Cultural Architects and Organizational Heroes

1 Frances Frei, *Uncommon Service: How to Win by Putting Customers at the Core of Your Business* (Harvard Business School Press, 2012), p .23.

2 Margot Morrell and Stephanie Capparell, *Shackleton's Way: Leadership Lessons from the Great Antarctic Explorer* (Nicholas Brealey Publishing, 2003), p. 45.

4.i – The Influence and Power of Peers

1 Solomon E. Asch, 'Opinions and Social Pressure', *Scientific American* 193, 5 (1955), pp. 31–5; Harold Guetzkow, *Groups, Leadership and Men* (Carnegie Press, 1951), pp. 177–90.

2 Vernon Allen and John Levine, 'Social Support and Conformity: The Role of Independent Assessment of Reality', *Journal of Experimental Social Psychology* 7 (1971), pp. 48–58.

3 Eriksson and Railo, *Sven-Göran Eriksson*, p. 84.

4 Ancelotti, *Quiet Leadership*, pp. 40–1.

5 'Ferguson advice to Blair', *Guardian*, 22 October 2013; Alastair Campbell, *Winners: And How They Succeed* (Pegasus, 2015).

6 Balagué, *Pep Guardiola*, p. 84.

7 Sir Alex Ferguson, *Managing My Life* (Hodder, 2000), p. 234; Hughes, *How to Think*.

8 Roy Keane with Roddy Doyle, *The Second Half* (W&N, 2015), pp. 52–3.

9 Ancelotti, *Quiet Leadership*, pp. 40–1.

10 *These Football Times*, 10 January 2016: http://thesefootballtimes. co/2016/01/10/lionel-messi-religion-and-the-meaning-of-watching-sport/

11 Canut, *Els Secrets del Barça*.

12 Balagué, *Messi*, p. 314.

13 Hughes, interview with Soriano and Begiristain.

14 Iniesta, *The Artist*, p. 274.

15 Thomas Brenner and Nichola J. Vriend, 'On the behavior of proposers in ultimatum games', *Journal of Economic Behavior & Organization* 61, 4 (2006), pp. 617–31.

4.ii – Developing Cultural Architects

1 Martí Perarnau, *Senda de Campeones (Path of Champions) – From La Masia to Camp Nou* (Salsa Books, 2011).

2 James March, *A Primer on Decision Making: How Decisions Happen* (Free Press, 1994).

3 Iniesta, *The Artist*, p. 241.

4 Balagué, *Pep Guardiola*, p. 92.

5 I. R. Faber et al., 'Assessing personal talent determinants in young racquet sport players: a systematic review', *Journal of Sports Sciences* 34, 5 (2016), pp. 395–410; B. C. H. Huijgen et al., 'Cognitive Functions in Elite and Sub-Elite Youth Soccer Players Aged 13 to 17 Years', *PLOS One* 10, 12 (2015); B. C. H. Huijgen et al., 'Multidimensional performance characteristics in selected and deselected talented soccer players', *European Journal of Sport Science* 14, 1 (2015), pp. 2–10; T. Toering et al., 'Self-regulation of learning and performance level of elite youth soccer players', *International Journal of Sport Psychology* 43, 4 (2012), pp. 312–25; M. T. Elferink-Gemser et al., 'The marvels of elite sports: how to get there?' *British Journal of Sports Medicine* 45, 9 (2011), pp. 683–7; L. Jonker et al., 'Differences in self-regulatory skills among talented athletes: The significance of competitive level and type of sport', *Journal of Sports Sciences* 28, 8 (2010), pp. 901–8.

6 Angela Duckworth, *Grit: The Power of Passion and Perseverance* (Vermilion, 2016); L. S. Blackwell, K. H. Tvzesniewski and C. S. Dweck, 'Implicit Theories of Intelligence Predict Achievement Across an Adolescent Transition: A Longitudinal Study and an Intervention', *Child Development* 78, 1 (2007), pp. 246–63.

7 Balagué, *Pep Guardiola*, pp. 106–7.

8 Hughes, interview with Soriano and Begiristain.

4.iii – Group Norms

1 Anita Williams Woolley et al., 'Evidence for a Collective Intelligence Factor in the Performance of Human Groups', *Science* 330, 6004 (2010), pp. 686–8.

2 Ibid.

3 Balagué, *Messi*, p. 554; Leo Messi interview with Martin Souto, TyC Sports, March 2013.

4 Wright Thompson, 'Outside the Lines': http://www.espn.co.uk/espn/eticket/story?page=Lionel-Messi

5 Hughes, interview with Valdes.

6 Hunter, *Barça*, p. 34.

7 Simon Baron-Cohen et al., 'Another Advanced Test of Theory of Mind: Evidence from Very High Functioning Adults with Autism or Asperger Syndrome', *Journal of Child Psychology and Psychiatry* 38, 7 (1997), pp. 813–22; Simon Baron-Cohen et al., 'The "Reading the Minds in the Eyes" Test, Revised Version: A Study with Normal Adults, and Adults with Asperger Syndrome or High-Functioning Autism', *Journal of Child Psychology and Psychiatry* 42, 2 (2001), pp. 241–51.

8 Mazafer Sherif, *The Psychology of Social Norms* (Octagon Books, 1965); Amy C. Edmondson, 'Learning from Mistakes is Easier Said than Done: Group and Organizational Influences on the Detection and Correction of Human Error', *Journal of Applied Behavioral Science* 32, 1 (1996), pp. 5–28; Amy C. Edmondson, 'Psychological Safety and Learning Behavior in Work Teams', *Administrative Science Quarterly* 44, 2 (1999), pp. 350–83; Amy C. Edmondson, Roderick M. Kramer and Karen S. Cook, 'Psychological Safety, Trust, and Learning: A Group-level Lens', in Roderick Kramer and Karen Cook (eds.), *Trust and Distrust in Organizations: Dilemmas and Approaches* (Russell Sage Foundation, 2004), pp. 239–72; Amy C. Edmondson, 'The Competitive Imperative of Learning', *Harvard Business Review* 86, 7–8 (1986), pp. 60–7.

9 David Kantor, *Reading the Room: Group Dynamics for Coaches and Leaders* (John Wiley & Sons, 2012).

10 Hughes, interview with Soriano.

11 Ibid.

12 Hunter, *Barça*, pp. 204–31.

13 Thierry Henry column, *Sun*, 18 December 2016.

14 Hughes, interview with Soriano.

15 R. D. Chute and E. L. Wiener, 'Cockpit/cabin communication: I. A tale

of two cultures', *International Journal of Aviation Psychology* 5, 3 (1995), pp. 257–76; R. D. Chute and E. L. Wiener, 'Cockpit/cabin communication: II. Shall we tell the pilots?', *International Journal of Aviation Psychology* 6, 3 (1996), pp. 211–31; J. K. Burgoon, 'Relational message interpretations of touch, conversational distance, and posture', *Journal of Nonverbal Behaviour* 15, 4 (1991), pp. 233–59.

16 Hughes, interview with Soriano and Begiristain.
17 'Football isn't a science'.
18 Iniesta, *The Artist*, p. 259.

5. Authentic Leadership

5.i – Cultural Compatibility

1 Pep Guardiola, Lu Martin and Miguel Rico, *La meva gent, el meu futbol (My people, My football)*, (Edecasa, 2001).
2 Simon Kuper and Stefan Szymanski, *Soccernomics* (Nation Books, 2014).
3 Jeff Borland and Jenny Lye, 'Matching and Mobility in the Market for Australian Rules Football Coaches', *Industrial and Labor Relations Review* 50, 1 (1996), pp. 145–58.
4 John Carlin, 'Guardiola to Munich', *Financial Times*, 18 January 2013.
5 Ibid.
6 Balagué, *Pep Guardiola*, p. 94.
7 Carlin, 'Guardiola to Munich'.

5.ii – Authentic Leadership

1 Notes taken from William T. Pounds, Professor of Organization Studies, MIT, interview: https://www.youtube.com/watch?v=XTd4h9FmZuM
2 Gabriele Marcotti, *Capello: The Man Behind England's World Cup Dream* (Bantam, 2010), p. 23.
3 Balagué, *Pep Guardiola*, p. 12.
4 Ibid., pp. 153–5.
5 Ibid.
6 Jim Collins, *Good to Great* (Random House Business Books, 2001).
7 Hunter, *Barç*, p. 72.
8 Peter Bregman, *18 Minutes: Find Your Focus, Master Distraction and Get the Right Things Done* (Orion, 2012).
9 Hunter, *Barça*, pp. 167–8.

10 Robert H. Waterman, Jr. and Tom Peters, *In Search of Excellence: Lessons from America's Best-run Companies* (HarperBusiness, 1982).

5.iii – Consistency

1 Balagué, *Pep Guardiola*, p. 112.
2 Ibid., p. 116.
3 Hughes, *How to Think*, p. 94.
4 M. Synder, E. D. Tanke and E. Berscheid, 'Social Perception and Interpersonal Behavior: On the Self-fulfilling Nature of Social Stereotypes', *Journal of Personality and Social Psychology* 35, 9 (1977), pp. 656–66.
5 Rory Smith, 'The Five Months in Mexico that Shaped Pep Guardiola's Philosophy', *New York Times*, 19 October 2016.
6 Martí Perarnau, *Pep Guardiola: The Evolution* (Arena Sport, 2016), p. 73.
7 Damian Hughes, interview with Pere Guardiola.
8 Ariel Senosian, *Lo Suficientemente Loco: Una Biografía de Marcelo Bielsa* (Ediciones Corregidor, 2012).
9 Cruyff, *My Turn*, p. 236.
10 Max Brooks, *World War Z* (Gerald Duckworth & Co., 2007); Max Brooks, *The Zombie Survival Guide: Complete Protection from the Living Dead* (Gerald Duckworth & Co., 2013).

5.iv – Transparency

1 Joel Brockner and Batia M. Wisenfeld, 'An Integrative Framework for Explaining Reactions to Decisions: Interactive Effects of Outcomes and Procedures', *Pyschological Bulletin* 120, 2 (1996), pp. 189–208.
2 Hunter, *Barça*, p. 75.
3 Iniesta, *The Artist*, pp. 123–5.
4 Clive Woodward, *Winning!* (Hodder & Stoughton, 2004).

5.v – Authentic Leadership Summary

1 Alan Deutschman, *Change or Die: The Three Keys to Change at Work and in Life* (Collins Publishers, 2007).

6. The X Spot

1 Hunter, *Barça*, p. 17.
2 Iniesta, *The Artist*, p. 161.
3 Jane E. Allen, 'Adrenaline-Fuelled Sprint Makes Some Marathons Deadly', ABC News, 21 November 2011: http://abcnews.go.com/Health/

HeartDisease/marathon-deaths/story?id=15000378#.UAwJoY5alvY;
Shawn Achor, *Before Happiness: Five Actionable Strategies to Create a
Positive Path to Success* (Virgin Books, 2013), pp. 34–6.
4 Hughes, interview with Valdes.
5 Hunter, *Barça*, p. 17.
6 Hughes, interview with Soriano.

Bibliography

Achor, Shawn, *Before Happiness: Five Actionable Strategies to Create a Positive Path to Success* (Virgin Books, 2013)

Aguilar, Paco, interview: http://www.bundesliga.com/en/news/ Bundesliga/0000256824.jsp

Ancelotti, Carlo, *Quiet Leadership: Winning Hearts, Minds and Matches* (Portfolio Penguin, 2017)

Baker, Stan, *Our Competition is the World* (Lulu Publishing, 2012)

Balagué, Guillem, *Pep Guardiola: Another Way of Winning: The Biography* (Orion, 2016)

Balagué, Guillem, *Messi* (Orion, 2014)

Bandura, Albert, *Self Efficacy: The Exercise of Control* (Worth Publishers, 1997)

Beer, Michael, Eisenstat, Russell A. and Spector, Bert, *The Critical Path to Corporate Renewal* (Harvard Business School Press, 1990)

Bock, Laszlo, *Work Rules! Insights from Inside Google That Will Transform the Way You Live and Lead* (Twelve, 2015)

Brady, Chris and Bolchover, David, *90 Minute Manager* (Prentice Hall, 2004)

Bregman, Peter, *18 Minutes: Find Your Focus, Master Distraction and Get the Right Things Done* (Orion, 2012)

Brooks, Max, *The Zombie Survival Guide: Complete Protection from the Living Dead* (Gerald Duckworth & Co., 2013)

Brooks, Max, *World War Z* (Gerald Duckworth & Co., 2007)

Bryant, Adam, 'Google's Quest to Build a Better Boss', *New York Times*, 12 March 2011

Campbell, Alastair, *Winners: And How They Succeed* (Pegasus, 2015)

Campbell, Joseph, *The Hero with a Thousand Faces (Collected Works of Joseph Campbell)* (New World Library, 2012)

Canut, Lluís, *Els Secrets del Barça* (Columna, 2010)

Carlin, John, 'Best Team Ever', *Financial Times*, 12 March 2012

Catmull, Ed, *Creativity, Inc.: Overcoming the Unseen Forces That Stand in the Way of True Inspiration* (Bantam Press, 2014)

Collins, J. C. and Porras, J. I., *Built to Last: Successful Habits of Visionary Companies* (HarperCollins Publishers, 1994)

Collins, Jim, *Good to Great* (Random House Business Books, 2001)

Coram, R., *Boyd: The Fighter Pilot Who Changed the Art of War* (Back Bay Books, 2004)

Coyle, Daniel, *The Talent Code: Greatness isn't born. It's grown* (Arrow, 2010)

Cruyff, Johan, *My Turn: The Autobiography* (Macmillan, 2016)

Deutschman, Alan, *Change or Die: The Three Keys to Change at Work and in Life* (Collins Publishers, 2007)

Dubner, Stephen. J. and Levitt, Steven D., *Think Like a Freak: Secrets of the Rogue Economist* (Penguin, 2015)

Duckworth, Angela, *Grit: The Power of Passion and Perseverance* (Vermilion, 2016)

Duhigg, Charles, *The Power of Habit: Why We Do What We Do and How to Change* (Random House Books, 2013)

Durkheim, Émile and Fields, Karen, *The Elementary Forms of Religious Life* (Simon & Schuster, 1995)

Eriksson, Sven-Göran and Railo, Willi, *Sven-Göran Eriksson: On Management* (Carlton Books, 2002)

Ferguson, Sir Alex, *Managing My Life* (Hodder, 2000)

Festinger, Leon, *A Theory of Cognitive Dissonance* (vol. 2) (Stanford University Press, 1962)

Forsyth, Donelson, *Group Dynamics* (Cengage Learning, 2009)

Frankl, V. E., *Man's Search for Meaning* (Simon & Schuster, 1997)

Frei, Frances, *Uncommon Service: How to Win by Putting Customers at the Core of Your Business* (Harvard Business School Press, 2012)

Gambetta, Vern, *The Gambetta Method: Common Sense Training for Athletic Performance* (Gambetta Sports Training Systems, 2002)

Gibbons, Barry, *If You Want to Make God Really Laugh Show Him Your Business Plan* (Capstone, 1999)

Goetz, Thomas, *The Decision Tree: How to Make Better Choices and Take Control of Your Health* (Rodale, 2011)

Goetz, Thomas, *Wired* Magazine, 19 June 2011: https://www.wired.com/2011/06/ff_feedbackloop/

Goldsmith, Marshall, *Triggers: Sparking Positive Change and Making it Last* (Profile Books, 2016)

Gollwitzer, Peter M., Milne, Sarah, Sheeran, Paschal and Webb, Thomas L., 'Implementation Intentions and Health Behaviours', in M. Conner and

P. Norman (eds.), *Predicting Health Behaviour: Research and Practice with Social Cognition Models* (2nd edition) (Open University Press, 2005)

Grant, Adam, *Give and Take: Why Helping Others Drives Our Success* (W&N, 2014)

Guardiola, Pep, Martin, Lu and Rico, Miguel, *La meva gent, el meu futbol (My people, My football)* (Edecasa, 2001)

Guetzkow, Harold, *Groups, Leadership and Men* (Carnegie Press, 1951)

Guillit, Ruud, *How to Watch Football* (Viking, 2016)

Handy, Charles, *The Empty Raincoat: Making Sense of the Future* (Random House Business, 1995)

Hebb, Donald, *The Organisation of Behaviour* (John Wiley & Sons, 1949)

Honigstein, Raphael, *Das Reboot: How German Football Reinvented Itself and Conquered the World* (Yellow Jersey, 2016)

Hughes, Damian, *How to Think Like Sir Alex Ferguson: The Business of Winning and Managing Success* (Aurum Press, 2014)

Hughes, Damian, *Liquid Leadership: Inspirational Lessons from the World's Great Leaders* (Capstone, 2009)

Hughes, Damian, *The Five STEPS to a Winning Mindset* (Macmillan, 2016)

Hunter, Graham, *Barça: The Making of the Greatest Team in the World* (BackPage Press, 2012)

Ibrahimovic, Zlatan, *I am Zlatan* (Penguin, 2013)

Iniesta, Andrés, *The Artist: Being Iniesta* (Headline, 2016)

James, William, *The Principles of Psychology* vols. I and II (Dover Publications, new edition 2000)

Kanter, Rosabeth Moss, *Evolve! Succeeding in the Digital Culture of Tomorrow* (Harvard Business School Press, 2001)

Kanter, Rosabeth Moss, *Leadership for Change: Enduring Skills for Change Masters*, Harvard Business School Note 9-304-06 (Harvard Business School Press, 2006)

Kantor, David, *Reading the Room: Group Dynamics for Coaches and Leaders* (John Wiley & Sons, 2012)

Katwala, Amit, *The Athletic Brain* (Simon & Schuster, 2016)

Keane, Roy, with Roddy Doyle, *The Second Half* (W&N, 2015)

King, Dr Martin Luther, *Where Do We Go from Here: Chaos or Community?* (Beacon Press, 2010)

Kuper, Simon, *The Football Men: Up Close With The Giants of the Modern Game* (Simon & Schuster, 2012)

Kuper, Simon and Szymanski, Stefan, *Soccernomics* (Nation Books, 2014)

Lee, Fred, *If Disney Ran Your Hospital: 9 1/2 Things You Would Do Differently* (Second River Healthcare Press, 2004)

Liker, J. K., *The Toyota Way – 14 Management Principles from the World's Greatest Manufacturer* (McGraw-Hill, 2003)

Lowe, Sid, *Fear and Loathing in La Liga* (Yellow Jersey, 2014)

March, James, *A Primer on Decision Making: How Decisions Happen* (Free Press, 1994)

Marcotti, Gabriele, *Capello: The Man Behind England's World Cup Dream* (Bantam, 2010)

Maslow, A., *Motivation and Personality* (New York, 1954)

Maurer, Robert, *One Small Step Can Change Your Life: The Kaizen Way* (Workman, 2004)

McManaman, Steve, *Four Years with Real Madrid* (Simon & Schuster, 2005)

Merryman, Ashley and Bronson, Po, *Top Dog: The Science of Winning and Losing* (Ebury Press, 2014)

Messi, Leo, interview with Martin Souto, TyC Sports, March 2013

Morrell, Margot and Capparell, Stephanie, *Shackleton's Way: Leadership Lessons from the Great Antarctic Explorer* (Nicholas Brealey Publishing, 2003)

Ohno, Taiichi, *Toyota Production System: Beyond Large-Scale Production* (Productivity Press, 1988)

Owen, Mark and Maurer, Kevin, *No Easy Day: The Only First-hand Account of the Navy Seal Mission that Killed Osama bin Laden* (Penguin, 2013)

Parrado, Nando, *Miracle in the Andes: 72 Days on the Mountain and My Long Trek Home* (Orion, 2007)

Perarnau, Martí, *Pep Confidential: Inside Guardiola's First Season at Bayern Munich* (Arena Sport, 2014)

Perarnau, Martí, *Pep Guardiola: The Evolution* (Arena Sport, 2016)

Perarnau, Martí, *Senda de Campeones (Path of Champions) – From La Masia to Camp Nou* (Salsa Books, 2011)

Pixar Story Rules, Pixar Touch Blog, 15 May 2011

Ramachandran, V. S. and Blakeslee, S., *Phantoms in the Brain: Probing the Mysteries of the Human Mind* (William Morrow and Company, 1998)

Riley, Pat, *The Winner Within: A life plan for team players* (Putnam's Sons, 1993)

Roberts, Kevin, *Lovemarks: The Future Beyond Brands* (Power House Books, 2006)

Ross, Lee and Nisbett, Richard E., *The Person and the Situation* (Pinter & Martin, 2011)

Schein, Edgar, *Organizational Culture and Leadership* (John Wiley & Sons, 2010)

Schwartz, Barry, *The Paradox of Choice: Why More is Less* (Harper Perennial, 2005)

Senosian, Ariel, *Lo Suficientemente Loco: Una Biografía de Marcelo Bielsa* (Ediciones Corregidor, 2012)

Sherif, Mazafer, *The Psychology of Social Norms* (Octagon Books, 1965)

Sinek, Simon, *Start With Why* (Penguin, 2011)

Violan, Miguel Angel, *Pep Guardiola: The Philosophy That Changed the Game* (Meyer & Meyer Sport, 2014)

Waterman, Jr., Robert, H. and Peters, Tom, *In Search of Excellence: Lessons from America's Best-run Companies* (Harper Business, 1982)

Wooden, John and Jamison, Steve, *The Wisdom of Wooden: My Century On and Off the Court* (McGraw-Hill Contemporary, 2010)

Woodward, Clive, *Winning!* (Hodder & Stoughton, 2004)

Zak, Paul J., *Trust Factor: The Science of Creating High-Performance Companies* (AMACOM, 2017)

Zander, Rosamund Stone and Zander, Benjamin, *The Art of Possibility: Transforming Professional and Personal Life* (Penguin Books, 2002)

Academic Papers

'Americans Know Big Macs Better than Ten Commandments', Reuters.com (12 October 2007)

'Motive Marketing: Ten Commandments Survey', Kelton Research (September 2007)

Allen, Jane E., 'Adrenaline-Fuelled Sprint Makes Some Marathons Deadly', ABC News, 21 November 2011: http://abcnews.go.com/Health/ HeartDisease/marathon-deaths/story?id=15000378#.UAwJoY5alvY

Allen, Vernon and Levine, John, 'Social Support and Conformity: The Role of Independent Assessment of Reality', *Journal of Experimental Social Psychology* 7 (1971), pp. 48–58

Asch, Solomon E., 'Opinions and Social Pressure', *Scientific American* 193, 5 (1955), pp. 31–5

Baddeley, A. D. and Longman, D. J. A., 'The Influence of Length and Frequency of Training Session on the Rate of Learning to Type', *Ergonomics* 21 (1978), pp. 627–35

Baron, James N. and Hannan, Michael T., 'Organizational Blueprints for Success in High-Tech Start-Ups: Lessons from the Stanford Project on Emerging Companies', *California Management Review* 44, 3 (2002), pp. 8–36

Baron, James N. and Hannan, Michael T., 'Organizational Blueprints for Success in High-Tech Start-Ups: Lessons from the Stanford Project on

Emerging Companies', *IEEE Engineering Management Review* 31, 1
(2003), p. 16

Baron, James N. and Hannan, Michael T., 'The Economic Sociology of
Organizational Entrepreneurship: Lessons from the Stanford Project
on Emerging Companies', in Victor Nee and Richard Swedberg
(eds.), *The Economic Sociology of Capitalism* (Russell Sage, 2002),
pp. 168–203

Baron, James N., Burton, Diane M. and Hannan, Michael T., 'The Road
Taken: Origins and Evolution of Employment Systems in Emerging
Companies', *Industrial and Corporate Change* 5, 2 (1996), pp. 239–75

Baron, James N., Hannan, Michael T. and Burton, Diane M., 'Building
the Iron Cage: Determinants of Managerial Intensity in the Early Years
of Organizations', *American Sociological Review* 64, 4 (1999), pp. 527–47

Baron-Cohen, Simon et al., 'Another Advanced Test of Theory of Mind:
Evidence from Very High Functioning Adults with Autism or Asperger
Syndrome', *Journal of Child Psychology and Psychiatry* 38, 7 (1997),
pp. 813–22

Baron-Cohen, Simon et al., 'The "Reading the Minds in the Eyes" Test',
revised version: 'A Study with Normal Adults, and Adults with Asperger
Syndrome or High-Functioning Autism', *Journal of Child Psychology and
Psychiatry* 42, 2 (2001), pp. 241–51

Barsade, Sigal G., 'The Ripple Effect: Emotional Contagion and Its
Influence on Group Behavior', *Administrative Science Quarterly* 47, 4
(2002), pp. 644–75

Blackwell, L. S., Tvzesniewski, K. H. and Dweck, C. S., 'Implicit Theories
of Intelligence Predict Achievement Across an Adolescent Transition:
A Longitudinal Study and an Intervention', *Child Development* 78, 1
(2007), pp. 246–63

Borland, Jeff and Lye, Jenny, 'Matching and Mobility in the Market for
Australian Rules Football Coaches', *Industrial and Labor Relations Review*
50, 1 (1996), pp. 143–58

Brenner, Thomas and Vriend, Nichola J., 'On the behavior of proposers in
ultimatum games', *Journal of Economic Behavior & Organization* 61, 4
(2006), pp. 617–31

Brockner, Joel and Wisenfeld, Batia M., 'An Integrative Framework for
Explaining Reactions to Decisions: Interactive Effects of Outcomes and
Procedures', *Psychological Bulletin* 120, 2 (1991), pp. 189–208

Burgoon, J. K., 'Relational message interpretations of touch, conversational
distance, and posture', *Journal of Nonverbal Behavior* 15, 4 (1991),
pp. 233–59

Chute, R. D. and Wiener, E. L., 'Cockpit/cabin communication: I. A tale of two cultures', *The International Journal of Aviation Psychology* 5, 3 (1995), pp. 257–76

Chute, R. D. and Wiener, E. L., 'Cockpit/cabin communication: II. Shall we tell the pilots?', *The International Journal of Aviation Psychology* 6, 3 (1996), pp. 211–31

Collins, James C. and Porras, Jerry L., 'Building Your Company's Vision', *Harvard Business Review* 74, 5 (1996), pp. 65–77

Davenport, Thomas H., Harris, Jeanne and Shapiro, Jeremy, 'Competing on Talent Analytics', *Harvard Business Review* 88, 10 (2010), pp. 52–8, 150

Druskat, Vanessa Urch and Wolff, Steve B., 'Building the Emotional Intelligence of Groups', *Harvard Business Review* 79, 3 (2001), pp. 80–90, 164

Edmondson, Amy C., 'Learning from Mistakes is Easier Said than Done: Group and Organizational Influences on the Detection and Correction of Human Error', *The Journal of Applied Behavioral Science* 32, 1 (1996), pp. 5–28

Edmondson, Amy C., 'Psychological Safety and Learning Behavior in Work Teams', *Administrative Science Quarterly* 44, 2 (1999), pp. 350–83

Edmondson, Amy C., 'The Competitive Imperative of Learning', *Harvard Business Review* 86, 7–8 (1986), pp. 60–7

Edmondson, Amy C., Kramer, Roderick M. and Cook, Karen S., 'Psychological Safety, Trust, and Learning: A Group-level Lens', in Roderick Kramer and Karen Cook (eds.), *Trust and Distrust in Organizations: Dilemmas and Approaches* (Russell Sage Foundation, 2004), pp. 239–72

Elferink-Gemser, M. T., Jordet, G., Coelho-E-Silva, M. J. and Visscher, C., 'The marvels of elite sports: how to get there?', *British Journal of Sports Medicine* 45, 9 (2011), pp. 683–7

Faber, I. R., Bustin, P. M. J., Oosterveld, F. G. J., Elferink-Gemser, M. T. and Nijhuis-Van Der Sanden, M. W. G., 'Assessing personal talent determinants in young racquet sport players: a systematic review', *Journal of Sports Sciences* 34, 5 (2016), pp. 395–410

Fields, R. Douglas, 'Myelination: An Overlooked Mechanism of Synaptic Plasticity?', *Neuroscientist* 11, 6 (2005), pp. 528–31

Fields, R. Douglas, 'White Matter Matters', *Scientific American* 298 (2008), pp. 54–61

Gollwitzer, P., 'Implementation Intentions: Strong Effects of Simple Plans', *American Psychologist* 54 (1999), pp. 493–503

Graybiel, Ann. M., 'Habits, Rituals, and the Evaluative Brain', *Annual Review of Neuroscience* 31 (2008), pp. 359–87

Graybiel, Ann. M., 'The Basal Ganglia and Chunking of Action Repertoires', *Neurobiology of Learning and Memory* 70, 1–2 (1998), pp. 119–36

Huijgen, B. C. H., Elferink-Gemser, M. T., Lemmink, K. A. P. M. and Visscher, C., 'Multidimensional performance characteristics in selected and deselected talented soccer players', *European Journal of Sport Science* 14, 1 (2015), pp. 2–10

Huijgen, B. C. H., Leemhuis, S., Kok, N. M., Verburgh, L., Oosterlaan, J., Elferink-Gemser, M. T. and Visscher, C., 'Cognitive Functions in Elite and Sub-Elite Youth Soccer Players Aged 13 to 17 Years', *PLOS One* 10, 12 (2015)

Iyengar, Sheena S. and Lepper, Mark R., 'When Choice is Demotivating: Can One Desire Too Much of a Good Thing?', *Journal of Personality and Social Psychology* 79, 6 (2000), pp. 995–1006

Jonker, L., Elferink-Gemser, M. T. and Visscher, C., 'Differences in self-regulatory skills among talented athletes: The significance of competitive level and type of sport', *Journal of Sports Sciences* 28, 8 (2010), pp. 901–8

Kahn, William A., 'Psychological Conditions of Personal Engagement and Disengagement at Work', *Academy of Management Journal* 33, 4 (1990), pp. 692–724

Knoch, D., Brugger, P. and Regard, M., 'Suppressing Versus Releasing a Habit: Frequency-Dependent Effects of Prefrontal Transcranial Magnetic Stimulation', *Cerebral Cortex* 15, 7 (2005), pp. 885–7

Kuper, Simon, 'Barcelona's Seven Secrets to Success', *The Blizzard*, Issue 15

Leotti, Lauren A. and Delgado, Mauricio R., 'The Inherent Reward of Choice', *Psychological Science* 22, 10 (2011), pp. 1310–18

Leotti, Lauren A. and Delgado, Mauricio R., 'The Value of Exercising Control over Monetary Gains and Losses', *Psychological Science* 25, 2 (2014), pp. 596–604

Leotti, Lauren A., Iyengar, Sheena S. and Ochsner, Kevin N., 'Born to Choose: The Origins and Value of the Need for Control', *Trends in Cognitive Sciences* 14, 10 (2010), pp. 457–63

Levitt, Theodore, 'Marketing Myopia' (1960; Harvard Business School Press, 1 June 2008)

Maslow, A., 'A Theory of Human Motivation', *Psychological Review* 50, 4 (1943), pp. 370–96

McPherson, Gary E. and Renwick, James M., 'Interest and Choice: Student-Selected Repertoire and Its Effect on Practising Behaviour', *British Journal of Music Education* 19, 2 (2002), pp. 173–88

Miller, E. M., 'Intelligence and Brain Myelination: A Hypothesis', *Personality and Individual Differences* 17, 6 (1994), pp. 803–32

Naito, E. and Hirose, S., 'Efficient Foot Motor Control by Neymar's Brain', *Frontiers in Human Neuroscience* 8, 594 (2014), pp. 1–6

Neal, David T., Wood, Wendy and Quinn, Jeffrey M., 'Habits – a Repeat Performance', *Current Directions in Psychological Science* 15, 4 (2006), pp. 198–202

Pounds, William T., Professor of Organization Studies, MIT, interview: https://www.youtube.com/watch?v=XTd4h9FmZuM

Patall, Erika A., Cooper, Harris and Robinson, Jorgianne Civey, 'The Effects of Choice on Intrinsic Motivation and Related Outcomes: A Meta-Analysis of Research Findings', *Psychological Bulletin* 134, 2 (2008), pp. 270–300

Pujol, J., Soriano-Mas, C., Ortiz, H., Sebastién-Gallés, N., Losilla, J. M. and Deus, J., 'Myelination of Language-Related Areas in the Developing Brain', *Neurology* 66, 3 (2006), pp. 339–43

Salmon, D. P. and Butters, N., 'Neurobiology of Skill and Habit Learning', *Current Opinion in Neurobiology* 5, 2 (1995), pp. 184–90

Shields, D. L. L. et al., 'Leadership, Cohesion and Team Norms Regarding Cheating and Aggression', *Sociology of Sport Journal* 12, 3 (1995), pp. 324–36

Silverberg, D., 'Sir Richard Branson's Virgin Territory', digitaljournal.com, 22 April 2005

Singer, Wolf, 'Neuronal Synchrony: A Versatile Code for the Definition of Relations?', *Neuron* 24, 1 (1999), pp. 49–65

Sosis, Richard and Alcorta, Candace, 'Signaling, Solidarity, and the Sacred: The Evolution of Religious Behaviour', *Evolutionary Anthropology* 12, 6 (2003), pp. 264–74

Synder, M., Tanke, E. D. and Berscheid, E., 'Social Perception and Interpersonal Behavior: On the Self-fulfilling Nature of Social Stereotypes', *Journal of Personality and Social Psychology* 35, 9 (1977), pp. 656–66

Terry, Deborah J., Hogg, Michael A. and White, Katherine M., 'The Theory of Planned Behaviour: Self-identity, Social Identity and Group Norms', *British Journal of Social Psychology* 38, 3, (1999), pp. 225–44

Thompson, Wright, 'Outside the Lines': http://www.espn.co.uk/espn/eticket/story?page=Lionel-Messi

Toering, T., Elferink-Gemser, M. T., Jordet, G., Pepping, G-J. and Visscher, C., 'Self-regulation of learning and performance level of elite youth soccer players', *International Journal of Sport Psychology* 43, 4 (2012), pp. 312–25

Woolley, Anita Williams et al., 'Evidence for a Collective Intelligence Factor in the Performance of Human Groups', *Science* 330, 6004 (2010), pp. 686–8

Websites

http://thesefootballtimes.co/2016/01/10/lionel-messi-religion-and-the-meaning-of-watching-sport/

http://www.football365.com/news/portrait-of-an-icon-xavi

http://www.keytothekingdombook.com/wordpress/2012/08/the-forgotten-tale-of-walt-disneys-three-little-pigs/

http://www.martiperarnau.com/